Approaches to Prepositions

Tübinger Beiträge zur Linguistik

herausgegeben von Gunter Narr

358

Gisa Rauh (ed.)

Approaches to Prepositions

gnv Gunter Narr Verlag Tübingen

CIP-Titelaufnahme der Deutschen Bibliothek

Approaches to prepositions / Gisa Rauh (ed.). – Tübingen : Narr, 1991
(Tübinger Beiträge zur Linguistik ; 358)
ISBN 3–8233–4213–4

NE: Rauh, Gisa [Hrsg.]; GT

Dischingerweg 5 · D-7400 Tübingen 5

Gedruckt auf säurefreiem und alterungsbeständigem Werkdruckpapier.

Druck: Laupp + Göbel, Nehren

Verarbeitung: Geiger, Ammerbuch-Poltringen
Printed in Germany

ISBN 3–8233–4213–4

Contents

Preface 7

Bibliography on prepositions
Angelika Huppertz 9

***Together* – a preposition?**
Colin Foskett 29

Prepositions and prepositional phrases: a contrastive analysis
Norbert Fries 53

Präpositionen und Objektkonzepte
Ein kognitiv orientiertes, zweistufiges Modell für die Semantik lokaler Präpositionen
Priska-Monika Hottenroth 77

On the reanalysis of verbs as prepositions
Ekkehard König und Bernd Kortmann 109

A two-level approach to projective prepositions
Ewald Lang 127

Prepositional forms in the lexicon: problems and suggestions
Gisa Rauh 169

The lexical meaning of the French preposition *contre*
Marie-Theres Schepping 225

Getting round to *(a)round*: towards the description and analysis of a "spatial" predicate
Rainer Schulze 253

On the lexical meaning of prepositions: a study of *above, below* and *over*
Barbara Wege 275

List of contributors 297

Preface

Prepositions belong to the "small" words of a language and as such they have been neglected in the past. It is only recently, and in part due to the intention to implement natural language on a computer, that they have received more attention. One result is that the elements of the category preposition have proved to be extremely heterogeneous and problematic with respect to both their semantic and their syntactic properties.

In November 1988 the editor of this volume organized a conference on prepositions at the University of Wuppertal. The aim of the conference was to shed more light on the problematic category preposition by bringing together colleagues who had worked on prepositions independently and who had dealt with different aspects of this category from different points of view. Thus, an essential part of the concept behind the conference was to provide an opportunity for specialists on prepositions to present their diverging approaches to syntactic or semantic aspects, basing their analyses on languages of their own choice. Most of the contributions to this volume have grown out of papers delivered at the conference in Wuppertal.

The diversity of the articles that make up this volume mirrors the diversity of the contributions at the conference. Thus, semantic aspects of prepositions are considered in the studies by E. Lang, M.-P. Hottenroth, M. T. Schepping, R. Schulze and B. Wege; with English (R. Schulze, B. Wege), French (M.-P. Hottenroth, M. T. Schepping) and German (E. Lang) as the languages under investigation. The contributions by C. Foskett, N. Fries, E. König and B. Kortmann, and G. Rauh on the other hand, are predominantly syntactic in orientation, dealing with prepositions in English, and, in the paper by N. Fries, German and Greek. In view of this variety and the different theoretical approaches adopted, no attempt has been made to group the contributions thematically, and they appear in alphabetical order (according to the author's name).

I should like to thank all those who have made the publication of this book possible. Not all of them can be mentioned by name, but special thanks are due to the authors for allowing publication of their papers in this volume, and additionally to Angelika Huppertz for compiling a general bibliography of prepositions. I am particularly grateful to Colin Foskett, who was very much involved in the preparation of this book, not only as a contributor, but also as a translator and an informant on questions concerning data and formulation in English. Thanks are also due to Martin Othmar and Frank Otterbein, who were largely responsible for preparing the manuscript for printing.

Last but not least I must thank the University of Wuppertal for providing the financial support for the conference on prepositions in November 1988 without which this volume would not have been possible.

Wuppertal, August 1990 **Gisa Rauh**

Bibliography on prepositions

Angelika Huppertz
(Wuppertal)

In the course of the Colloquium on Prepositions on 25th and 26th November, 1988, it became obvious that a general interest in this word class had developed during the recent years. It was therefore decided that the bibliographical data that had accumulated as a result of the work done in the Wuppertal research project on prepositions (under Gisa Rauh) should be revised and updated in order to make it accessible to anyone interested in the topic.

In the early stages of the project the very extensive

Guimier, C. 1981. *Prepositions: An Analytical Bibliography.* Amsterdam: Benjamins.

was used as a survey of relevant publications. However, it is the tragic fate of all bibliographies that they rapidly become out of date. Hence, this publication, which includes those items not found in Guimier (1981) as well as those published after 1981. The aim of this bibliography is to list the majority of books and articles on prepositions published over the last ten or fifteen years. It does *not* attempt to provide a complete survey of the material but should be regarded and used as a sequel to Guimier (1981).

The user of this bibliography should not be surprised to find the titles of books and articles on topics other than prepositions, for example on verbs, adverbs, particles etc. The results of research on e.g. the valency of verbs may serve as a model for research on prepositions.

This bibliography does not claim to be exhaustive, but tries to reflect in the choice of items included the problem areas of the word class, under the headings of syntax and semantics on the one hand, and from the viewpoint of other linguistic fields such as psycholinguistics, computer linguistics, research on language teaching etc. on the other hand.

The bibliography is to be seen as an independent part of this publication as e.g. it neither includes all the references mentioned or cited in the other articles nor does it set out to avoid duplicating them.

Many of the titles included are taken from the MLA (Modern Language Association of America, International Bibliography of Books and Articles on the Modern Languages and Literatures) and Bibliographie Linguistischer Literatur (Frankfurt a.M.), others are from lists compiled during the last few years in our research project.

I must thank all of my colleagues and fellow students who have helped by bringing along anything interesting about prepositions without knowing that this would become a published work one day - *today*.

A. H.

Abkarian, G.G. 1982. Comprehension of Deictic Locatives: The Object 'behind' It. *Journal of Psycholinguistic Research* 11: 229-245.

Abkarian, G.G. 1983. More Negative Findings for Positive Prepositions. *Journal of Child Language* 10: 415-429.

Ahnert, L., F. Klix and H.-D. Schmidt. 1980. The Acquisition of Local Prepositions in Early Childhood. *Zeitschrift für Psychologie mit Zeitschrift für Angewandte Psychologie* 188: 226-234.

Allerton, D.J. 1982. *Valency and the English Verb*. London: Academic Press.

Altenberg, B. 1984. Causal Linking in Spoken and Written English. *Studia Linguistica* 38: 20-69.

Amano, M. 1982. On P-Stranding. *Studies in English Literature* 59: 265-278.

Anderman, G. 1985. Linguistics and Modern Language Teaching - A Typological Approach. *IRAL, International Review of Applied Linguistics in Language Teaching* 23: 60-64.

Anderson, W.E. 1972. *Das englische Verb: Ein Arbeitsbuch für Studenten und Lehrer*. Heidelberg: Quelle & Meyer.

Anglin, J.M. 1971. *The Growth of Word Meaning*. Cambridge, Mass.: MIT Press.

Aoun, J. and D.W. Lightfoot. 1984. Government and Contraction. *Linguistic Inquiry* 15: 465-473.

Arlin, M. 1983. Children's Comprehension of Semantic Constraints on Temporal Prepositions. *Journal of Psycholinguistic Research* 12: 1-15.

Armstrong, S.L., H. Gleitman and L.R. Gleitman. 1983. What Some Concepts Might not Be. *Cognition* 13: 263-308.

Baardewijk-Rességuier, J. van. 1983. La Non-Alternance entre Syntagme Prépositionnel et Adjectif de Relation. *Cahiers de Lexicologie* 43: 73-84.
Bailey, C.-J. 1986. Where English Cannot Put a Preposition before a Relative or Interrogative Pronoun. In Leitner, G. (ed.). *The English Reference Grammar: Language and Linguistics, Writers and Readers*. Tübingen: Niemeyer. 156-177.
Bardovi-Harlig, K. 1987. Markedness and Salience in Second-Language Acquisition. *Language Learning: A Journal of Applied Linguistics* 37: 385-407.
Bartsch, R. 1972. *Adverbialsemantik. Die Konstitution logisch-semantischer Repräsentationen von Adverbialkonstruktionen*. Frankfurt a.M.: Athenäum.
Becker, J.D. 1975. The Phrasal Lexicon. In Nash-Webber, B. and R. Schank (eds.). *Theoretical Issues in Natural Language Processing. Papers from an Interdisciplinary Workshop in Computational Linguistics, Psychology, Linguistics, Artificial Intelligence, 10-13 June, 1975, Cambridge, MA*. Cambridge, Mass.: Yale Univ. Mathematical Soc. Sciences Board. 70-73.
Bennis, H., R. Prins and J. Vermeulen. 1983. Lexical-Semantic versus Syntactic Disorders in Aphasia: The Processing of Prepositions. *Publikaties van het Instituut voor Algemene Taalwetenschap* 40: 1-32.
Bergeder, F. 1914. *Die periphrastische Form des englischen Verbums im 17. Jahrhundert*. Halle: Kaemmerer.
Bibovic, L. 1984. The Structural Possibilites of Serbo-Croatian Related to the English Structure Adjective + Prepositional Sentential Complement. *Linguistica* 24: 369-382.
Block, H.U. 1984. *Maschinelle Übersetzung komplexer französischer Nominalsyntagmen ins Deutsche*. Tübingen: Niemeyer.
Bloom, L., J. Tackeff and M. Lahey. 1984. Learning 'to' in Complement Constructions. *Journal of Child Language* 11: 391-406.
Boggess, L.C. 1978. *Computational Interpretation of English Spatial Prepositions*. Ph.D. Diss., University of Illinois at Urbana-Champaign.
Bolinger, D. 1971. *The Phrasal Verb in English*. Cambridge, Mass.: Harvard University Press.
Borsley, R.D. 1983. A Note on Preposition Stranding. *Linguistic Inquiry* 14: 338-343.
Borsley, R.D. 1986. Prepositional Complementizers in Welsh. *Journal of Linguistics* 22: 67-84.
Bossong, G. 1980. Questions de Linguistique Chinoise: Réflexions Critiques au Sujet du Livre de Claude Hagège, 'Le Problème des Prépositions et la Solution Chinoise'. *Lingua* 51: 233-250.
Bourquin-Launey, M.-C. 1984. De la Traduction Automatique à la Réflexion Linguistique: La Traduction de la Préposition Anglaise 'through'. *Contrastes* A4: 81-99.
Breindl, E. 1989. *Präpositionalobjekte und Präpositionalobjektsätze im Deutschen*. Tübingen: Niemeyer.
Bresnan, J. (ed.). 1982. *The Mental Representation of Grammatical Relations*. Cambridge, Mass.: MIT Press.
Bridgeman, L.I. (ed.). 1965. *More Classes of Verbs in English*. Bloomington, Ind.: Indiana University.

Brinker, K. 1972. *Konstituentenstrukturgrammatik und operationale Satzgliedanalyse. Methodenkritische Untersuchungen zur Syntax des einfachen Satzes im Deutschen.* Frankfurt a.M.: Athenäum.

Brown, C.H. 1983. Where Do Cardinal Direction Terms Come from? *Anthropological Linguistics* 25: 121-161.

Brugman, C.M. 1983. *Story of 'over'.* Trier: L.A.U.T.

Buren, P. van and Smith, M.Sh. 1985. The Acquisition of Preposition Stranding by Second Language Learners and Parametric Variation. *Second Language Research* 1: 18-46.

Burger, H., A. Buhofer and A. Sialm. 1982. *Handbuch der Phraseologie.* Berlin: de Gruyter.

Buscha, J. 1984. Zur Syntax der Präpositionen. *Deutsch als Fremdsprache* 21: 145-151.

Buyssens, E. 1987. The Preposition 'for' with an Infinitive Clause. *English Studies* 68: 336-347.

Calbert, J.P. 1973. *Modality and Case Grammar.* Trier: L.A.U.T.

Cervoni, J. 1984. Prépositions et Continuum. *Modèles Linguistiques* 6: 87-98.

Chiu-ming, L. and H. Ching-hua. 1981. 'Except' or 'Except for'? *English Language Teaching Journal* 35: 260-263.

Clark, E.V. 1971. On the Acquisition of the Meaning of 'before' and 'after'. *Journal of Verbal Learning and Verbal Behavior* 10: 266-275.

Clark, E.V. 1972. Some Perceptual Factors in the Acquisition of Locative Terms by Young Children. In Paranteau, P.M., J.N. Levi and G.C. Phares (eds.). *Papers from the 8th Regional Meeting, Chicago Linguistic Society.* Chicago: Chicago Linguistic Society. 431-439.

Clark, H.H. 1970. The Primitive Nature of Children's Relational Concepts. In Hayes, J.R. (ed.). *Cognition and the Development of Language.* New York: Wiley. 269-278.

Clark, H.H. and R.A. Stafford. 1969. Memory for Semantic Features in the Verb. *Journal of Experimental Psychology* 80: 326-334.

Closs-Traugott, E. 1974. Explorations in Linguistic Elaboration: Language Change, Language Acquisition, and the Genesis of Spatio-Temporal Terms. In Anderson, J.M. and C. Jones (eds.). *Historical Linguistics I.* Amsterdam: North-Holland. 263-314.

Coker, P.L. 1978. Syntactic and Semantic Factors in the Acquisition of 'before' and 'after'. *Journal of Child Language* 5: 261-277.

Colombo, L. and G.B. Flores d'Arcais. 1984. The Meaning of Dutch Prepositions: A Psycholinguistic Study of Polysemy. *Linguistics* 22: 51-98.

Colombo, L. and P.H.K. Seymour. 1983. Semantic and Pragmatic Factors in the Representation of 'Near' and 'Far'. *Journal of Psycholinguistic Research* 12: 75-92.

Conner, P.S. and R.S. Chapman. 1985. The Development of Locative Comprehension in Spanish. *Journal of Child Language* 12: 109-123.

Couper-Kuhlen, E. 1979. *The Prepositional Passive in English: A Semantic-Syntactic Analysis, with a Lexicon of Prepositional Verbs.* Tübingen: Niemeyer.

Courtney, R. 1983. *Longman Dictionary of Phrasal Verbs.* Harlow, Essex: Longman.

Cox, Th.J. 1983. Teaching the Unteachable: Prepositional Complementizers in French. *The French Review: Journal of the American Association of Teachers of French* 57: 168-178.

Crowell, T.L., Jr. [4]1975. *A Glossary of Phrases with Prepositions: with Exercises*. Frankfurt a.M./Berlin/München: Diesterweg.

Csillag, E., A. Károlyi and A. Nagy. 1983. Die deutschen Präpositionen und ihre ungarischen Entsprechungen - Didaktische Möglichkeiten der Bekämpfung der Interferenz der Muttersprache -. *Deutsch als Fremdsprache* 20: 230-234.

Cuyckens, H. 1984. 'At': a Typically English Preposition. *Papers and Studies in Contrastive Linguistics* 19: 49-64.

Cuyckens, H. 1984. The Deictic vs. Non-Deictic Ambiguity in the Spatial Uses of Prepositions. *Lingvisticae Investigationes* 8: 187-194.

Cuyckens, H. 1988. Spatial Prepositions in Cognitive Semantics. In Hüllen, W. and R. Schulze (eds.). *Understanding the Lexicon: Meaning, Sense and World Knowledge in Lexical Semantics*. Tübingen: Niemeyer. 316-328.

Czepluch, H. 1981. *Syntaktische Funktionen im Englischen: Elemente einer 'Funktionalen Autonomen Syntax'*. Tübingen: Narr.

Czepluch, H. and H. Janßen (eds.). 1983. *Syntaktische Struktur und Kasusrelation*. Tübingen: Narr.

Declerck, R. 1978. An Unexpected Implication of 'Nouns and Noun Phrases' (Bach 1968). *Linguistics* 211: 11-21.

Dekeyser, X. 1988. Preposition Stranding and Relative Complementizer Deletion: Implicational Tendencies in English and the Other Germanic Languages. *Leuvense Bijdragen: Tijdschrift voor Germaanse Filologie* 77: 161-181.

Demonte, V. 1987. C-Command, Prepositions, and Predication. *Linguistic Inquiry* 18: 147-157.

Denison, D. 1985. Why Old English Had no Prepositional Passive. *English Studies* 66: 189-204.

Dill, L.B. 1986. *English Prepositions: The History of a Word Class*. Ph.D. Diss., University of Georgia.

Dirven, R. 1981. Spatial Relations in English. *Anglistik und Englischunterricht* 14: 103-132.

Donaldson, A. 1982. On Restructuring and Preposition Stranding. *Cahiers Linguistiques d'Ottawa* 10: 81-100.

Dowty, D.R. 1979. *Word Meaning and Montague Grammar: The Semantics of Verbs and Times in Generative Semantics and in Montague's PTQ*. Dordrecht: Reidel.

Döpke, W. 1985. *Kasus, Sachverhalte und Quantoren: Ein Beitrag zur formalen Semantik natürlicher Sprachen*. Tübingen: Narr.

Droop, H.G. 1977. *Das präpositionale Attribut. Grammatische Darstellung und Korpusanalyse*. Tübingen: Narr.

Dugas, A. and L. Cusson. 1985. Les Prépositions des Dénominations Complexes. *Revue Québécoise de Linguistique* 4: 159-165.

Ebneter, Th. 1984. Die Adverbien und Präpositionen des Ortes und der Richtung im Romanischen von Vaz/Obervaz. *Zeitschrift für Romanische Philologie* 100: 387-407.

Emonds, J. 1984. The Prepositional Copula 'as'. *Linguistic Analysis* 13: 127-144.

Emonds, J.E. 1985. *A Unified Theory of Syntactic Categories*. Dordrecht: Foris Publications.

Emons, R. 1974. *Valenzen englischer Prädikatsverben*. Tübingen: Niemeyer.

Engel, U. and H. Schumacher. 1976. *Kleines Valenzlexikon deutscher Verben*. Tübingen: Narr.

Erdmann, P. 1986. Die For-to-Konstruktion im Britischen (BrE) und Amerikanischen Englisch (AmE). *Arbeiten aus Anglistik und Amerikanistik* 11: 139-158.

Eroms, H.-W. 1981. *Valenz, Kasus und Präpositionen: Untersuchungen zur Syntax und Semantik präpositionaler Konstruktionen in der deutschen Gegenwartssprache*. Heidelberg: Winter.

Fehling, D. 1980. The Origins of European Syntax. *Folia Linguistica Historica* 1: 353-387.

Felix, S.W. 1972. *Syntaktische Analyse englischer verbaler Gruppen*. Ph.D. Diss., Univ. Kiel, Phil. Fak.

Féneyrol, Ch. and E. Stegentritt. 1982. Komplementanalyse und komplexe Sätze im Französischen. In Kühlwein, W. and A. Raasch (eds.). *Stil: Komponenten - Wirkungen*. Volume 2. Tübingen: Narr.

Fillmore, C.J. 1968. Lexical Entries for Verbs. *Foundations of Language* 4: 373-393.

Fillmore, C.J. 1969. Toward a Modern Theory of Case. In Reibel, D.A. and S.A. Shane (eds.). *Modern Studies in English. Readings in Transformational Grammar*. Englewood Cliffs, New Jersey: Prentice-Hall. 361-375.

Fillmore, C.J. 1969. Verbs of Judging: An Exercise in Semantic Description. *Papers in Linguistics* 1: 91-117.

Fillmore, C.J. 1971. Some Problems for Case Grammar. In O'Brien, R.J. (ed.). *Report on the Twenty-Second Annual Round Table Meeting on Linguistics and Language Studies*. Washington, D.C.: Georgetown University Press. 33-56.

Fillmore, C.J. 1982. Towards a Descriptive Framework for Spatial Deixis. In Jarvella, R.J. and W. Klein (eds.). *Speech, Place, and Action. Studies in Deixis and Related Topics*. Chichester: Wiley. 31-59.

Fillmore, C.J. 1983. Commentary on the Papers by Klein and Talmy. In Pick, H.L.,Jr. and L.P. Acredolo (eds.). *Spatial Orientation: Theory, Research, and Application*. New York/London: Plenum Press. 313-320.

Finlay, I.F. 1986. Random Thoughts on Language, 13. *Linguist* 25: 101-102.

Fischer, W. 1982. *Die englischen Präpositionen und präpositionalen Ausdrücke: Deutsch-Englische Einzelsätze und Wendungen zu deren Erlernung, Einübung und Kontrolle*. Bad Honnef: Keimer.

Flores d'Arcais, G.B. 1985. Children's Recognition of Function Words. In Hoppenbrouwers, G., P. Seuren and T. Weijters (eds.). *Meaning and the Lexicon*. Dordrecht: Foris Publications. 124-131.

Folsom, M.H. 1966. *The Syntax of Substantive and Non-Finite Satellites to the Finite Verb in German*. The Hague: Mouton.

Fraser, B. 1974. *The Verb-Particle Combination in English*. Tokyo: Taishukan Publishing Company.

Freckleton, P. 1984. Des 'That Clauses' Prépositionelles en Anglais. *Lingvisticae Investigationes* 8: 285-303.

Freeman, N.H., C.G. Sinha and J.A. Stedmon. 1981. The Allative Bias in Three-Year-Olds Is almost Proof against Task Naturalness. *Journal of Child Language* 8: 283-296.

French, M.A. 1985. Markedness and the Acquisition of Pied-Piping and Preposition Stranding. In Falk, L., K. Flikeid and M. Harry (eds.). *Papers from the Ninth Annual Meeting of the Atlantic Provinces Linguistic Association, November 8-9, 1985*.
52-64.

Friederich, W. 1973. *Probleme der Semantik und Syntax des englischen Gerundiums*. München: Hueber.

Friederich, W. and H. Nuffer. 1976. Übersetzungssystematik: Sprachtypisches als Übersetzungshilfe. *Lebende Sprachen* 21: 103-106.

Friederici, A.D. 1982. Syntactic and Semantic Processes in Aphasic Deficits: The Availability of Prepositions. *Brain and Language* 15: 249-258.

Friederici, A.D. 1983. Children's Sensitivity to Function Words During Sentence Comprehension. *Linguistics* 21: 717-739.

Friederici, A.D. 1985. Vom Umgang mit Funktionswörtern während des Spracherwerbs. *Unterrichtswissenschaften* 1: 17-29.

Fries, C.C. 1952. *The Structure of English. An Introduction to the Construction of English Sentences*. New York: Harcourt, Brace and World.

Fries, N. 1988. Deutsche Präpositionen und Präpositionalphrasen aus der Sicht der Angewandten Linguistik. *Deutsch als Fremdsprache* 25: 331-336.

Fries, N. 1988. *Präpositionen und Präpositionalphrasen im Deutschen und im Neugriechischen: Aspekte einer kontrastiven Analyse Deutsch - Neugriechisch*. Tübingen: Niemeyer.

Gallais-Hamonno, J. 1984. Le Rôle des Pré-Postpositions dans le Texte Scientifique Anglais. *Special Language/Fachsprache* 6: 140-148.

Gawron, J.M. 1986. Situations and Prepositions. *Linguistics and Philosophy* 9: 327-382.

Geis, J.E. 1970. *Some Aspects of Verb Phrase Adverbials in English*. Ph.D. Diss., University of Illinois at Urbana-Champaign.

Geis, M.L. 1987. On Situation Adverbs. *Working Papers in Linguistics* 35: 177-185.

Gerling, M. and N. Orthen. 1979. *Deutsche Zustands- und Bewegungsverben: Eine Untersuchung zu ihrer semantischen Struktur und Valenz*. Tübingen: Narr.

Glas, R. 1982. Disambiguierung deutscher Präpositionen. In Fix, H., A. Rothkegel and E. Stegentritt (eds.). *Sprachen und Computer. Festschrift zum 75. Geburtstag von Hans Eggers, 9 Juli 1982*. Dudweiler: AQ Verlag. 263-274.

Goldberg, J. 1985. A Nonsolution for a Problem of PP-Extraction. *Linguistic Inquiry* 16: 478-481.

Goodluck, H. 1986. Children's Knowledge of Prepositional Phrase Structure: An Experimental Test. *Journal of Psycholinguistic Research* 15: 177-188.

Gordon, W.T. and G.W. Patterson. 1979. Prepositional Loss in English. *Journal of English Linguistics* 13: 1-23.

Gosztonyi, A. 1976. *Der Raum: Geschichte seiner Probleme in Philosophie und Wissenschaft*. Freiburg: Alber.

Grady, M. 1970. *Syntax and Semantics of the English Verb Phrase*. The Hague: Mouton.

Gregory, St. 1981. La Préposition a(h)ier en Ancien Français. Romania: *Revue Consacrée à l'Etude des Langues et des Literatures Romanes* 102: 543-549.

Grieve, R., R. Hoogenraad and D. Murray. 1977. On the Young Child's Use of Lexis and Syntax in Understanding Locative Instructions. *Cognition* 5: 235-250.

Grimm, H.-J. 1981. Zum Artikelgebrauch in deutschen Funktionsverbgefügen mit Präpositionen. *Deutsch als Fremdsprache* 18: 333-337.

Grodzinsky, Y. 1988. Syntactic Representations in Agrammatic Aphasia: The Case of Prepositions. *Language and Speech* 31: 115-134.

Gross, M. 1976. Sur quelques Groupes Nominaux Complexes. In Chevalier, J.-C. and M. Gross (eds.). *Méthodes en Grammaire Française*. Paris: Klincksieck. 97-119.

Guillet, A. 1984. Prépositions de Lieu et Verbes Supports. *Revue Québécoise de Linguistique* 13: 59-93.

Guimier, C. 1981. Prepositions: *An Analytical Bibliography*. Amsterdam: Benjamins.

Gunnarson, K.-Å. 1982. Trois Constructions à Dépendance entre Sujet et PP. *Lingvisticae Investigationes* 6: 45-81.

Günther, H. 1974. *Das System der Verben mit be- in der deutschen Sprache der Gegenwart: Ein Beitrag zur Struktur des Lexikons der deutschen Grammatik*. Tübingen: Niemeyer.

Haan, P. de. 1988. A Corpus Investigation into the Behaviour of Prepositional Verbs. In Kyto, M., O. Ihalainen and M. Rissanen (eds.). *Corpus Linguistics, Hard and Soft*. Amsterdam: Rodopi. 121-135.

Handschack, J. 1988. 'Auftrags' - eine neue Präposition? *Sprachpflege: Zeitschrift für gutes Deutsch* 37: 84.

Hantson, A. 1983. 'For', 'with' and 'without' as Non-Finite Clause Introducers. *English Studies: A Journal of English Language and Literature* 64: 54-66.

Harleman Stewart, A. 1976. The Development of the Verb-Phrase Complement with Verbs of Physical Perception in English: Historical Linguistics as a Source of Deep Structures. *Journal of English Linguistics* 10: 34-53.

Hawkins, B.W. 1984. *The Semantics of English Spatial Prepositions*. Ph.D. Diss., University of California, San Diego.

Helbig, G. (ed.). 1977. *Beiträge zur Klassifizierung der Wortarten*. Leipzig: VEB Verlag Enzyklopädie.

Heringer, H.-J. 1968. Präpositionale Ergänzungsbestimmungen im Deutschen. *Zeitschrift für Deutsche Philologie* 87: 426-457.

Heringer, H.-J. 1985. The Verb and Its Semantic Power: Association as a Basis for Valency Theory. *Journal of Semantics* 4: 79-99.

Herrlitz, W. 1973. *Funktionsverbgefüge vom Typ 'in Erfahrung bringen': Ein Beitrag zur generativ-transformationellen Grammatik des Deutschen*. Tübingen: Niemeyer.

Herskovits, A. 1980. On the Spatial Uses of Prepositions. In Sondheimer, N.K. (pref.). *The 18th Annual Meeting of the Association for Computational Linguistics and Parasession on Topics in Interactive Discourse*. Menlo Park, CA: SRI International. 1-5.

Herskovits, A. 1981. On the Spatial Uses of Prepositions in English. *Lingvisticae Investigationes* 5: 303-327.

Herskovits, A. 1982. *Space and the Prepositions in English: Regularities and Irregularities in a Complex Domain*. Ph.D. Diss., Stanford University.

Herskovits, A. 1986. *Language and Spatial Cognition: An Interdisciplinary Study of the Prepositions in English*. Cambridge: CUP.

Herslkund, M. 1984. Particles, Prefixes and Preposition Stranding. *Nydanske Studier & Almen Kommunikationsteori* 14: 34-71.

Heuer, K. 1977. *Untersuchung zur Abgrenzung der obligatorischen und fakultativen Valenz des Verbs*. Frankfurt a.M./Bern/Las Vegas: Lang.

Heydrich, W. 1981. Einige Möglichkeiten der Repräsentation und Explikation von 'mit', 'ohne' und 'für' im Rahmen von DiSynFC. In Heydrich, W. (ed.). *Grundelemente der semantischen Struktur von Texten, V: Lexikoneinträge*. Hamburg: Buske. 115-148.

Hietaranta, P.S. 1983. Which 'for' Is It? *Neuphilologische Mitteilungen* 84: 228-232.

Hildebrand, J. 1987. The Acquisition of Preposition Stranding. *Canadian Journal of Linguistics* 32: 65-86.

Hinrichs, E.W. 1984. Attachment of Articles and Prepositions in German: Simple Cliticization or Inflected Prepositions. *Working Papers in Linguistics* 29: 127-138.

Hinrichs, E.W. 1986. Verschmelzungsformen in German: A GPSG Analysis. *Linguistics* 24: 939-955.

Hochster, A. 1976. Verbal Complements and Lexical Filtering. *Acta Linguistica Hafniensia* 16: 21-43.

Hoekstra, T. 1980. The Freezing Principle and Stranded Prepositions. In Zonneveld, W. and F. Weermann (eds.). *Linguistics in the Netherlands 1977-79*. Dordrecht: Foris Publications. 321-335.

Hornstein, N. and A. Weinberg. 1981. Case Theory and Preposition Stranding. *Linguistic Inquiry* 12: 55-91.

Huckert, E. 1978. Automatische Synthese französischer Nominalgruppen. In Conte, M.-E., A.G. Ramat and P. Ramat (eds.). *Wortstellung und Bedeutung, Akten des 12. Linguistischen Kolloquiums Pavia 1977*. Volume 1. Tübingen: Niemeyer. 269-278.

Ijaz, I.H. 1985. *Native Language and Cognitive Constraints on the Meaning Ascribed to Select English Spatial Prepositions by Advanced Adult Second Language Learners of English*. Ph.D. Diss., University of Toronto (Canada).

Ikegami, Y. 1969. *The Semological Structure of the English Verbs of Motion*. New Haven, Conn.: Ling. Automation Project, Yale U.

Ishihara, R. 1985. Absolute Phrases and Preposition Stranding. *Linguistic Analysis* 15: 129-136.

Jackendoff, R.S. 1972. *Semantic Interpretation in Generative Grammar*. Cambridge, Mass.: MIT Press.

Jaksche, H., A. Sialm and H. Burger (eds.). 1981. *Reader zur sowjetischen Phraseologie*. Berlin: de Gruyter.

Jarvella, R.J. and W. Klein (eds.). 1982. *Speech, Place, and Action: Studies in Deixis and Related Topics*. Chichester: Wiley.

Jaworska, E. 1986. Prepositional Phrases as Subjects and Objects. *Journal of Linguistics* 22: 355-374.

Jaworska, E. 1988. Intransitive Prepositions in Polish. *Papers and Studies in Contrastive Linguistics* 24: 171-182.

Jayaseelan, K.A. 1983. Prepositions as Deletion-Triggers. *Linguistic Analysis* 11: 429-437.

Jenkins, F.M. 1980. Mixing Adjectives and Prepositional Phrases in Postnominal Position. *The French Review* 53: 696-702.

Johnston, J.R. 1984. Acquisition of Locative Meanings: 'behind' and 'in front of'. *Journal of Child Language* 11: 407-422.

Jones, N. and I. Scherff. 1970. *English Phrasal Verbs*. München: Hueber.

Joos, M. 1964. *The English Verb. Form and Meanings*. Madison/Milwaukee/London: The Univ. of Wisconsin Press.

Jorgensen, E. 1975. Notes on the Group 'for + (Pro)Noun + 'to'-Infinitive'. *English Studies* 56: 129-139.

Kaluza, H. 1981. The Particle: Preposition Contrasts in English. *Kwartalnik Neofilologiczny* 28: 213-224.

Kaluza, H. 1984. English Verbs with Prepositions and Particles. *International Review of Applied Linguistics in Language Teaching* 22: 109-113.

Kayne, R.S. 1980. De Certaines Différences entre le Français et l'Anglais. *Langages* 60: 47-64.

Kayne, R.S. 1981. On Certain Differences between French and English. *Linguistic Inquiry* 12: 349-371.

Kikuo, Y. 1980. The Adverbial Accusative of Duration and Its Prepositional Equivalent: Part 1, Old and Middle English. *Hitotsubashi Journal of Arts & Sciences* 21: 1-39.

Kilby, D. 1984. *Descriptive Syntax and the English Verb*. London: Croom Helm.

Kim, I.-S. 1982. A Study of the History of English Preposition Stranding. *Language Research* 18: 59-81.

Kirsner, R.S. 1988. Prepositional versus 'Bare' Indirect Objects in the Written Dutch of Novels and Newspapers; Held at University of Michigan, Ann Arbor, 12-14 June 1986. In Broos, T.J. (ed.). *Papers from the Third Interdisciplinary Conference on Netherlandic Studies*. Lanham, MD: UP of America. 279-296.

Kjellmer, G. 1985. A Preposition Vanishes. In Backman, S. and G. Kjellmer (eds.). *Papers on Language and Literature: Presented to Alvar Ellegard and Eric Frykman*. Goteborg: ACTA Univ. Gothoburgensis. 233-244.

Klein, E. 1978. *Verbal Complement Structures in English: The Role of Syntactic and Semantic Factors in Explaining Acceptability Phenomena.* Trier: L.A.U.T.

Klein, P.W. 1984. Apparent Correspondences in Spanish to English Infinitival 'to'. *Hispania* 67: 416-419.

Koopman, H. 1984. *The Syntax of Verbs: From Verb Movement Rules in the Kru Languages to Universal Grammar.* Dordrecht: Foris Publications.

Kotschi, Th. 1981. Verbvalenz im Französischen. In Kotschi, Th. (ed.). *Beiträge zur Linguistik des Französischen.* Tübingen: Narr. 80-122.

Kraus, R. 1978. Die Präposition 'bei' in technisch-wissenschaftlichen Texten (D-E). *Lebende Sprachen* 23: 8-12.

Krzeszowski, T.P. 1986. Prototypes and Equivalence. *Papers and Studies in Contrastive Linguistics* 21: 5-20.

Kucera, H. and K. Trnka. 1975. *Time in Language: Temporal Adverbial Constructions in Czech, Russian and English.* Ann Arbor, Mich.: University of Michigan - LithoCrafters, Inc.

Kuczaj, S.A.,II, and M.P. Maratsos. 1975. On the Acquisition of 'front', 'back', and 'side'. *Child Development* 46: 202-210.

Kunsmann, P. 1973. *Verbale Gefüge: Transformationsgrammatische Untersuchungen im Deutschen und Englischen.* München: Hueber.

Kupferman, L. 1981. Le Mouvement des Groupes Prépositionnels. *Linguisticae Investigationes* 5: 39-73.

Lagace, M.F. 1987. L'Analyse Semantique de sans (que): Retour de la Présupposition? *Revue Quebecoise de Linguistique Theorique et Appliquée* 6: 169-182.

Lamiroy, B. 1981. Les Prépositions 'a' et 'para' devant l'Infinitif Complément d'un Verbe de Mouvement en Espangnol. *Lingvisticea Investigationes* 5: 75-90.

Lamiroy, B. 1983. *Les Verbes de Mouvement en Français et en Espagnol: Etude Comparée de Leurs Infinitives.* Amsterdam: Benjamins.

Lang, E. 1977. *Semantik der koordinativen Verknüpfung.* Berlin (DDR): Akademie-Verlag.

Lang, E. 1984. *The Semantics of Coordination.* Amsterdam: Benjamins.

Langendoen, D.T. 1970. *Essentials of English Grammar.* New York: Holt, Rinehart and Winston.

Langenscheidt-Redaktion. (1978) ^{8}1986. *Englische Präpositionen: Bedeutung und korrekter Gebrauch der englischen Verhältniswörter. Bearbeitet von der Langenscheidt-Redaktion.* Berlin/München/Wien/Zürich: Langenscheidt.

Larson, R.K. 1987. 'Missing Prepositions' and the Analysis of English Free Relative Clauses. *Linguistic Inquiry* 18: 239-266.

Le Flem, D.C. 1987. De + Infinitif: Preposition ou Complementiseur? *Revue Langues et Linguistique* 13: 121-145.

Leclère, Ch. 1979. Syntactic Datives and Ethic Dative. *Journal of Linguistic Calculus* 1/2: 122-147.

Lee, K.-D. 1981. The Meaning of the Preposition 'on'. *Language Research* 17: 199-214.

Leech, G. and J. Svartvik. 1975. *A Communicative Grammar of English.* London: Longman.

Leech, G.N. 1969. *Towards a Semantic Description of English.* London: Longman.

Lehmus, U. 1983. *Attribut oder Satzglied? Untersuchungen zum postnominalen Präpositonalausdruck unter einem syntaktischen, semantischen und kommunikativ-pragmatischen Aspekt.* Helsinki: Suomalainen Tiedeakatemia.

Lehrer, A. 1974. *Verb and Adverb Interaction: A Problem for Semantic Interpretation.* Trier: L.A.U.T.

Leys, O. 1989. Aspekt und Rektion räumlicher Präpositionen. *Deutsche Sprache: Zeitschrift für Theorie, Praxis, Dokumentation* 17: 97-113.

Liefrink, F. 1973. *Semantico-Syntax.* London: Longman.

Lindkvist, K.-G. 1978. Some Notes on 'at' as a Preposition of Place in English. In Ryden, M. and L.A. Bjork (eds.). *Studies in English Philology, Linguistics and Literature Presented to Alarik Rynell, 7 March 1978.* Stockholm: Almqvist & Wiksell. 102-107.

Lindner, S.J. 1981. *A Lexico-Semantic Analysis of English Verb Particle Constructions with 'out' and 'up'.* Ph.D. Diss., University of California, San Diego.

Lindner, S.J. 1983. *A Lexico-Semantic Analysis of English Verb Particle Constructions.* Trier: L.A.U.T.

Lutzeier, P.R. 1985. Sprachliche Vermittler von Räumlichkeit: Zur Syntax und Semantik lokaler Präpositionen. In Schweizer, H. (ed.). *Sprache und Raum: Psychologische und linguistische Aspekte der Aneignung und Verarbeitung von Räumlichkeit; Ein Arbeitsbuch für das Lehren von Forschung.* Stuttgart: Metzler. 90-110.

Mack, J.L. 1981. The Comprehension of Locative Prepositions in Nonfluent and Fluent Aphasia. *Brain and Language* 14: 81-92.

Mackenzie, J.L. and M. Hannay. 1982. Prepositional Predicates and Focus Constructions in a Functional Grammar of English. *Lingua* 56: 43-57.

MacRae, A.J. 1976. Movement and Location in the Acquisition of Deictic Verbs. *Journal of Child Language* 3: 191-219.

Madrid-Rey, H.L. 1987. *Learning the English Preposition System: A Pedagogical Study of an English/Spanish Contrastive Analysis.* Ph.D. Diss., D.A. State University of New York at Stony Brook.

Maling, J. 1985. Preposition-Stranding and Oblique Case. *Cornell Working Papers in Linguistics* 7: 149-161.

Maling, J. and A. Zaenen. 1985. Preposition-Stranding and Passive. *Nordic Journal of Linguistics* 8: 197-209.

Marcantonio, A. 1981. The Distribution of 'a' and 'da' in Italian Causative Constructions. *Journal of Italian Linguistics* 6: 1-33.

Mathews, W.R. 1978. *Semantic Aspects of Verbal Grammaticization.* Ph.D. Diss., University of California, San Diego.

Mazurkewich, I. 1984. The Acquisition of the Dative Alternation by Second Language Learners and Linguistic Theory. *Language Learning* 34: 91-109.

Mazurkewich, I. 1985. Syntactic Markedness and Language Acquisition. *Studies in Second Language Acquisition* 7: 15-35.

Mazurkewich, I. and L. White. 1984. The Acquisition of the Dative Alternation: Unlearning Generalizations. *Cognition* 16: 261-283.

McCloskey, J. 1986. Right Node Raising and Preposition Stranding. *Linguistic Inquiry* 17: 183-186.

McNamara, T.P. 1986. Mental Representations of Spatial Relations. *Cognitive Psychology* 18: 87-121.

Meador, H.E. 1987. *Sign Language Use of Hearing-Impaired Children Whose Home and School Sign Language Is a Manual English System*. Ph.D. Diss., University of Michigan.

Mehdi, M.F. 1981. *The Interference of Arabic in the Use of English Prepositions*. Ph.D. Diss., The University of Texas at Austin.

Mikosch, I. 1987. *Die Präpositionen in gesprochener Sprache: Vorkommen und Funktion untersucht an Tonbandaufnahmen aus Baden-Württemberg, Bayrisch-Schwaben und Vorarlberg*. Tübingen: Niemeyer.

Miller, J. 1985. *Semantics and Syntax: Parallels and Connections*. Cambridge: CUP.

Morgan, L.Z. 1987. In/A: Contrasting English and Italian Locative Preposition Usage. *Canadian Journal of Italian Studies* 10: 151-163.

Morrow, D.G. 1985. Prepositions and Verb Aspect in Narrative Understanding. *Journal of Memory and Language* 24: 390-404.

Mougeon, R., M. Bélanger, M. Canale and S. Ituen. 1977. L'Usage de la Préposition 'sur' en Franco-Ontarien. *Canadian Journal of Linguistics* 22: 95-124.

Mukattash, L. 1984. Errors Made by Arab University Students in the Use of English Prepositions. *Glottadidactica* 17: 47-64.

Mungan, G. 1986. *Die semantische Interaktion zwischen dem präfigierenden Verbzusatz und dem Simplex bei Partikel- und Präfixverben*. Frankfurt a.M.: Lang.

Napoli, D.J. and J. Nevis. 1987. Inflected Prepositions in Italian. *Phonology* 4: 195-209.

Ney, J.W. 1981. *Semantic Structures for the Syntax of Complements and Auxiliaries in English*. The Hague: de Gruyter.

Nilsen, D.L.F. 1972. *English Adverbials*. The Hague/Paris: Mouton.

Nilsen, D.L.F. and A.P. Nilsen. 1975. *Semantic Theory: A Linguistic Perspective*. Rowley, Mass.: Newbury House Publ., Inc.

O'Grady, W. 1985. Thematic Dependency and Semantic Interpretation. *Canadian Journal of Linguistics* 30: 159-177.

Ojanen, A.-L. 1985. Use and Non-Use of Prepositions in Spatial Expressions in the Dialect of Cambridgeshire. In Viereck, W. (ed.). *Focus On England and Wales*. Amsterdam: Benjamins. 179-212.

Ojeda, A.E. 1983. On Oblique Relativization in Spanish. *Papers from the Nineteenth Regional Meetings, Chicago Linguistic Society* 19: 329-337.

Palmer, F.R. 1965. *A Linguistic Study of the English Verb*. London: Longman.

Palmer, L. and B. Spolsky. 1975. *Papers on Language Testing. 1967-1974*. Washington, D.C.: Tesol Publications.

Pavesi, M. 1987. Lexical Simplification in Spatial Prepositions. *Rassegna Italiana di Linguistica Applicata* 19: 97-107.

Peronard, M. 1985. Spanish Prepositions Introducing Adverbial Constructions. *Journal of Child Language* 12: 95-108.

Persson, I. 1975. *Das System der kausativen Funktionsverbgefüge*. Lund: Gleerup.

Philipose, S.C. 1984. *A Contrastive Study of Case in English and Malayalam: Proposals for a Theory of Nuclear Case Relations*. Frankfurt a.M.: Lang.

Piaget, J. and B. Inhelder. 1971. *Die Entwicklung des räumlichen Denkens beim Kinde*. Stuttgart: Klett.

Piérart, B. and J. Costermans. 1979. A Multi-Dimensional Analysis of Some French Prepositions of Space Localization. *International Journal of Psycholinguistics* 6: 45-57.

Plann, S. 1988. Prepositions, Postpositions and Substantives. *Hispania* 71: 920-926.

Platzack, Ch. 1978. The Swedish Prepositions 'pa' and 'i' Followed by Measure Phrases. *Working Papers* 16: 105-120.

Polomska, M. 1988. A Case for 'Acquisitional Strategies': Some Methodological Observations on Investigation into Second Language Learners' Initial State. *Second Language Research* 4: 110-132.

Postal, P.M. and G.K. Pullum. 1982. The Contraction Debate. *Linguistic Inquiry* 13: 122-138.

Poutsma, H. 1926. *A Grammar of Late Modern English: For the Use of Continental, especially Dutch, Students. Part II: The Parts of Speech. Section II: The Verb and the Particles*. Groningen: Noordhoff.

Qian, Ch. 1984. The Use of WITH + Absolute Clause. *Waiguoyu* 6: 16-19.

Qvonje, J.I. 1980. Die Grammatikalisierung der Präposition 'na' im Bulgarischen. *Folia Linguistica Historica* 1: 317-351.

Rachmankulova, I.E. 1980. Zur Verbalsemantik in polysyntaktischen Satzmodellen. *Zeitschrift für Phonetik, Sprachwissenschaft und Kommunikationsforschung* 33: 179-184.

Radden, G. 1981. Die übertragenen Bedeutungen der englischen Raumpräpositionen. *Anglistik und Englischunterricht* 14: 133-179.

Radden, G. 1985. Spatial Metaphors Underlying Prepositions of Causality. In Paprotte, W. and R. Dirven (eds.). *The Ubiquity of Metaphor: Metaphor in Language and Thought*. Amsterdam: Benjamins. 177-207.

Rauh, G. 1989. Präpositionengesteuerte Metaphorik. In Habel, Ch., M. Herweg and K. Rehkämper (eds.). *Raumkonzepte in Verstehensprozessen: Interdisziplinäre Beiträge zu Sprache und Raum*. Tübingen: Niemeyer. 249-282.

Rauh, G. 1990. Präpositionen: Eine geschlossene Klasse? *Wuppertaler Arbeitspapiere zur Sprachwissenschaft* 7: 33-63.

Richards, M.M. 1976. 'Come' and 'Go' Reconsidered: Children's Use of Deictic Verbs in Contrived Situations. *Journal of Verbal Learning and Verbal Behavior* 15: 655-665.

Riemsdijk, H. van. 1984. On Pied-Piped Infinitives in German Relative Clauses. In Toman, J. (ed.). *Studies in German Grammar* 21. Dordrecht: Foris Publications. 165-192.

Riiho, T. 1980. De la Formation des Systèmes Prépositifs Romans. *Neuphilologische Mitteilungen* 81: 353-360.

Ritzke, J. 1979. Präpositionalgruppen in der automatischen Syntaxanalyse des Französischen. In Velde, M. van de and W. Vandeweghe (eds.). *Sprachstruktur, Individuum und Gesellschaft*. Tübingen: Niemeyer. 103-112.

Ritzke, J. 1981. Problèmes de l'Analyse Automatique des Prépositions du Français. In Schwarze, Ch. (ed.). *Analyse des Prépositions. IIIe Colloque Franco-Allemand de Linguistique Théorique du 2 au 4 Février 1981 á Constance*. Tübingen: Niemeyer. 139-157.

Ritzke, J. 1982. Zur automatischen Analyse adverbialer Relationen. In Fix, H., A. Rothkegel and E. Stegentritt (eds.). *Sprachen und Computer. Festschrift zum 75. Geburtstag von Hans Eggers, 9. Juli 1982*. Dudweiler: AQ-Verlag. 287-307.

Ritzke, J. 1984. 'Mit'-Phrasen als Objekte. *Deutsch als Fremdsprache* 21: 351-356.

Ritzke, J. 1984. Bestimmung und Beschreibung von französischen Temporaladverbien auf automatischem Wege. In Figge, U.L. (ed.). *Romanistik und Datenverarbeitung 1981*. Dudweiler: AQ-Verlag. 39-60.

Ritzke, J. 1985. 'Mit'-Phrasen außerhalb des Objektbereiches, ihre Antonymie- und Synonymiebeziehungen. *Deutsch als Fremdsprache* 22: 40-46.

Ritzke, J. 1986. *Die französische Präpositionalphrase und ihre automatische Analyse*. Dudweiler: AQ-Verlag.

Roegiest, E. 1982/83. 'A' et 'par' dans la Construction Factitive: L'EGLF dans la Perspective de la Linguistique Contemporaine. *Travaux de Linguistique: Publications du Service de Linguistique Française de l'Université de l'Etat à Gand* 9/10: 127-143.

Rohrer, C. (ed.). 1978. *Papers on Tense, Aspect and Verb Classification*. Tübingen: Narr.

Rosenbaum, P.S. 1967. *The Grammar of English Predicate Complement Constructions*. Cambridge, Mass.: MIT Press.

Rothkegel, A. 1973. *Feste Syntagmen: Grundlagen, Strukturbeschreibung und automatische Analyse*. Tübingen: Niemeyer.

Russell, P. 1988. Preverbs, Prepositions and Adverbs: Sigmatic and Asigmatic. *Transactions of the Philological Society* 86: 144-172.

Ryckman, T. and M. Gottfried. 1981. Some Informational Properties of Prepositions. *Lingvisticae Investigationes* 5: 169-214.

Sadzinski, R. 1983. Komposition 'Präposition + Substantiv' im Deutschen aus kontrastiver Sicht. *Zeitschrift für germanistische Linguistik* 11: 78-81.

Saile, G. 1984. *Sprache und Handlung: Eine sprachwissenschaftliche Untersuchung von Handhabe-Verben, Orts- und Richtungsadverbialen am Beispiel von Gebrauchsanweisungen*. Braunschweig: Vieweg.

Sanchez, F. 1986. 'Of'-Reduction in Black English: A Quantitative Study. In Sankoff, D. (ed.). *Diversity and Diachrony*. Amsterdam: Benjamins. 59-72.

Savary, R. 1984. *Ordre Langagier, Champ Spatial et Emplois (Figures): Prépositions, Cas et Verbes en Allemand et en Français*. Tübingen: Niemeyer.

Schaeder, B. 1985. Die Beschreibung der Präpositionen im einsprachigen deutschen Wörterbuch; Akten des Essener Kolloquiums zur Grammatik im Wörterbuch, 28.-30.6.1984. In Bergenholtz, H. and J. Mugdan (eds.). *Lexikographie und Grammatik*. Tübingen: Niemeyer. 278-307.

Schellinger, W. 1988. Zu den Präposition-Artikel-Verschmelzungen im Deutschen. *Linguistische Berichte* 115: 214-228.

Schlesinger, I.M. 1979. Cognitive Structures and Semantic Deep Structures: The Case of the Instrumental. *Journal of Linguistics* 15: 307-324.

Schooneveld, C.H. van. 1982. The Extension Feature in Russian. *International Journal of Slavic Linguistics and Poetics* 25/26: 445-457.

Schopf, A. 1979. Das präpositionale Passiv des Englischen und die neuere Linguistik. *Linguistische Berichte* 63: 56-83.

Schröder, J. 1978. Überlegungen zu zwei weiteren Untergruppen von Präpositionen im lokalen Bereich. *Deutsch als Fremdsprache* 15: 356-361.

Schröder, J. 1978. Zum Zusammenhang von Lokalität und Direktionalität bei einigen wichtigen deutschen Präpositionen. *Deutsch als Fremdsprache* 15: 9-15.

Schröder, J. 1979. Semantischer Instrumental in deutschen Präpositionalgefügen mit adverbialem Charakter. *Deutsch als Fremdsprache* 16: 321-328.

Schröder, J. 1983. Präpositionen in Kausaladverbialien. *Deutsch als Fremdsprache* 20: 78-86.

Schumacher, H. (ed.). 1976. *Untersuchungen zur Verbvalenz. Eine Dokumentation über die Arbeit an einem deutschen Valenzlexikon*. Tübingen: Narr.

Schumacher, H. 1982. Zur maschinellen Erstellung eines Valenzregisters. In Fix, H., A. Rothkegel and E. Stegentritt (eds.). *Sprachen und Computer. Festschrift zum 75. Geburtstag von Hans Eggers, 9. Juli 1982*. Dudweiler: AQ-Verlag. 129-148.

Schumacher, H. and N. Trautz. 1976. Bibliographie zur Valenz und Dependenz. In Schumacher, H. (ed.). *Untersuchungen zur Verbvalenz. Eine Dokumentation über die Arbeit an einem deutschen Valenzlexikon*. Tübingen: Narr. 314-343.

Schwarze, Ch. (ed.). 1981. *Analyse des Prépositions. IIIe Colloque Franco-Allemand de Linguistique Théorique du 2 au 4 Février 1981 á Constance*. Tübingen: Niemeyer.

Schwarze, Ch. 1981. La Pré-Position de la Préposition. In Schwarze, Ch. (ed.). *Analyse des Prépositions. IIIe Colloque Franco-Allemand de Linguistique Théorique du 2 au 4 Février 1981 á Constance*. Tübingen: Niemeyer. 215-223.

Schwarze, Ch. 1985. Die Behandlung von Präpositionen in der lexikalisch-funktionalen Grammatik. In Klenk, U. (ed.). *Kontextfreie Syntaxen und verwandte Systeme: Vorträge eines Kolloquiums in Ventron (Vogesen) im Oktober 1984*. Tübingen: Niemeyer. 1-18.

Schweisthal, K.G. (ed.). 1971. *Grammatik, Kybernetik, Kommunikation: Festschrift für Alfred Hoppe*. Bonn: Dümmler.

Schweizer, H. (ed.). 1985. *Sprache und Raum: Psychologische und linguistische Aspekte der Aneignung und Verarbeitung von Räumlichkeit; Ein Arbeitsbuch für das Lehren von Forschung*. Stuttgart: Metzler.

Sciullo, A.-M. and S. Robidoux. 1985. Vers une Théorie des Representations Lexicales. *Revue Quebecoise de Linguistique* 4: 147-157.
Seppänen, A. 1981. Two Points of English Verb Syntax. *Neuphilologische Mitteilungen* 82: 386-399.
Seppänen, A. 1984. On an Analysis of the 'For-NP-to-V' Structure. *Neuphilologische Mitteilungen* 85: 242-253.
Seppänen, A. 1987. Some Problems in the Analysis of Verb Complementation. In Kahlas-Tarkka, L. (ed.). *Neophilologica Fennica: Societé Neophilologique 100 Ans/ Neuphilologischer Verein 100 Jahre/ Modern Language Society 100 Years.* Helsinki: Soc. Neophilol.. 467-488.
Seron, X. and G. Deloche. 1981. Processing of Locatives 'in', 'on', and 'under' by Aphasic Patients: An Analysis of the Regression Hypothesis. *Brain and Language* 14: 70-80.
Seuren, P.A.M. 1973. *Predicate Raising and Dative in French and Sundry Languages.* Trier: L.A.U.T.
Seyfert, G. 1976. *Zur Theorie der Verbgrammatik.* Tübingen: Narr.
Shorr, D.N. and P.S. Dale. 1981. Prepositional Marking of Source-Goal Structure and Children's Comprehension of English Passives. *Journal of Speech and Hearing Research* 24: 179-184.
Shumaker, N.W. 1977. *A Conceptual Analysis of Spatial Location as Indicated by Certain English Prepositions.* Ph.D. Diss., University of Georgia.
Siegel, M.E.A. 1983. Problems in Preposition Stranding. *Linguistic Inquiry* 14: 184-188.
Simon-Vandenbergen, A.-M. 1980/81. The Preposition 'over' in Newspaper Headlines. *Studia Germanica Gandensia* 21: 171-184.
Slotkin, A.R. 1985. Absent 'without': Adjective, Participle, or Preposition. *American Speech* 60: 222-227.
Smith, M.B. 1988. The Semantics of Case-Assignment by Two-Way Prepositions in German: Toward an Empirically More Adequate Account; Papers from Second Symposium on Germanic Ling., University of Illinois at Urbana-Champaign, 3-4 Oct. 1986. In Antonsen, E.H. and H.H. Hock (eds.). *Germanic Linguistics, II.* Bloomington: Indiana University Ling. Club.
Sobin, N. 1981. On Adv/PP-First Reductions. *Linguistic Inquiry* 12: 488-491.
Stepanova, M.D. and G. Helbig. 1978. *Wortarten und das Problem der Valenz in der deutschen Gegenwartssprache* = Casti Reci i Problema Valentnosti v Sobremennom Nemeckom Jazyke. Leipzig: Bibliographisches Institut.
Stillings, N.A. 1975. Meaning Rules and Systems of Inference for Verbs of Transfer and Possession. *Journal of Verbal Learning and Verbal Behavior* 14: 453-470.
Svartvik, J. 1988. English Prepositions in Applied Linguistics. In Klegraf J. and D. Nehls (eds.). *Essays on the English Language and Applied Linguistics on the Occasion of Gerhard Nickel's 60th Birthday.* Heidelberg: Julius Groos. 397-406.
Sweetser, E.E. 1986. Polysemy vs. Abstraction: Mutually Exclusive or Complementary? In Nikiforidou, V., M. VanClay, M. Niepokuj and D. Feder (eds.). *Proceedings of the Twelfth Annual Meeting of the Berkeley Linguistics Society, February 15-17, 1986.* Berkeley: Berkeley Linguistics Society. 528-538.
Szlek, S. 1980. *Logisch-semantische Untersuchungen zu ausgewählten Handlungsverben im Deutschen.* Lauterburg: Kümmerle.

Takahasi, T. 1985. Die gotischen Präpositionen, Adverbien und Verbalpräfixe zur Bezeichnung von Intra-Extra-, Supra-Infra- und Ante-Post-Verhältnissen. In Heintz, G. and P. Schmitter (eds.). *Collectanea Philologica: Festschrift für Helmut Gipper zum 65. Geburtstag, I & II.* Baden-Baden: Valentin Koerner. 777-792.

Takahaski, G. 1969. Perception of Space and the Function of Certain English Prepositions. *Language Learning* 19: 217-234.

Takami, K.-I. 1988. Preposition Stranding: Arguments against Syntactic Analyses and an Alternative Functional Explanation. *Lingua* 76: 299-335.

Talmy, L. 1983. How Language Structures Space. In Pick, H.L.,Jr. and L.P. Acredolo (eds.). *Spatial Orientation: Theory, Research, and Application.* New York: Plenum Press. 225-282.

Tang, W. 1985. Grammatical Ambiguity: Syntactic Function of Prepositional Phrases. *Waiguoyu* 3: 40-43.

Tanz, C. 1980. *Studies in the Acquisition of Deictic Terms.* Cambridge: CUP.

Teigeler, P. 1972. *Satzstruktur und Lernverhalten.* Bern/Stuttgart/Wien: Huber.

Tekinay, A. 1984/85. Die Wiedergabe der deutschen Präpositionen im Türkischen. *Muttersprache* 95: 20-29.

Teubert, W. 1979. *Valenz des Substantivs: Attributive Ergänzungen und Angaben.* Düsseldorf: Schwann.

Thelin, N.B. 1983. Die Semantiko-Syntax präpositionloser Substantivverbindungen im Bulgarischen und der theoretische Status der typologischen Gegenüberstellung 'Analytisch': 'Synthetisch'. *Die Welt der Slaven: Halbjahresschrift für Slavistik* 28: 250-260.

Thiel, M. 1982. *Zur Verwendung der Kasusgrammatik im faktenorientierten 'Information Retrieval' von Textdaten.* Tübingen: Niemeyer.

Tobin, Y. 1981. Participation Systems, Prepositions and Deep Structure Case as Decoding Devices for Modern Hebrew. *Review of Applied Linguistics* 54: 45-63.

Tomasello, M. 1987. Learning to Use Prepositions: A Case Study. *Journal of Child Language* 14: 79-98.

Trost, P. 1982. Zur Bedeutung von 'über' und 'über-'. *Zeitschrift für Germanistik* 3: 156-157.

Vandeloise, C. 1984. *Description of Space in French.* Ph.D. Diss., University of California, San Diego.

Vandeloise, C. 1985. Audelà des Descriptions Géométriques et Logiques de l'Espace: Une Description Fonctionelle. *Lingvisticae Investigationes* 9: 109-129.

Vandeloise, C. 1985. Les Prépositions SUR/SOUS et la Relation Porteur/Porte. *Leuvense Bijdragen* 74: 457-481.

Vandeloise, C. 1986. L'avant/l'arriere et le devant/le derriere. *Revue Quebecoise de Linguistique* 16: 281-308.

Vanparys, J. 1984. Source Metaphors in English. *Journal of Pragmatics* 8: 395-410.

Vater, H. 1985. *Einführung in die Nominalphrasensyntax des Deutschen.* Trier: L.A.U.T.

Verkuyl, H.J. 1978. Thematic Relations and the Semantic Representations of Verbs Expressing Change. *Studies in Language* 2: 199-233.

Vidalenc, J.-L. 1984. Approche Contrastive des Prépositions Françaises et Anglaises. In Cherchi, L. (ed.). *Contrastivité en Linguistique Anglaise*. Saint-Etienne: Centre Interdisciplinaire d'Etude et de Recherches sur l'Expression Contemp.. 35-50.

Vidalenc, J.-L. 1986. Prépositions: Lexies ou cas? In Verrac, M. and M. Pagnoux (foreword). *Lexique - Grammaire: Domaine Anglais*. Saint-Etienne: Centre Interdisciplinaire d'Etude et de Recherches sur l'Expression Contemp., Univ. de Saint-Etienne. 25-39.

Vinet, M.-T. and P. Baldi. 1984. Preposition-Complementizers in French. *Papers from the XIIth Linguistic Symposium on Romance Languages*. Amsterdam: Benjamins. 105-117.

Vivès, R. 1982. Une Analyse Possible de Certains Compléments Prépositionnels. *Lingvisticae Investigationes* 6: 227-233.

Wade, T. 1983. *Prepositions in Modern Russian*. Durham: University of Durham.

Washabaugh, W. 1980. From Preposition to Complementizer in Caribbean English Creole. In Day, R.R. (ed.). *Issues in English Creoles: Papers from the 1975 Hawaii Conference*. Heidelberg: Groos. 97-109.

Watson, G. 1985. *Pronouns and Prepositional Phrases*. Ph.D. Diss., Yale University.

Weigand, E. 1980. Wortarten als grammatische Kategorien. In Tschauder, G. and E. Weigand (eds.). *Perspektive: Textintern; Akten des 14.Linguistischen Kolloquiums Bochum.* Volume 1. Tübingen: Niemeyer. 197-209.

Weissenborn, J. and W. Klein. (eds.). 1982. *Here and There: Cross-Linguistic Studies on Deixis and Demonstration*. Amsterdam: Benjamins.

Wesche, B. 1986/87. At Ease with 'at'. *Journal of Semantics: An International Journal for the Interdisciplinary Study of the Semantics of Natural Language* 5: 385-398.

Wesche, B. 1987. A Close Look at AT: Darstellung des Bedeutungsfeldes; Akten des 21. Ling. Kolloquiums, Groningen 1986. In Abraham, W. and R. Århammer (eds.). *Linguistik in Deutschland*. Tübingen: Niemeyer. 119-133.

Wollmann, A. 1985. Der Ausdruck der Zeit durch Präpositionalphrasen und Tempus. *Anglistik und Englischunterricht* 27: 137-155.

Wood, F.T. 1970. *English Prepositional Idioms*. London: Macmillan.

Wunderlich, D. 1982. Sprache und Raum. - 2. Teil - *Studium Linguistik* 13: 37-59.

Wunderlich, D. 1982. Sprache und Raum. *Studium Linguistik* 12: 1-19.

Wunderlich, D. 1984. Zur Syntax der Präpositionalphrasen im Deutschen. *Zeitschrift für Sprachwissenschaft* 3: 65-99.

Wunderlich, D. 1985. Raum, Zeit und das Lexikon. In Schweizer, H. (ed.). *Sprache und Raum: Psychologische und linguistische Aspekte der Aneignung und Verarbeitung von Räumlichkeit; Ein Arbeitsbuch für das Lehren von Forschung*. Stuttgart: Metzler. 66-90.

Wunderlich, D. 1985. Raumkonzepte: Zur Semantik der lokalen Präpositionen. In Ballmer, T.T. and R. Posner (eds.). *Nach-Chomskysche Linguistik: Neuere Arbeiten von Berliner Linguisten*. Berlin: de Gruyter. 340-351.

Wunderlich, D. 1985. Über die Argumente des Verbs. *Linguistische Berichte* 97: 183-227.

Yamakawa, K. 1982. The Adverbial Accusative of Duration and Its Prepositional Equivalent, II: Early Modern English. *Hitotsubashi Journal of Arts & Sciences* 23: 1-52.

Zwicky, A.M. 1987. French Prepositions: No Peeking. *Phonology* 4: 211-227.

Together - a preposition?

Colin Foskett
(Wuppertal)

0. Introduction

In this study I investigate the claim that *together* is not an adverb but a preposition, more precisely an intransitive preposition. Section one outlines traditional and more recent approaches to the problem of classification into word classes and to the defining characteristics of adverbs and prepositions. In sections two, three and four I adopt the X-bar framework and apply it to a selection of the 300 occurrences of *together* in the LOB corpus. Section two considers *together* as a VP adjunct, and section three examines the claim that *together* can occupy the PP position of verb complement and NP adjunct. In section four I discuss the internal structure of a phrasal category headed by *together*, in particular the possible specifiers of such a phrase. In the final section some conclusions are drawn about the syntactic category of *together* and the relationship between adverbs and PPs.

Since this study is a synchronic one, the introduction is an appropriate place to make a few necessary remarks on the history of the word *together*. Like a considerable number of prepositions, adverbs and conjunctions (e.g. *abroad*, *away*, *because*, *before*, *downstairs*, *towards* etc.) *together* is historically complex, consisting of an unstressed preposition or adverb prefixed to another word, typically a noun. In the case of *together* the first element is the Modern English preposition *to* and the second an obsolete noun (OE *gædere*) meaning "fellowship". The absence of a determiner is a common feature of such complex forms (cf. *downstairs*, *in place of*, *instead of*). Thus, diachronically *together* is a prepositional phrase, which is a historical explanation for the absence of a complement position. The original local meaning of *together* is reflected in the common dictionary definition ("into one company, into one gathering") and it is the local meaning that predominates in Modern English. The LOB corpus contains very few examples where *together* is purely temporal (e.g. The whole congregation will say together in sincerity...).

Since one of the typical functions of prepositional phrases is as an adverbial, in modern grammatical terminology as a VP adjunct, it is not difficult to see how *together* should be classified as an adverb, especially once its internal PP structure was obscured by the loss of the noun that it historically contains.

1.1. Categories

The word *together* is generally classified as an adverb in grammars and dictionaries. This is the word-class given in the OED and by Quirk et al. (1985), who call *together* a prepositional-adverb, which is one of their three groups of so-called particles. However, as has often been pointed out, the traditional class of adverbs in English is heterogeneous and ill-defined, with many of its members "adverbs by default" rather than on the basis of positive evidence. In the classical tradition of the theory of the "parts of speech", adverbs are typically characterized negatively, as forms that neither conjugate nor decline, and the functional criterion that an adverb modifies a verb, adjective or adverb is a very general one, grouping together a disparate class of items that are by no means distributionally equivalent. The traditional classification into parts of speech is described in Robins (1966), Lyons (1966) and Huddleston (1984). In this approach syntax plays a subsidiary role in the classification of the major parts of speech (traditionally the open-class elements verb, noun, adjective and adverb), but in modern grammatical theory the role of syntax is central, and this is reflected by the replacement of the term part of speech, word class or form class by syntactic category. In as far as they have dealt with adverbs at all, recent studies have tended to concentrate on the more "central" adverbs of manner (the -ly adverbs), where the morphological parallel to semantically equivalent adjectives supports the view that adverbs are verbal modifiers and can be viewed as positional variants of adjectives, which are nominal modifiers (see e.g. Emonds (1976:152)).

Prepositions are traditionally defined as words that govern a noun or pronoun and indicate a relation between this and another word, which can be a verb, an adjective or another noun (see e.g. Curme (1935:87)). Clearly, *to-*

gether does not satisfy this condition, as it can never be followed by a noun which it governs. However, recent work within the framework of X-bar syntax has led to a new evaluation of the category preposition. It is no longer regarded as a closed class, but is seen as a major category alongside the categories verb, noun and adjective/adverb. It has been shown that these four word-level categories can each be analysed as consisting of a combination of the syntactic features [± N] and [± V] in a way that enables important generalisations to be made. Following this approach, it has been claimed (e.g. by Emonds (1976:172-6) and Jackendoff (1977:78-9)) that *together*, *away*, *across* etc. are all prepositions, and that *together* and *away* are intransitive prepositions. There are good reasons for distinguishing a subclass of intransitive prepositions, as can be seen from the following examples:

(1) John walked across the road.

(2) John walked across.

(3) John walked away.

In traditional grammar *across* is a preposition in (1) but an adverb in (2), and *away* is an adverb in (3). Recognizing the problem of classification, some linguists (e.g. Bolinger 1971, Quirk et al. 1985) talk of prepositional-adverbs in sentences like (2). This label indicates that there is a close relationship between some members of the traditional preposition and adverb classes (Bolinger even has a further class of so-called "adpreps"), a relationship that reflects the adverbial origin of many prepositions as well as the adverbial function of PPs (see 1.2.). Including *across*, *away*, *together* etc. among the class of prepositions rather than the adverb class neatly solves the problem with *across* and reinforces the parallels between prepositions and verbs. These two categories share the feature [- N] and both may have NP complements to which they assign case. Verbs are subcategorized according to their complement structures, and the same subclassification can be applied to prepositions, giving an exact parallel between (1)-(3) above and (4)-(6) below:[1]

---

1 The notion of prepositions without a complement was put forward long ago by Jespersen (Jespersen (1924:87-8)), who drew exactly the same parallel with verbs and used the term particle to avoid making the traditional distinction between adverbs, prepositions and conjunctions.

(4) John is eating an apple.

(5) John is eating.

(6) John is sleeping.

There are, of course, compelling morphological and syntactic reasons for regarding transitive and intransitive verbs as members of the same category (inflexion, concord, co-ordination, word order, uses of the same verb in intransitive/ergative or middle/transitive patterns etc.) whereas in the case of transitive and intransitive prepositions the arguments must be of a different kind (see Emonds (1972) and (1985) for a summmary).

One consequence of enlarging the class of prepositions by including such words as *away*, *back*, *downstairs*, *forwards*, *indoors*, *together* is that the heterogeneity of the adverb class is reduced by a number of "single word adverbs" which are untypical members of the adverb class in various ways (e.g. in not allowing a typical adverbial specifier such as *so* or *very*). The class of prepositions, on the other hand, is brought more into line with the other major categories, for example in that there are now cases where the head of the phrase can stand alone. The class of prepositions now consists of three subclasses, to which Emonds (1985:254) gives the subcategorization features:

+ __ NP	(e.g. *at*, *of*, *for*, *with*)
+ __ (NP)	(e.g. *across*, *down*, *in*, *over*, *up*)
+ __	(e.g. *apart*, *ahead*, *away*, *together*)

From these few examples it seems that the first group contains established or "central" prepositions (typical members of the traditional class). These occur with the so-called prepositional verbs (*look at*, *search for* etc.) but tend not to enter into phrasal verb/verb particle constructions, and the claim that prepositions are the syntactic heads of their PPs (but, by implication are lacking in semantic content) applies particularly to this class. The second group contains prepositions with a syntactically optional complement, and the members of this group figure significantly in phrasal verbs, where many of them show a tendency to develop idiomatic meanings (*to run s.th. down*, *to take s.o. in*). The third group also contains forms which may occur in phrasal verbs, but these tend not to have idiomatic meaning; this is the case, for example, with *together*. The members of this group cannot be followed directly by an NP, an intervening preposition from the first group must occur, as in *ahead of his rivals*, *apart from her*, *away from his friends*, *together with this evidence*. Members of the second and third groups share some features, in particular, they may be followed by the sequence P + NP. The structure of the resulting larger PP (e.g. *down to the bottom*, *across to the other side*, *away from his friends*, *ahead of his rivals*) is not the same in all cases. A classification into types will be attempted in 1.2.

1.2. Functions and positions

(a) Functions

The terms adverb, preposition, adverbial phrase (ADVP), and prepositional phrase (PP) denote categories. These categories can be described or defined in terms of features (± N ± V) for word level categories or in terms of their structure (e.g. PPs have a preposition as their head and allow certain categories as specifier, adjunct or complement). However, prepositions and adverbs (or PPs and ADVPs) also have functions, typical functions, within the sentence, and here there is considerable overlap, since both are prototypically adjuncts. Traditional grammar recognized the functional overlap between adverbs and prepositional phrases by according to the latter adverbial function and distinguishing different adverbial classes such as time, place, manner, degree etc. The following shows the most important of these traditional adverbial functions and examples of syntactic realizations:

TYPE OF ADVERBIAL	Adverb Phrase	Prepositional Phrase	Noun
TIME	immediately	at two o'clock	this morning
PLACE	locally	in London	
DEGREE	sufficiently	to a sufficient extent	
MANNER	quietly	in a low voice	
MEANS	orally	through the mouth	
FREQUENCY	often	at frequent intervals	
DURATION	long	for a long time	
VIEWPOINT	frankly	in my opinion	
MODAL	perhaps		
CONNECTIVE	moreover	in addition	
REASON		because of this	

It is clear from the above that many of these traditional adverbial functions can be realized syntactically either by an adverb (or adverbial phrase) or by a prepositional phrase. As will be seen in section 5, a classification of this kind is necessary to explain coordination facts.

(b) Positions

In X-bar syntax, with its criterion of endocentricity, it is the category that is important, not the function. A PP position will be filled by a prepositional phrase, (which may just consist of an intransitive preposition) and an ADVP by an adverbial phrase (which may just consist of an adverb). There may, of course, be overlap in some cases (e.g. as a VP adjunct).

Given the conventions of X-bar syntax and the structure that is assumed to underlie all sentences, namely a structure of the following kind:

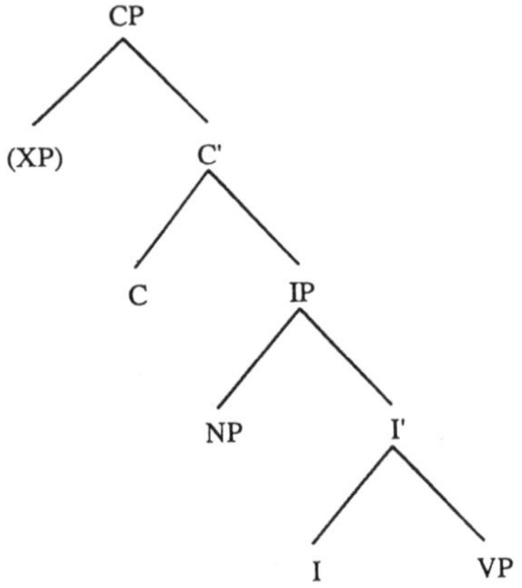

The [+N -V] and [-N +V] categories (noun and verb respectively) will occur as the heads of the subject NP and the VP. Further NP or VP positions may be generated within the NP subject or the VP. PP and ADVP positions will be generated lower down in the structure (within NPs or VPs), prototypically as adjuncts, but also as complements of appropriate head nouns or verbs.

Before considering whether *together* can fill PP or ADVP positions I shall first outline these positions and the possible structure of PPs and ADVPs. The possible positions for PPs are:

a complement of a verb	e.g. John went *to the cinema.*
a complement of a noun	e.g. the defeat *of the army*
a complement of an adjective	e.g. full *of water*
a complement of an adverb	e.g. independently *of us*
an adjunct in a VP	John arrived *after the match.*
an adjunct in a NP	the house *across the road*
an adjunct in an AP	strange *in some way*
a predicate	John is *in London*

PPs also occur within PPs (see the examples given above in 1.1.), and here there are at least two structures to be distinguished. In *Mary crawled from under the bed* the preposition *from* clearly has as its complement a PP. However, a different structure must be assumed if the first preposition is one of the second or third group. In *John was down in the cellar* it is the second preposition (*in*) that heads the PP complement of *be*, and *down* is probably a specifier, as Radford (Radford (1988:252-3)) claims. More problematic are cases involving a verb of motion, as in *John went down into the cellar*. Here, too, it is the second preposition (*into*) that is the head of the PP complement, but an analysis in which *down* is a specifier or adjunct within this PP makes wrong predictions about preposing. *Down John went into the cellar* is a perfectly natural sentence, yet the A-over-A Principle prohibits this if *down* is a preposition within the PP complement. And *down* does have prepositional rather than adverbial characteristics in this sentence, since it not only allows the prepositional specifier *right* (and not the adverbial specifier *so*), but can also have a complement - *John went down the stairs into the cellar*. This complement expresses PATH whereas the PP *into the cellar* contains the GOAL, which suggests that verbs of motion like *go* should be subcategorized for one or for two PPs as follows:

$$\begin{Bmatrix} \text{PATH} \\ \text{GOAL} \\ \text{PATH + GOAL} \end{Bmatrix}$$

This would allow *down* (or *down the stairs*) to be preposed. Examples of a rather different kind involving *together* will be encountered in 3.1.

For ADVPs the possible positions are:

a complement of a verb John treated Mary *badly*.

(There are very few verbs that are subcategorized for an ADVP complement.)

an adjunct in a VP John disappeared *quickly.*

There are various possible positions for an ADVP which is an adjunct within VP. These will be discussed in 2.

an adjunct in an AP	*completely* full of water
an adjunct in a PP	*completely* off the ground
an adjunct in an ADVP	*completely* independently of us

As the above outline of PP and ADVP positions indicates, it is as a VP adjunct that there is an obvious overlap, both in position and in function. Elsewhere these two phrasal categories occupy different positions in that PPs as adjuncts generally follow their heads, whereas ADVP adjuncts precede them.

The internal structure of PPs and ADVPs can be represented as follows:

SPECIFIER	HEAD	COMPLEMENT	ADJUNCT
right		NP	
NP		PP	
AP	preposition	(AP)	PP
ADVP		(ADVP)	
PP?		Ø	
very, quite, so etc.	adverb	PP	

In the following sections I shall use examples from the LOB corpus to test:

(a) whether *together* can occupy the PP or ADVP positions in structure of the kind given above (sections 2 and 3) and

(b) whether a phrasal category with *together* as its head has the characteristics of a PP or of an ADVP (section 4). This question reduces largely to a consideration of possible specifiers for *together*.

2. *Together* as a VP adjunct

The examples given in 1.2. of the traditional classes of adverbials show that many of them can be represented by an ADVP or by a PP. However, in most cases there is usually a prototypical category; thus for manner adverbials it is an ADVP (frequently a -ly form), whereas for place adverbials it is typically a PP. There are very few place adverbs apart from the proforms *here*, *there*, *where*, *anywhere* etc.

One important difference between ADVPs and PPs as VP adjuncts concerns their possible positions. As Jackendoff (Jackendoff (1977:73-5)) shows, there are, apart from initial position, which is not a base-generated one, four ADVP positions as against only one PP position. Jackendoff gives these four positions as:

1. at the end of the VP	Bill dropped the bananas quickly
2. at the beginning of the VP	Bill quickly dropped the bananas
3. before the ASPECT	John will completely have finished
4. before a PP complement	John gave the beans quickly to Bill

Since all these positions share the same semantic function, Jackendoff suggests that an ADVP is "transportable" and can appear in any position where it is a daughter of "V" (in his 3-bar analysis, see Jackendoff (1977:74)). This solution will handle the first three positions but not the fourth, for which Jackendoff suggests a rule of raising or lowering.

There are, however, restrictions on the kind of ADVP that can occur in these positions. Considering only the six traditional adverbial classes T(ime), P(lace), D(egree), M(anner), ME(ans), and F(requency), the following pattern emerges:

position 1	T	P	D	M	ME	F
position 2	T			M		F
position 3				M		F
position 4				M		

This distribution shows clearly why it is the manner adverbs that are frequently considered the prototypical or "central" members of the class. Apart from the fact that they are in the main derived from adjectives, they are the ones that occur in all four ADVP positions.

As pointed out in section 1.2., it is not only ADVPs that can function as adverbials, but also some NPs (time adverbial) and PPs. The NPs occur in position 1, and also in position 2, but by no means freely here - this stylistically marked position being typical of media reporting. Adverbial NPs are not found in positions 3 or 4. PPs, as Jackendoff observes, are restricted to postverbal position (position 1).

An important question concerning *together* as a VP adjunct is therefore its position(s). If it occurs only in position 1, then it behaves like a PP, but an ability to stand in the other positions would make it more like an ADVP. Despite its historically local meaning, *together* does not fit into any of the traditional adverbial classes, and thus no predictions can be made about possible positions, based on the pattern given above. The corpus contains a large number of examples where *together* is a VP adjunct and can or does appear in various positions in the sentence:

(7) __ the two children __ (2) walked together (4) across green fields __ (1)

(8) __ he and Maria had together (2) sat __ (4) on the little pebbly beach __ (1)

(9) so that __ they may together (2) receive __ the grace of God __ (1)

As shown in (7)-(9) above, *together* as a VP adjunct can occupy various positions, including the ADVP positions 1, 2 and 4, and can even stand between a verb and its complement, as in (9). This mobility of *together*, which is on the whole not shared by the other intransitive prepositions, shows that it has strong affinities with the adverb class.

3.1. *Together* as a PP verb complement

It has been pointed out, in particular by Emonds (e.g. Emonds (1985:257)) that words like *together*, *away* etc. can occupy the PP position of verbs that are subcategorized for a following NP and PP. These verbs exemplify the "scheme of motion" or the "scheme of rest" (Rauh (1988)) and semantically they involve an AFFECTED OBJECT together with a LOCATION ("scheme of rest") or one of the relations SOURCE, PATH and GOAL ("scheme of motion"). A typical verb is *put*, and Emonds (1985:257) gives the example:

(10) John put some toys in the garage /downstairs /away /down /together /back /out etc.

If downstairs /away /down /together /back /out etc. are classified as intransitive prepositions, and thus as heads of PPs, subcategorization facts about verbs like *put* will be easier to state.

However, there are a number of important differences between the structures verb + NP + PP and verb + NP + P. One of them is the much discussed feature of phrasal verbs, namely that an intransitive preposition can precede the NP complement but a "full PP" cannot:

(11) John put away /down /back /out some toys.

(12) *John put in the garage some toys.

Sentence (12) is only possible with "Heavy NP Shift".

Independent principles require that a NP complement should precede a PP complement, and in order to account for sentences like (11), Emonds suggests a minor movement rule of Particle Movement (see Emonds (1985:255)) that moves an intransitive preposition to the left of a NP complement. His formulation of the rule:

V - NP - $[P]_{PP}$ 1 - 3 - 2

involves taking account of the internal structure of the PP, and there is a further restriction in that the NP complement of the verb may not be a pronoun. Emonds claims that the presence of a specifier in the PP will also block Particle Movement, and gives examples to confirm this. However, it is not difficult to find counterexamples to this claim:

(13) She dragged right in the two heavy boxes of chemicals.

(14) We cannot set totally aside a whole system of rules devised by Congress.

(both examples from Quirk et al. (1985:1395))

Presumably one could argue that these examples show "Heavy NP Shift" rather than Particle Movement, and certainly (14) does contain a "heavy" NP complement. However, it is unsatisfactory to have two different movement rules applying to what is basically the same structure leading to the same result, and it seems that an approach based purely on syntax cannot give a completely satisfactory answer. The order NP PP is more natural than the order PP NP given equal conditions (i.e. two pronouns or two NPs of similar internal structure), and semantically too an AFFECTED OBJECT is more closely associated with the verb than a SOURCE, PATH or GOAL. However, factors such as complexity or length, and less clearly definable pragmatic ones such as information value may lead to final position for one of the constituents irrespective of its syntactic status (cf. the notions of "end-focus" and "end-weight" in Quirk (1985) and Bolinger's concept of "semantic spreading" (Bolinger (1971:ch.4))).

I have so far excluded *downstairs* and *together* from the discussion because they bring additional problems. ?*John put downstairs some toys* is unusual and seems to require a "Heavy NP" complement. (Some confirmation of this is provided by Cowie/Mackin (1975), whose entry for e.g. *kick downstairs* is given the pattern *B1*, meaning that a "short object" must precede the particle). *Together* also shows a marked preference for post-NP complement position (see the discussion of the LOB examples for confirmation), although there are some perfectly acceptable examples where *together* is followed by a "non-Heavy" NP complement, such as *He put together a convincing case*. It seems likely that *downstairs* is excluded from pre-NP position because it is still recognizably a PP, consisting of a preposition and a noun, rather than the bare preposition required by Emonds' rule. The preference that *together* shows for the post-NP position in such structures is probably similarly due to its historical status as a preposition plus noun.

Although the discussion so far has tended to support the view that the PP complement position of a verb like *put* can be filled by an intransitive preposition such as *together*, there is a complication in that both an intransitive preposition and a "full PP" can occur in the same sentence:

(15) John put some toys { away / back / down / downstairs / together } in the garage.

There is some evidence that it is the intransitive preposition that occupies the PP complement position in (15) and that *in the garage* is an adjunct. It must follow (and cannot precede) the intransitive preposition, and a time adjunct can intervene between the two: *John put some toys away yesterday in the garage*. Furthermore, the preposition *into* (which can be the head of a complement PP after *put* but cannot head a prepositional place adjunct) is not possible in this position:

(16) *John put the envelope away into his pocket.

It can be concluded from this that *away* in (16) occupies the PP complement position and that a further PP can only be an adjunct within this PP.

The LOB corpus contains over 30 examples in which *together* occupies the PP complement position of a verb which is subcategorized for an NP and a PP complement. The verbs represented in the corpus are the following:

add, bind, bring, connect, fasten, gather, glue, hold, join, keep, link, nail, put, press, screw, sew, rivet, weld

Typical examples from the corpus are:

(17) The women sewed skins together for clothing.

(18) Gently press cut edges together.

(19) by bringing together both sides of the motor industry

Just as in the examples with *put* above (e.g. (15)), *together* fills the PP position of the [NP PP] frame, and a following PP can only be an adjunct. Thus in (19) *together* can be replaced by a phrase such *to the negotiating table* (*by bringing both sides of the motor industry to the negotiating table*) but both may not occur (**by bringing both sides of the motor industry together to the negotiating table*). The second PP can only be an adjunct as in:

(20) by bringing both sides of the motor industry together at the negotiating table

(21) by bringing both sides of the motor industry to the negotiating table together

In (21) *together* is an adjunct with a temporal meaning.

The examples in the corpus show a clear two-to-one preference for the NP PP order seen in (17) and (18), and (19) is typical of the smaller group in that it could be said to show a "Heavy NP" complement. This supports the claim made earlier that *together* tends to follow the NP complement in such structures.

Semantically the verbs in this group all involve an AFFECTED OBJECT being brought into contact with something (a kind of GOAL). As a result, the transitive prepositions that head a PP complement tend to be one of a small set implying contact (e.g. *against*, *on*, *with*, as in *he pressed his nose against the glass*, *she sewed the button on the coat*). When the PP position is filled by *together*, the NP complement is notionally plural, consisting either of a grammatically plural NP, as in the examples above, or of a notionally plural one, as in *She sewed the jacket together*, *Pull yourself together*. There is no longer an AFFECTED OBJECT and a GOAL, but instead two or more entities (at least notionally), of equal syntactic status. Thus one consequence of the occurrence of *together* in such structures is that two (or more) NP arguments are collapsed into one. As a conclusion it can be stated that *together* can fill a PP verb complement position of appropriate verbs and refers to a "final position or state", and here there are strong similarities with those adjectives which can function as the particles of phrasal verbs - *push the door open*, *pull the rope tight*.

3.2. *Together* as an NP adjunct

As outlined in 1.2., one of the functions of a PP is that of a nominal modifier within an NP. PPs occur as postnominal adjuncts in phrases like *a man of honour*, *a book on syntax*, *a present for John*, *the house across the road* etc. A postnominal PP that refers to place or time (such as *on the table*, *after lunch*) may be a nominal or verbal adjunct (or even a verb complement) depending on the verb in question:

Have you read the book on the table?	(NP adjunct)
He saw a book on the table.	(VP adjunct)
The speech after dinner was too long.	(NP adjunct)
He gave a speech after dinner.	(VP adjunct)

Preposing is a test that will reliably distinguish PP adjuncts within a VP from those within an NP, since the latter are not preposable.

Postposition is usual for PP adjuncts within an NP, although there are PPs that can stand in prenominal position - *an out of work teacher*, *an off the cuff remark*, *an out of the way place*, *an after dinner speech*. Such expressions are PPs formally, but their position and function is that of an adjective and they may exhibit adjectival features, e.g. gradability, as in *a very out of the way place*.

"Central" adverbs do not occur as postnominal modifiers at all, and thus if *together* can be shown to be a postnominal modifier, this will support the analysis as a preposition. However, some grammars (e.g. Quirk et al. (1985)) classify elements such as *ahead*, *back*, *downstairs*, *above*, *below*, *yesterday* in postnominal position as adverbs. Examples are:

the meal afterwards
the way ahead
the road back to the town
the people behind (us)

(Quirk et al. (1985:895))

As already pointed out, this position is not at all typical of adverbs, and it is more natural to classify these elements as (transitive or intransitive) prepositions (cf. especially the last example with the optional complement). Just like the postnominal "full NP's", these are adjuncts of place or time, and as with the earlier examples, it is possible here too to find a verb that naturally fits the context and can be added, leading to a VP adjunct/complement analysis:

the meal they had afterwards	(adjunct)
the way that lies ahead	(complement)
the road that leads back to the town	(complement?)
the people that were behind (us)	(complement)

The adjectival affinities commented on earlier are apparent here too in the case of *above*, where prenominal position is also possible - *the quotation above, the above quotation* - but only if *above* has no complement - **The above the diagram quotation.*

There are a number of examples in the corpus where *together* has the status of an adjunct within NP:

(22) they would have time to make a proper start to their life together

(23) that he and Angelina would have plenty of time together in the future

(24) when he calls for her before an evening out together

(24) when he calls for her before an evening out together

(25) I didn't want to spoil your last tender moments together

(24) shows stacking of two postnominal adjuncts.

There are further examples which at first sight may seem similar, but where the existence of alternative positions for *together* suggests that it is an ADVP and an adjunct within a VP. Typical cases are:

(26) we went for a last walk together

(27) where she and John spent their happiest hours together

(28) you can go and have a drink together afterwards

In (26) *together* can stand initially or between *went* and *for*, and is thus a VP adjunct of the kind discussed in 2. The introduction of a semantically empty verb here allows *walk* to appear as a noun and thus be modified by the adjective *last*. (27) and (28) are similar cases, and the alternative word order in (28), namely *have a drink afterwards together*, is a clear indication that *together* is a VP adjunct, just like *afterwards*. Although as they stand (26)-(28) must be viewed as containing a VP adjunct, they can easily be converted into sentences where this is no longer possible without invoking a process of ellipsis:

(26a) I was thinking of our last walk together

(27a) Their happiest hours together were over

(28a) He suggested a drink together

and (23)-(25) are readily converted into the VP adjunct type by the addition of the verb *spend*. In fact, there is a range of "activity" nouns or nouns denoting a period of time that all behave in this way:

(have) a meal together	eat/dine together
(have) a drink together	drink together
(have) a game together	play together
(have) a dance together	dance together
(have/spend) time together	

Thus, although *together* occurs as a postnominal NP adjunct, it does so only with certain head nouns, namely those that denote activities or refer to a period of time. However, it was noted at the beginning of this section that there is often a relationship between PP adjuncts within a NP and the same PP adjuncts within a VP. It is only the prepositions of group one (as in *a man of honour*, *a present for John*) that do not exhibit this relationship.

Two further cases in which *together* functions as an NP adjunct are documented in the corpus. First, there are a number of examples of coordinated NPs followed by *together* in the meaning "considered together, considered as a whole". (In dictionaries this is usually given as a separate meaning in the entry for *together*):

(29) no man and wife together were to pay more than 20 shillings

(30) the area of the box and spilt sand together should not exceed 50 per cent

Here too there are related structures in which *together* is a VP adjunct, and the verb that must be supplied (in the passive) is *consider* or *take*. Sentences in which such a verb is actually present also occur in the corpus:

(31) the house and layout taken together

Although the position of *together* in sentences like (29) and (30) is clearly that of an NP adjunct, these examples are unlike typical NP adjuncts in not being equivalent in function to defining relative clauses (e.g. to *no man and wife who are together*). Such examples correspond rather to adverbial clauses of condition (*no man and wife if/when/as long as they are considered together*)). This illustrates a further link between the category PP and traditional adverbial function.

Finally, it is possible for *together* to occur postnominally in so-called "small clauses" after certain verbs and to modify the subject of these clauses:

(32) I suppose them in the car together

Without going into the controversial issues of the status of small clauses and their appropriate analysis (cf. Stowell (1981) and Chomsky (1986:16), it seems plausible that *them in the car together* in (32) is a clause of some kind, parallel to the equivalent clauses *that they are in the car together/them to be in the car together*, and that *them* is the subject of this small clause. Since, however, there is no verb and thus no VP, these PPs (as I assume them both to be) must be either nominal modifiers (cf. Chomsky's adjunction-to-subject analysis of small clauses) or, following Stowell, the heads of the small clauses.

4.1. The structure of phrases headed by *together*

The internal structure of ADVPs and PPs was outlined at the end of section 1. Since *together* lacks a complement position, this section will be concerned primarily with the specifier position. Despite more recent claims by Fukui (1986) and Bierwisch (1988) that PPs lack a specifier position, I here follow Jackendoff (1973) and Riemsdijk (1978:45-8), in assuming that the category PP does have a specifier position, which can be filled by a number of phrasal categories. Riemsdijk's rule for the "Specifier of P'" (as he calls it) is:

$$Spec_{P'} \longrightarrow \{N''', A''', P''', M\}$$

(M consists of elements such as *right*, *only*, *even*, *still*. NPs in the specifier position are typically measure phrases, APs as specifier have words such as *close*, *far* etc. as their heads, and the PPs that occur as specifier are *up*, *down* etc.). In more recent literature (e.g. Emonds (1985:257-8)) *right* is taken as the typical specifier within PPs containing a local or temporal preposition.

ADVPs, however, are like APs in allowing as specifier a determiner such as *very*, *so*, *too*, *rather*, *quite*. The range of ADVP specifiers shows that "central" adverbs tend to be like some adjectives in being gradable. Jackendoff (1977:146) extends the list of specifiers, adding *as*, *this*, *that*, *how*.

Support for the view that *together* is a preposition comes from the fact that in some cases at least it may be preceded by *right*:

(33) Put your feet right together!

Since **very together* is impossible, *together* cannot be a "central" adverb, if it is an adverb at all.

The LOB corpus does not contain any examples where *together* is preceded by *right*, but there are a number of cases of *close together* or *closely together*, and these examples will be discussed and an attempt made to characterize their structure. Before doing so, however, I shall briefly consider *close* as a potential specifier of a PP headed by *to*.

Specifier status for *close* within a PP is claimed by Riemsdijk (1978:46). He gives no examples, but what he says would presumably apply to sentences like the following:

(34) The men stood close to the window.

Assuming that the phrasal category is the double bar level, the PP in this sentence would have the following structure:

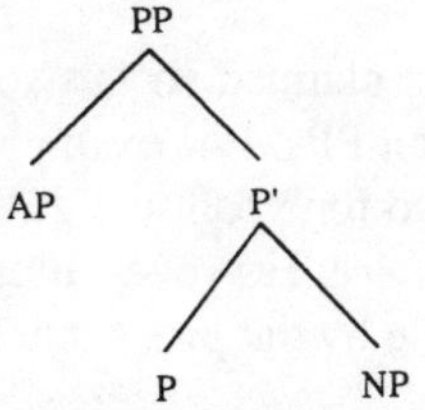

However, this analysis is problematic; firstly, in that specifiers tend to be optional, and secondly in the light of the common assumption that *there* is a pro P'. Since *the men stood there* is grammatical but *_the men stood close there_ is not, *close* should be within P' and *to the window* should not be a P' in this sentence. One way to satisfy these conditions is to analyse *close to* as a P constituent (a complex preposition). Some support for this comes from distributional evidence - *to* is not in contrast with any other preposition (except perhaps *by*) but *close to* is distributionally equivalent to a range of prepositions. The structure below makes correct predictions about *there*-replacement:

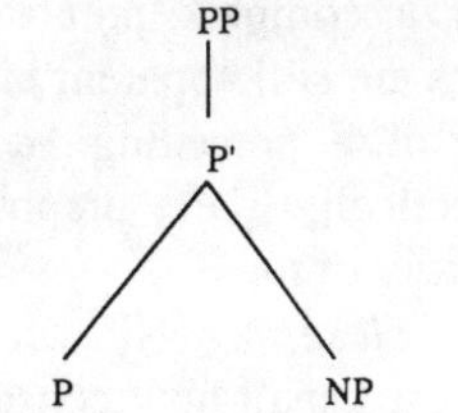

Although it is here analysed as part of a complex preposition, *close* has characteristics of an AP, in particular it can be preceded by the specifier *very*.

There is some further support for the analysis above from the behaviour of *near*, which is semantically equivalent to *close*. *Near* occurs in sentences like (35) and (36), with or without a following *to*:

(35) The men stood near to the window.

(36) The men stood near the window.

Such (more or less) free variation is exhibited by a few other prepositions - *alongside* (*of*), *opposite* (*to*), *outside* (*of*). In (35) *near* is traditionally an adverb, but in (36) it is a preposition. Here it combines prepositional and adjectival/adverbial properties in that it has an NP complement yet at the same time can be preceded by *very*.

However, despite what has been claimed so far, some non-literal *close to* phrases seem to be APs rather than PPs. For example, *close to tears* cannot follow a verb that is subcategorized for a following PP (*stand*, *go* etc.) and is not replaceable by the pro-P-bar *there*. However, it can follow copular verbs like *seem*, *be* etc. and is replaceable by the pro-A-bar *so*:

(37) Jane was close to tears but Mary was even more so.

This suggests that *close to tears* is an AP, with *close* as its head, though the status of *to* is unclear. *To tears* does not have typical PP characteristics, so it might be argued that *close to* is an adjective with *tears* as its complement

It seems then that the sequence *close to* + NP can fill either a PP or an AP position (the latter perhaps in fixed phrases with metaphorical meaning), and that *close to* can be either an adjective or a preposition. A diachronic study of this combination (and of similar ones like *near* (*to*), *high up*, *low down*, *next to*, *nearby* etc.) might confirm what can only be suggested here, namely that *close to* is an example of a complex preposition in the making. Adjectival/adverbial characteristics are still apparent in some uses (e.g. *close to tears*) and in the possibility of a preceding *very*, *so* etc. However, frequently *close to* behaves syntactically like a preposition, but there is no clear evidence that *close* is a specifier of *to*.

Having shown that the sequence *close to* + NP can have prepositional as well as adjectival/adverbial features, I shall now consider some of the LOB examples of *close together*.

There are cases where the subcategorization frame of the verb and the omissibility of *close* require that *close together* is a PP. For example, this is true of:

(38) The same couple sitting close together

The fact that *there* can replace *close together* but not *together* shows that *close* is best treated as part of a complex preposition (as in (34)).

PP status can likewise be demonstrated for:

(39) small black eyes set close together

since *set* is subcategorized for a following NP and a PP complement.

More problematic are examples like the following:

(40) with three trombones high up and close together

Coordination suggests that the phrases *high up* and *close together* are of the same category, but tests yield conflicting results as to the kind of category. In both cases neither element is omissible, and both kinds of specifier are possible:

right high up	right close together
very high up	very close together

However, a specifier cannot intervene between the two words:

*high right up	*close right together

As argued in section 2, postnominal position is typical of a PP adjunct rather than an ADVP. There is a further parallel to the examples considered there in that in (49) too it is possible to supply a verb (*playing high up and close together*) which would make the phrases in question VP adjuncts.

The following two examples from the LOB corpus show *close together* as APs in which *together* is not the head of the phrase but a complement of the adjective *close*. In

(41) the contractions became stronger and much closer together

coordination and subcategorization facts demonstrate that *close together* must be considered an AP and not a PP. Finally,

(42) some exhibits which are very close together in merit

contains a verb (*be*) which is subcategorized for a following AP or a PP. Omissibility of *together* is evidence that *close* is the head of the phrase, and *in merit* is an adjunct within the AP (it can precede the head of the phrase - *some exhibits which are in merit very close together*). *Together* is therefore best treated as a PP complement of *close* in this case, giving an analysis like that suggested for *close to tears*.

5. Conclusion

It has been shown that the mobility exhibited by *together* is more typical of adverbs than of prepositions, but that *together* can occupy typical PP positions and take the typical PP specifier *right*. Thus, the classification as a preposition is justified. However, as an intransitive preposition (historically a P'), *together* is not a "central" member of the category, and it is one that shows affinities with the adverb/adjective class, for example in occurring as a VP adjunct. *Together* can even be coordinated with an adverb of manner (i.e. one of the "central" adverbs), as the following example from the corpus shows:

(43) transmission brakes of the disc variety operate together or independently

(The fact that different categories can be coordinated as VP adjuncts is pointed out in Quirk et al. (1985:969)).

One possible conclusion is, therefore, as Jacobson states:

> Adverbs shade imperceptibly into prepositions and vice versa. (Jacobson (1977:42))

PPs and ADVPs are prototypical adjuncts, and just as there is no clear boundary between them, so there are members of the preposition and of the adverb classes which resemble the third group of adjuncts, namely the adjectives. The classification of English *a*-adjectives/adverbs (*abroad*, *asleep* etc.) and the use of PPs as adjectives (mentioned in 3.2.) are examples. It is therefore not surprising to find that *together* also shows adjectival characteristics, for example in taking the typical adjective suffix *-ness*, and even in occurring prenominally (in rather recent informal English):

She's a really together person
(*Dictionary of Contemporary English*, London: Longman 1987)

These additional factors support the view that categories are not watertight compartments, and that *together* is an example of a peripheral member of the class of prepositions.

References

Bierwisch, M. 1988. "On the Grammar of Local Prepositions". In: Bierwisch, M./W. Motsch/I. Zimmermann (eds.). 1988. *Syntax, Semantik und Lexikon*. Berlin: Akademie Verlag. 1-65.

Bolinger, D. 1971. *The Phrasal Verb in English*. Cambridge, Mass.: Harvard University Press.

Chomsky, N. 1986. *Barriers*. Cambridge, Mass.: MIT Press.

Cowie, A.P./R. Mackin. 1985. *Oxford Dictionary of Current Idiomatic English. Vol. 1: Verbs with Prepositions & Particles*. Oxford: Oxford University Press.

Curme, G.O. 1935. *A Grammar of the English Language in Three Volumes. Vol. II: Parts of Speech and Accidence*. Boston: Heath.

Emonds, J.E. 1976. *A Transformational Approach to English Syntax. Root, Structure-Preserving, and Local Transformations*. New York: Academic Press.

Emonds, J.E. 1985. *A Unified Theory of Syntactic Categories*. Dordrecht: Foris Publications.

Fukui, N. 1986. *The Theory of Category Projection and its Application*. MIT Dissertation.

Hendrick, R. 1976. "Prepositions and the X' Theory". In: Emonds, J.E. (ed.). 1976. *Proposals for Semantic and Syntactic Theory*. UCLA Papers in Syntax 7. 95-122.

Huddleston, R. 1984. *Introduction to the Grammar of English*. Cambridge: Cambridge University Press.

Jackendoff, R. 1977. *X' Syntax: A Study of Phrase Structure*. Cambridge, Mass.: MIT Press.

Jacobson, B. 1977. "Adverbs, Prepositions and Conjunctions in English". *Studia Linguistica* 31 (1). 38-64.

Jespersen, O. 1924. *The Philosophy of Grammar*. London: George Allen & Unwin.

Johansson, St./G.N. Leech/H. Goodluck. 1978. *The Lancaster-Oslo/Bergen Corpus of British English, for Use with Digital Computers*. Department of English, University of Oslo.

Lyons, J. 1966. "Towards a Notional Theory of the Parts of Speech". *Journal of Linguistics* 2. 209-236.

Quirk, R./S. Greenbaum/G. Leech/J. Svartvik. 1985. *A Comprehensive Grammar of the English Language*. London: Longman.

Radford, A. 1988. *Transformational Grammar. A First Course*. Cambridge: Cambridge University Press.

Rauh, G. 1988. *Tiefenkasus, thematische Relationen und Thetarollen: Die Entwicklung einer Theorie von semantischen Relationen*. Tübingen: Gunter Narr.

Riemsdijk, H.C. van. 1978. *A Case Study in Syntactic Markedness. The Binding Nature of Prepositional Phrases*. Lisse: The Peter de Ridder Press.

Robins, R.H. 1966. "The Development of the Word Class System of the European Grammatical Tradition". *Foundations of Language* 2. 3-19.

Stowell, T. 1983. "Subjects across Categories". *The Linguistic Review* 2. 285-312.

Prepositions and prepositional phrases: a contrastive analysis

Norbert Fries
(Göttingen)

1. General

1.1. Projections

The framework of X-bar theory as it is conceived at the moment proposes general expansions of the form

(1) a. $[X^n [X^{n-1} [... [X^0]]]]$

b.

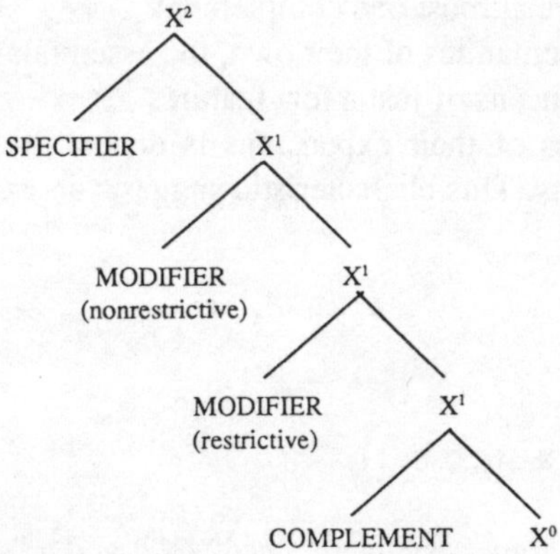

In dealing with expansions of the lexical class of prepositions (P) I assume here, following the argumentation in Bierwisch 1988 and Fries 1988a, that P expands maximally to P^1. One fact supporting this assumption could be that the lexical class P is one of the classes of lexemes that are marked -N and -V (see below 1.3.)

1.2. Functional elements

The principle of expansion may well apply not only to lexical classes such as noun (N), verb (V), adjective (A) and P but also to categories which have essentially syntactic-semantic functions. These categories may sometimes be represented by lexemes marked for such functions, and the lexical realization of such categories will then have predictable consequences for the S-structures in which they occur. Elements of this kind are called functional elements. The existence of at least one class of functional elements is relatively non-controversial - the class of complementizers. For the existence of other classes, e.g. D(eterminer) or I(nflection), cf. Abney 1986, Fukui 1986. For German, in particular, further arguments based on empirical work are needed if these categories are to be posited as the heads of NPs (which would then be DPs) or VPs (which would then be IPs).

Functional elements seem to show some common grammatical features; accounting for these is, however, a task for future research:

a. they form closed lexical classes, i.e. their number cannot be increased by means of regular word-formation patterns
b. they are often clitic or even without phonological form
c. they may have at most one complement
d. they have a semantics of their own, the essentials of which can be described by means of just a few features
e. the semantics of their expansions is denotationally determined by their complements. This characteristic suggests an expansion of the following kind:

(2)

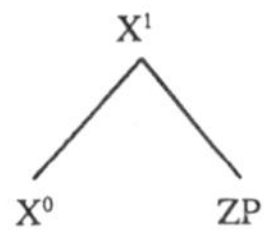

$X \in$ {COMP, ...}

splitting X^1 into a "syntactic head" (X^0) and a "semantic head" (ZP). The expansion of functional elements differs from the expansion of the major lexical categories N, V, A and P in that the syntactic and semantic heads do not coincide. One would, of course, have to specify precisely what the characteristics of semantic heads are.

It is important that transitive Ps (i.e. the class of lexemes traditionally called "prepositions") strongly resemble elements that are functional: changes in membership occur only as a result of diachronic processes (see below 1.4.), they frequently have clitic forms, they have maximally only one complement, and their meanings, especially the meanings of the commonly occurring Ps (which are also the oldest Ps), and especially in certain environments, can only be expressed in the form of a few feature specifications.

In environments where traditional grammar speaks of "prepositional objects", for example, (e.g. *Ich warte [auf ihn]. I am waiting [for him].*) they are subcategorization features (of the verb, noun or adjective) in a way similar to the distribution of complementizers as in *Ich frage ihn, [ob/*daß ...]. I ask him [whether/*that]*. Traditional grammar recognized this by classifying the phrases in question as "objects" (and not adverbials). The use of the term "object" also served to indicate the link between morphology (morphological case marking) and the P-element in question.

1.3. Projections of P

We assume that P-lexemes are contained in expansions of the form (3) (see 1.2. above):

(3)

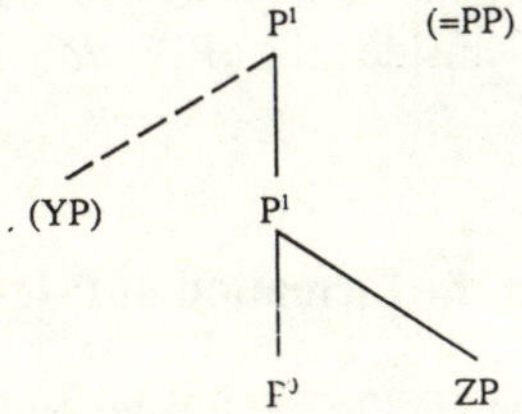

Representing the major lexical categories as combinations of features, we can give the following classification:

(4) N=[+N -V] A=[+N +V] V=[-N +V] P=[-N -V]

P-lexemes are thus given an essentially negative syntactic characterization (although it remains to be explained what "non-nominal" and "non-verbal" precisely mean. For German the morphological characteristic "non-inflecting" is a partial answer; a further feature may be the exclusion from regular word-formation processes); and furthermore they carry at least one further syntactic feature ([± DIR], see below), which is firstly responsible for specific characteristics of these lexemes, and secondly distinguishes the group of P-lexemes from other non-nominal and non-verbal classes of lexemes. Nor does the specification given in (4) enable P-lexemes to be distinguished from lexemes such as interjections, for example, or certain elements of interjections. It is assumed that each class of lexemes will be subclassified, by means of further syntactic features (for interjections cf. Fries 1988b,c,d).

Like the other major lexical classes, N, V and A, prepositions too are distinguished as either transitive or intransitive. The argument structures corresponding to these two subclasses can be represented as in (5):

(5) The argument structure of transitive and intransitive Ps:

transitive:	(e.g. *A unter B*) A under B	$\hat{y}\ \hat{x}$	$[\hat{x}$ UNDER $\hat{y}]$
intransitive:	(e.g. *A unten*) A underneath	$\hat{x}$	$[\hat{x}$ UNDER $\hat{y}]$
pronominal:	(e.g. *darunter*) underneath	$\hat{y}\ x$ *da*	$[\hat{x}$ UNDER $\hat{y}]$

We call $\hat{x}$ an "external argument" and $\hat{y}$ an "internal argument" of P ($\hat{x}$ is realised outside the PP, $\hat{y}$ inside the PP); *da* is a "morphologically incorporated argument" of P.

1.4. Diachronic processes in the formation of P-lexemes

The diachronic processes that lead to the formation of new P-lexemes have scarcely been investigated. A distinction is probably necessary here between the processes that produce new transitive P-lexemes and those that lead to intransitive P-lexemes. (6) - (8) list some of the forms:

(6) Lexemes with the structure $[N^0\text{-}P^0]$:
bergauf, heimzu, kopfüber, landaus, reihum, tagaus, tagsüber, talab, waldaus, zweifelsohne ...

(7) P^0 -hin- formations:
dahin, nahehin, nirgendhin, vornehin, daraufhin, hieraufhin, durchhin, überallhin, nebenhin, obenhin, zwischenhin, hintenhin, untenhin, fernhin, sohin, wohin, irgendwohin, hierhin, fernerhin, vorhin, linkshin, woandershin, rechtshin, dorthin, forthin, osthin

(8) P^0 -her- formations:
daher, ebendaher, nirgendher, jeher, nachher, beiher, umher, rundumher, ringsumher, nebenher, obenher, zwischenher, untenher, einher, fernher, woher, irgendwoher, hierher, weiterher, hinterher, vorher, bisher, linksher, rechtsher, seither, weither, zeither, dorther

Contrary to Bierwisch's claim (Bierwisch 1988), there are scarcely any general regularities to be observed here. This applies on the one hand to the stress contour of the form (those like (6) generally have the main stress on P^0); and on the other hand the features of the heads are not inherited in a predictable way, or it is not clear what the head of the form is. Cases like those under (9), where the feature [+DIR] is inherited, are not the norm, as is shown by formations such as *umher/herum*, *vorher/hervor*, *einher/herein*, which have various semantic idiosyncracies:

(9)

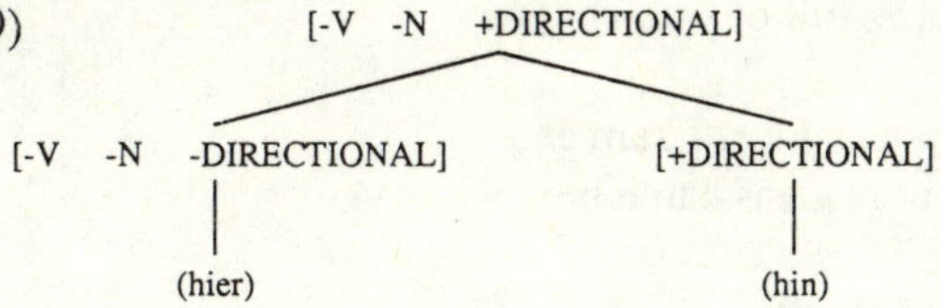

(*hierhin*)

Another way in which new P-lexemes can arise diachronically is by change of syntactic category (conversion), especially from A to P. Here again there is idiosyncratic semantic differentiation:

(10) Change $[X^0]$ ---> $[P^0]$:

(a) die [infolge ihrer Stellung ungeachteten] Mitglieder
(the as a result of their position disregarded members)

*die [der Konsequenzen ungeachteten] Ausführungen
![ungeachtet der Konsequenzen]
(the of the consequences irrespective statements)
([irrespective of the consequences])

(b) *der [innigsten Mitleids volle] Redner
(the of the most sincere sympathy full speaker)

[innigsten Mitleids voll] sprach er zu den Gästen
(of the most sincere sympathy full spoke he to the guests)

[voll größter Hochachtung]
(full of the greatest respect)

(c) *der [Wasser vollere] Mantel
(the of water full coat)

der Mantel ist [voller Wasser]
(the coat is full of water)

[voller neuer Ideen] kam er
(full of new ideas came he)

[voller Mitleid]
(full of sympathy)

Finally, syntactic restructuring is a further way in which new P-lexemes can be formed:

(11) [[in Anbetracht] dieses Vorfalls]
(in view of this occurrence)

[[im Zuge] der Verhandlung]
(in the course of the negotiations)

[dem Käufer [zu Lasten]]
(to the debit of the purchaser)

Complex prepositions ("präpositionswertige Fügungen", see Beneš 1974) arise essentially as a result of restructuring of full PPs. Structures that are synchronically like (12a) develop diachronically into structures like (12b):

(12) a.

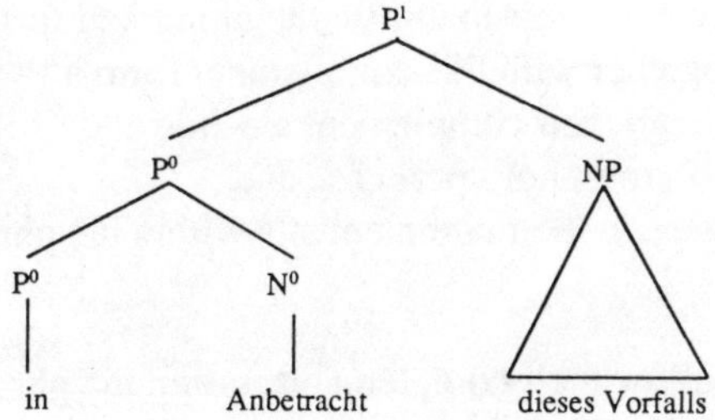

b.

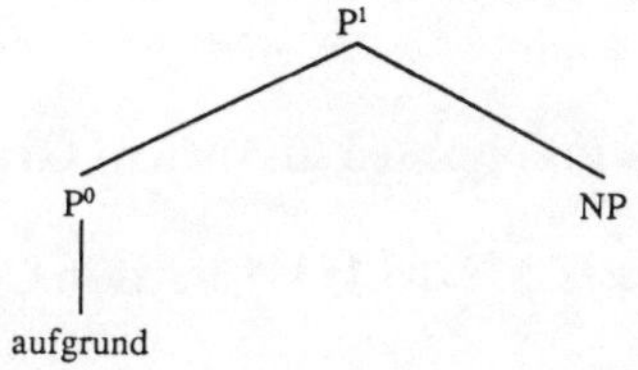

Both transitive and intransitive P-lexemes can be created in this way, see the examples under (13). Because of their diachronic origin, the transitive ones always govern the genitive case:

(13) Lexemes with the structure [P^0 - X^0]:

transitive: *aufgrund, aufseiten, infolge, zufolge, mitsamt, zuliebe, inmitten ...*

intransitive: *abhanden, vorhanden, zuhauf, imstande, insbesondere, an Hand, an Land, zu Ende ...*

2. The specification of Ps

P-lexemes receive different lexical specifications in different languages, and these specifications account for the distribution of the particular lexemes. In traditional approaches this kind of differentiation is reflected in "parts-of-speech classifications", for example. The specifications for German and Modern Greek are given in 2.1. and 2.2. respectively:

2.1. German

"PrePs" = P^0s which

(a) have a complement (in the unmarked form an NP) and
(b) together with this complement form a P^1 phrase and
(c) assign their complement a θ-role and, if the complement is an NP, morphological case and
(d) precede their complements within the phrase

"PostPs"

(d') follow their complements within the phrase

"AdvPs" = P^0s without a complement

2.2. Modern Greek [as opposed to Ancient Greek] (P{g}):

There are no "PostP{g}s"; "AdvP{g}s" are as in German.

"PrepP{g}s" = P^0s which

see above 2.1. (a) and (b), and

(c) in the unmarked form assign no case (structural accusative) but do assign a Θ-role and
(d) with pronominal complements allow only a so-called strong (non-clitic) form and
(e) are left-peripheral

To (d):

mázi (together (with)) is an intransitive P^0, and thus may not have a complement (cf. (1 b/e)). Phrases such as (1a) are accordingly to be interpreted as P^1-phrases with a cliticized (weak) pronoun, and phrases such as (1c) as [P^1-P^1]-structures.

me, on the other hand, is a transitive P^0, and thus requires a complement that can only be replaced by a strong pronoun (cf. (2)).:

(1) a. mazi mou
together with me-GEN.weak
b. *mazi mena
together with me-strong
c. mazi me mena
together with me-ACC.strong
d. *mazi me mou
together with me-GEN.weak
e. *mazi ton Kosta
together with (the) Kosta-ACC.

(2) a. me mena
with me-ACC.strong
b. *me mou
with me-GEN.weak
c. *me me
with me-ACC.weak
d. me ton Kosta
with (the) Kosta-ACC.

The above phrases have one of the structures given as (3) and (4) below:

(3)

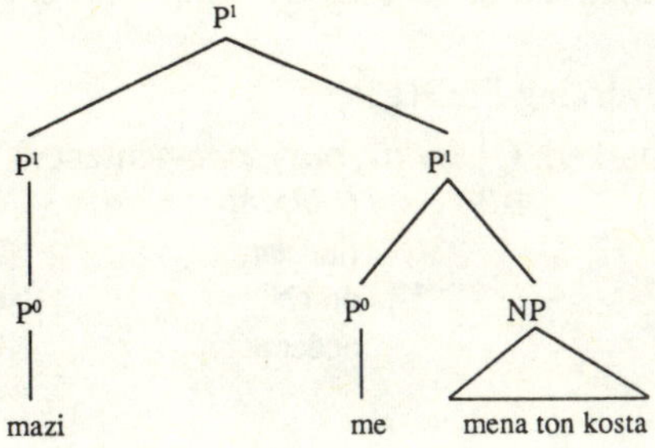

(4)

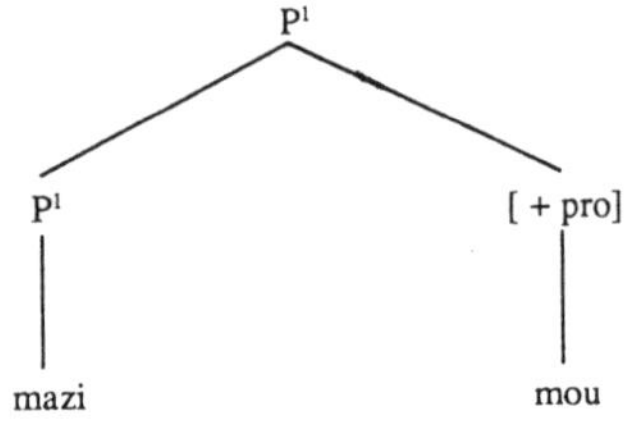

Structure (4) is an adequate representation not only of the syntactic properties of the PPs but also of their semantic and phonological properties. Thus PPs with a cliticized pronoun have a specific semantics which, for example, rules out non-animate referents for the pronoun. However, cliticization follows the general cliticization rules for Modern Greek, which apply to all expansions of [-V] categories. In such phrases, for example, the X^1-constituent has a primary stress, and a secondary stress on the final syllable. The syntactic and semantic properties of cliticized phrases can thus be captured by a clitic-rule such as (5):

(5) Distribution rule for genitive clitic pronouns:
[...[-V]^1 [+pro clitic/GENITIVE]]
[pro] is possessive

To (c):

The P-lexemes taken from the Katharevousa ('high' variety) assign morphological case in the Dhimotiki ('low' variety), too; however, these lexemes sometimes assign structural case. This is an area that requires detailed empirical research and, in particular, I have not included in (6) those prepositions that occur only in fixed expressions or in certain registers, namely the words *vasi* (because of), *dhia* (through, via), *ek* (out of, from), *enanti* (opposite, against), *entos* (within), *enopion* (in front of, in the light of), *epi* (on, during, concerning), *katopi* (after, according to), *pro* (before), *iperano* (beyond). Prepositions such as *exaitias* (on account of) that must be treated as new formations in accordance with what is said in 1.4. are not included either.

(6) case-governing PreP{g}s
(strongly marked, C^1 = *oti-*, *pos-*, *pou*-sentence)

Mod. Gk.	*[αDIR]*	*GERMAN*	*COMPLEMENT TYPES*
anti(s)	-	(an)statt	NP-GEN./NP-ACC., P^1, *na*-C.
dhiamesou	+	durch	NP-GEN.
ektos	-	außer	NP-GEN./NP-ACC., P^1

enantion	+	entgegen	NP-GEN.
iper		für, zugunsten	NP-GEN./NP-ACC.
kata	+	gemäß, gegen	NP-GEN./NP-ACC.
logo	-	wegen, aufgrund	NP-GEN.
meta	-	nach, hinter	NP-GEN./NP-ACC., P^1, C^1
meso	+	durch	NP-GEN.
metaxi		zwischen	NP-GEN.
para		bei, trotz	NP-GEN./NP-ACC., C^1

(7) non-case-governing PreP{g}s (structural accusative)

apo		von	NP, P^1
choris	-	ohne	NP, *na*-C.
dhichos	-	ohne	NP, *na*-C.
isame	+	bis	NP
jia	+	für	NP, P^1, *na*-C.
me	-	mit	NP
mechri	+	bis	NP, P^1, C^1, *na*-C.
os	+	bis	NP, P^1, C^1, *na*-C.
prin	-	vor	NP, P^1, *na*-C.
pros	+	zu, nach	NP
se		in, zu	NP

3. Simple/complex PPs

In traditional grammar PPs were distinguished functionally as "prepositional objects" or as "adverbials" largely on the basis of their external distribution. Internally, non-adverbial PPs differ from adverbial PPs in that the latter can in general have a relatively complex structure, whereas the former cannot:

(1) a. ich verschenke das Buch [an Maria]
   (I present the book [to Mary])
b. das Essen wurde [von uns] gegessen
   (the food was eaten [by us])
c. dhino   to vivlio [s- ti Maria]
   give-I.SG. the book [to (the) Mary]
   (I give the book to Mary)
d. to fajito fagothike apo mas (=(b))

(2) a. ich steige [bis oben auf den Berg hinauf]
(I climb [to the top of the mountain])
b. Ich warte [etwa 10 Meter vor dem Kino]
(I wait [about 10 meters in front of the cinema])
c. er wartet [an der Ecke kurz vor dem Kino]
(He is waiting [on the corner just before the cinema])
d. anevika [mechri epano s- tin korifi tou vounou]
I climbed [to up on the top of the mountain]

Accordingly, prepositional objects, but also the *by* phrases in passives, generally have a "simple" structure like (3) (i.e. one permitting neither a PostP nor an AdvP, nor internal PP coordination or other modification; the P-complement seems to be essentially restricted to a [+ N] constituent); however, adverbial PPs may have complex internal structure, for example as in (4):

(3)

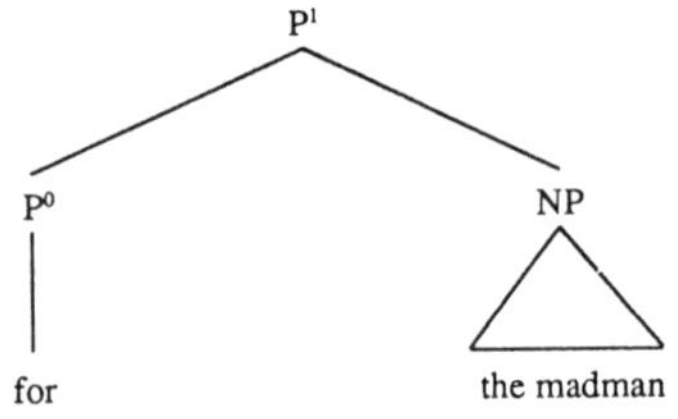

(4)

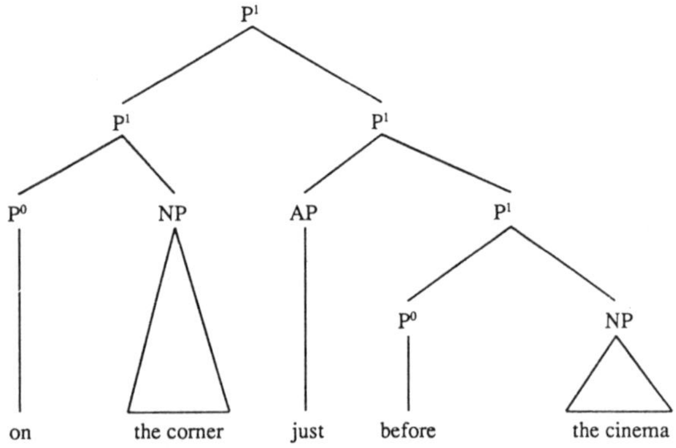

Moreover, the P-element of PPs with non-adverbial function must be one of a subset of the P-elements, and this subset is drawn from the historical P-lexemes. In German this subset is a group of 18 (or 19) P-lexemes that are here called "PreP&"; cf. (5) for German and (6) for Modern Greek;

(5) PreP&:
an auf aus bei durch für gegen in mit nach über um unter von vor wider zu zwischen außer
only in combinations with function verbs

(6) PreP&{g}:
apo jia me se

Semantically the "PPs with an obligatorily simple structure" differ from the "PPs with a potentially complex structure" in that the former do not assign a Θ-role (traditionally they are termed "synsemantic"), whereas the latter are "autosemantic" and, according to the view proposed here, assign a Θ-role. Thus PPs as in (7) are interpretable independently of their context as adverbials of a certain kind. The possible Θ-roles of such PPs are given under (8):

(7) the autosemantics of potentially complex PPs:

wegen der Länge meines Vortrags
(on account of the length of my talk)

inmitten des Mülls
(in the middle of the rubbish)

den ganzen Film über
(during the whole film)

mittels Schlaftabletten
(by means of sleeping pills)

(8) the Θ-roles of potentially complex PPs:
local, temporal, modal, causal, etc.

In the case of PPs that are obligatorily simple, there are also certain (unmarked) relationships between P^0s and certain Θ-roles:

(9) unmarked one-way relationships in PPs of simple structure:

Θ-role	*GERMAN*	*MODERN GREEK*
AGENT	*von*	*apo*
BENEFICIARY	*für*	*jia*
RECIPIENT	*an* +ACC	*se*
DONOR	*von*	*apo*

PreP& lexemes in particular are thus strongly functional. They are still the heads of their PPs syntactically, but semantically they are no longer the heads (they do not assign a Θ-role; they seem to form a closed class in that new PreP& lexemes cannot be formed by morphological processes. Interestingly, it is these lexemes that form P-correlates (*darüber lachen, daß* etc: laugh about it (the fact) that etc., cf. Fries 1985).

4. Information encoding by complex PPs: lexematic

General

Information can be encoded lexematically and/or in the structure. The following questions are of interest in contrastive linguistics: what means of encoding information does a language have? Which must it obligatorily make use of? What are the optional means? What means does the language use and what means does it not use?

A striking difference between German and Modern Greek is the fact that Modern Greek has only about 20 transitive P^0 lexemes (I am ignoring here those lexemes that can occur only in fixed expressions, cf. p. 7 and Hesse 1985), whereas German has over 200. As far as deictic phenomena are concerned, this means that Modern Greek has only intransitive deictic P^0 lexemes:

(1) Primary space deixis

	area around the speaker		excluding the area around the speaker:	
GERMAN	hier	da	dort	P
	hiesig	dasig	dortig	A
MOD GK	edho		eki	P
	edho		eki	A

(2) Secondary space deixis in GERMAN and MODERN GREEK

	vertical	horizontal α	horizontal ß	
GERMAN	über unter	vor hinter	rechts links	P-trans.
MOD GK	- -	- -	- -	
GERMAN	oben unten	vorn hinten	rechts links	P-intr.
MOD GK	pano kato	brosta piso	dhexia aristera	
GERMAN	ober unter	vorder hinter	recht link	A
MOD GK	pano kato	brostin- pisin-	dhexi- arister-	

Because of the small number of Modern Greek transitive P^0 lexemes and their low semantic specification, PPs with a simple structure cannot satisfactorily encode adverbial Θ-roles (see above). Complex phrases of the type (3) - (5) are used to encode important information, and here semantic idiosyncracies have developed which assign idiosyncratic meanings to certain combinations of intransitive and transitive P-lexemes in structures such as (5) (cf. (6)):

(3)

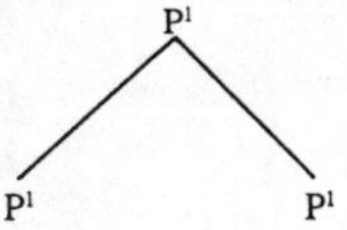

(4) pano apo to spiti
top of the house = above the house

(5)

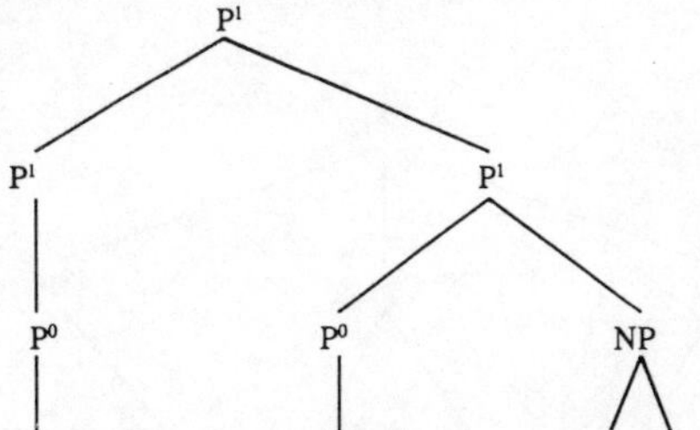

(6) semantic idiosyncracies:

AdvP{g}	*P^0 in P^1*	*GERMAN*
apenandi	apo/se	gegenüber
apeki	apo	jenseits
apo pera	apo	jenseits
brosta	apo/se	vor
dhipla	se	neben
exo	apo	draußen vor, außerhalb
	se	draußen an/in
istera	apo	nach
jiro	apo/se	um
kato	apo	unter
	se	unter
konta	se	in der Nähe von
makria	apo	fern von
mesa	se	innerhalb, in ... hinein
pano	apo	auf, hinauf
	se	über
piso	apo	hinter
	se	hinten an
simfona	me	gemäß, nach

This feature of Modern Greek provides a special argument against Bierwisch's suggested structure for PPs with measure phrases such as (7) (Bierwisch 1988):

(7)

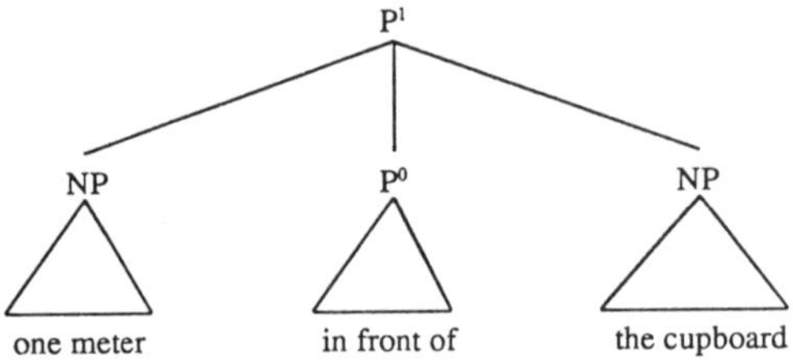

(as an alternative structure to [[NP-A^0{-overt}]-P^1

For Modern Greek structures such as (8) are required:

(8)

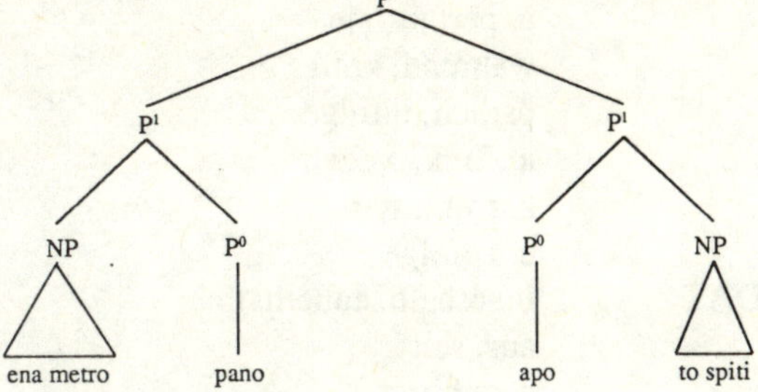

(8) is syntactically unsatisfactory because

(a) all P⁰s are left-peripheral
(b) *pano* is in other contexts unambiguously intransitive and, in particular, cannot take an NP-complement.

(9) is a syntactically satisfactory structure:

(9)

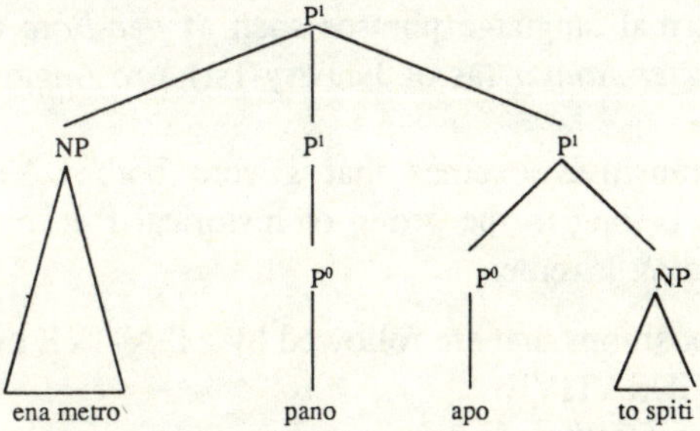

Measure phrases can thus not be interpreted as complements of P^0.

5. Information encoding by complex PPs: structural I [case opposition]

5.1. German

Of the possible case oppositions in German listed under (1) it is only the DATIVE-ACCUSATIVE opposition (and in the case of *entlang* the GENITIVE-DATIVE opposition) that is used to encode information:

(1) the case government of transitive P^0s in German:

1. NOM, ACC	à, per, pro, je
2. GEN only	während, kraft
3. GEN, *von*-NP	östlich, infolge
4. GEN, DAT	a. dank, wegen
	b. trotz, statt
	c. zufolge
5. GEN, *von*-NP, DAT	innerhalb, außerhalb
6. DAT only	aus, seit
7. DAT, ACC	a. auf, vor
	b. ab
	c. über
8. ACC only	für, um
9. GEN, DAT, ACC	a. entlang
	b. außer

For the details of (1) see Fries 1988a. According to the Duden (vol. IX, Mannheim, 1972) the prepositions under (1-1.) should all be followed by the accusative; in informal language phrases such as *per Bote* (by means of a messenger), *per erster Januar* (as of January 1st), *pro Angestellter* (per employee) occur.

The group of transitive lexemes that govern both DATIVE and ACCUSATIVE again belong to the group of historical P-lexemes and form a subgroup of the PreP& lexemes:

(2) Prepositions that are followed by a DATIVE or an ACCUSATIVE:
an, auf, außer, hinter, in, neben, über, unter, vor, zwischen

The DAT-ACC opposition encodes the syntactic-semantic relation [x-RELATION-y](-PREDICATE); [αDIR] refers to the internal argument of P^0 as far as case is concerned, and semantically to the external argument of P^0. The DAT-ACC opposition can be bound to the [±DIR] marking of P^0 (see Bierwisch 1988). (3) applies to German:

(3) [[-V -N, αDIR] [NP [-αobl, -gen]]]
(ACC = -obl, GEN/DAT = + obl)

The PPs concerned occur distributionally as in (4) (for details see Fries 1988a):

(4) [... X^0 [αDIR] ... [P [αDIR]]]

The preposition *auf* is an exception to (3), since it governs the ACC even when marked [-DIR]:

cf. [+ causal] *auf meinen Rat ging er*
(on my advice he went)
[+ modal] *Die Uhr geht auf die Sekunde genau*
(the clock keeps time to the second)
auf Pump, auf Staatskosten
(on borrowed money, at the expense of the state)

5.2. Modern Greek

General: The GEN-ACC-(DAT)-opposition of Ancient Greek:

(5) [-V -N αDIR ß C] [NP [-αobl, ß genitive]]
for: *amfí, epí, pará, perí, prós, ipó*
and with C as a complex of further features

(5) exists in Modern Greek only unsystematically and as a relic. It is systematic only in the case of the P^0 *kata*:

(6) a. kata tis gnomis mou [GENITIVE]
contrary to my opinion
b. kata tin gnomi mou [ACCUSATIVE]
according to my opinion
c. kata to Tübingen [ACCUSATIVE]
to Tübingen
d. kata tou Tübingen [GENITIVE]
at Tübingen
(e.g. the missiles are aimed at Tübingen)
e. *kata* [+adversative] ---> [+genitive]

The marking of P^0 as [αDIR] controls only PP distribution in Modern Greek; predicates such as *beno* are [+DIRECTION], others such as *ime* are [-DIRECTION]:

(7) a. pigame	[sto grafio]
we walked	[to the office]/[walked (about) in the office]
b. imaste	[sto grafio]
we were	[in the office]
c. beno	[sto grafio]
I enter	[the office]

Certain verbs of movement are restricted to SOURCE, PATH or GOAL for their place argument. *Erchome* (come), for example, is not restricted, *pernao* is restricted to PATH. Restriction correlates with the selection of the marking [∝DIR]:

(8) GOAL = PP [+DIR], SOURCE/PATH = PP [-DIR]

6. Information encoding by complex PPs: structural II [position]

This kind of structural variation is not possible in Modern Greek, and in German it is used only marginally to encode information. It involves those P-lexemes that are marked as both PreP and PostP (see outline under (2)), giving rise to variations such as those below under (1):

(1) a.

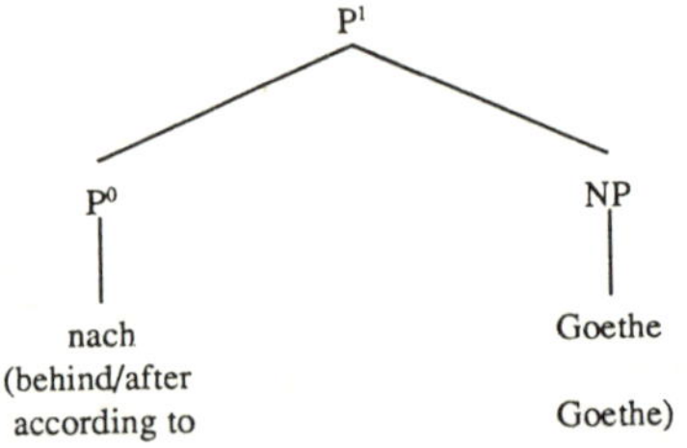

b.

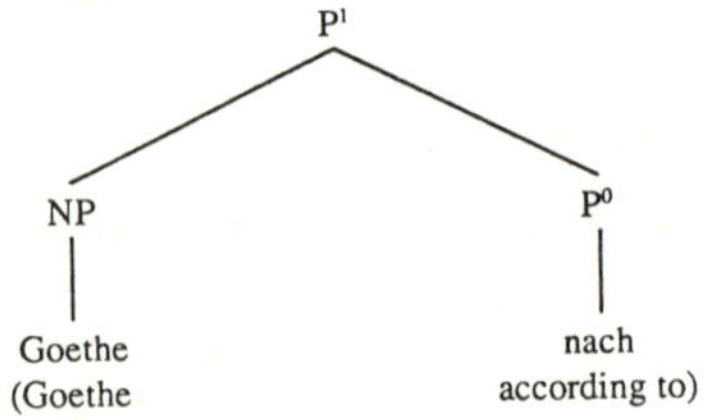

(2) *LEXEME* *case governed as PreP* *case governed as PostP*

durch	ACC	ACC
entgegen	DAT	DAT
entlang	DAT, GEN	DAT, ACC
entsprechend	DAT	DAT
gegenüber	DAT	DAT
gemäß	DAT	DAT
halber	-	GEN
nach	DAT	ACC
über	DAT, ACC	ACC
unbeschadet	GEN	GEN
ungeachtet	GEN	GEN
wegen	GEN, DAT	GEN (?DAT)
zufolge	GEN	DAT
zugunsten	GEN	DAT
zuliebe	-	DAT
zutrotz	-	DAT
zuungunsten	GEN	DAT
zuwider	-	DAT

(this does not include the *hin*- and *her*- lexemes nor other similar ones)

Any semantic differentiation between PreP and PostP is highly unsystematic and affects only 5 lexemes. Other cases seem to be accountable for in terms of analogy mechanisms (see Fries 1988a for details):

(3) semantic differentiation between PreP and PostP

	PreP	*PostP*
a. nach	[+local]	-
	[+temporal]	-
	[+causal]	[+causal, -final]
	[+modal]	-
b. wegen	[+causal, +final]	-
	[+causal, -final]	[+causal, -final]
c. durch	[+local]	-
	[+temporal]	[+temporal, +durative]
	[+medial]	-
	[+instrumental]	-
	[+causal]	-
d. über	[+local]	-
	[+temporal]	[+temporal, +durative]
	[+modal/+local]	-

Examples for *wegen*:

(4) a. Wegen ihres Dobermanns ließ sie sich scheiden.
(On account of her Doberman pinscher she got a divorce)
b. Wegen einer Flasche Wein laufe ich nicht 2 Kilometer.
(On account of a bottle of wine I'm not walking 2 kilometres)

(5) a. *Einer Flasche Wein wegen laufe ich nicht 2 Kilometer.
b. Wegen der Rückzahlung wende man sich an das zuständige Amt.
(For a refund apply to the appropriate office)
c. *Der Rückzahlung wegen wende man sich an das zuständige Amt.

entlang is a special case in that it governs a different morphological case as a PreP and as a PostP:

As a PreP: GEN/DAT, DAT with predicates that are [-DIRECTION]:

(6) a. ?? Entlang diesem Weg fuhr er mit dem Jeep.
(Along this way he drove his jeep)
b. Entlang dieses Weges fuhr er mit dem Jeep.

As a PostP DAT/ACC, DAT with predicates that are [-DIRECTION]:

(7) a. Dem Weg entlang stehen keine Nadelbäume.
(Along the way there are no pine trees)
b. ?? Den Weg entlang stehen keine Nadelbäume.

If the predicate is [+DIRECTION] *entlang* may also govern the DAT, and here there is a distinction between:

DAT: in a parallel direction
ACC: in a parallel direction or backwards and forwards

It is probably because of this that (7b) is, with idiolectal variation, relatively unacceptable.

(8) Rule: the distribution of *entlang*:
a. *entlang* [PreP]:
[-V -N, αDIR] [NP [+obl, αgenitive]]
b. *entlang* [PostP]:
Rule (5.-(3)), but not (5.-(4)):
DATIVE: parallel direction
ACCUSATIVE: a. parallel direction
b. backwards and forwards

Translated by Colin Foskett

References

Abney, S. (1986), *Functional Elements and Licensing*, Cambridge, (Ms.).

Beneš, E. (1974), "Präpositionswertige Präpositionalwendungen", SdG 34, 33-52.

Bierwisch, M. (1988), "On the grammar of local prepositions", in: M. Bierwisch, W. Motsch & I. Zimmermann (eds.), *Syntax, Semantik und Lexikon*, Berlin: Akademie-Verlag, 1-66. (STUDIA GRAMMATICA XXIV)

Fries, N. (1985), "Über S-2-Bar", ZS 4, 156-200.

Fries, N. (1988a), *Präpositionen im Deutschen und im Neugriechischen*, Tübingen: Niemeyer Verlag.

Fries, N. (1988b,c,d), "Interjektionen. Forschungsberichte 1, 2, 3", in: S & P 2, 9, 11. (Rosengren, I. (ed.), Forschungsberichte des Projektes *Sprache und Pragmatik*, Lund.)

Fukui, N. (1986), *A Theory of Category Projection and its Applications*, Cambridge, (Ms.).

Hesse, R. (1985), *Dansk-Græsk Præpositionsordbog med en indledning om de græske præpositioners syntaks*, Kobenhavn: Museum Tusculanums Forlag.

Präpositionen und Objektkonzepte

Ein kognitiv orientiertes, zweistufiges Modell für die Semantik lokaler Präpositionen

Priska-Monika Hottenroth
(Hamburg)

1. Vorbemerkungen

1.1. Zielsetzung und theoretischer Rahmen

Präpositionen haben sich bekanntlich bisher für semantische Theorien als besonders schwierig erwiesen. Der Grund dafür liegt einerseits in ihrer Mehrdeutigkeit, andererseits in der besonders engen semantischen Interaktion zwischen der Präposition und ihren Argumenten, aber auch Verben und anderen Kontextelementen.

Es ist das Ziel dieser Arbeit, am Beispiel der französischen Präposition *dans* einen Beitrag zur Entwicklung einer semantischen Theorie zu leisten, die dem Problem der Mehrdeutigkeit und Kontextabhängigkeit sprachlicher Ausdrücke wie der Präpositionen besser gerecht wird als bisherige semantische Theorien, vor allem die Polysemie- oder Monosemieansätze der strukturalistischen Semantik und der Wahrheitsbedingungssemantik.

Die Aufgabe für eine solche semantische Theorie der Präpositionen besteht darin, einerseits den spezifischen Bedeutungsbeitrag der Präposition zu bestimmen - und das bedeutet, ihn von den verschiedenen möglichen Kontexteinflüssen zu trennen - und andererseits die Bedingungen systematisch aufzuzeigen, die zur Verwendungsvariation der Präposition führen. D.h. es ist zu untersuchen, in welcher Weise die Bedeutung der Präposition mit den unterschiedlichen Kontextfaktoren interagiert. Eine spezielle Rolle kommt hierbei der Wechselwirkung zwischen der Präposition und den Argumentobjekten, besonders dem internen Argument zu.

Als theoretischer Rahmen für die semantische Analyse soll im Anschluß an neuere Entwicklungen in der kognitiv orientierten lexikalischen Semantik, speziell in Anlehnung an die Arbeiten von Bierwisch und Lang[1] von einem zweistufigen semantischen Modell ausgegangen werden.

Es werden jedoch nur die folgenden Grundannahmen übernommen:

Es wird unterschieden zwischen einer Ebene, auf der die lexikalischen Bedeutungen als das spezifisch sprachliche, lexikalische Wissen kodiert sind, und einer konzeptuellen Ebene, auf der unser Weltwissen sowie auch das situative und kontextuelle Wissen erfaßt und organisiert ist.

Die Interpretation sprachlicher Ausdrücke wird als Abbildung von semantischen Repräsentationen auf konzeptuelle Strukturen aufgefaßt.

Die semantische Repräsentation einer lexikalischen Einheit muß in möglichst abstrakter Form die Identifizierungsbedingungen für die Instantiierungen auf der konzeptuellen Ebene enthalten.

Die einzelnen Interpretationen eines mehrdeutigen sprachlichen Ausdrucks sind das Resultat der Verarbeitung der semantischen Repräsentation mit bestimmten relevanten Bereichen des konzeptuellen Wissens und mit dem relevanten situativen und kontextuellen Wissen.

Es wird dabei angenommen, daß dieser Verarbeitungsprozeß durch generelle, kognitiv fundierte, konzeptuelle Prinzipien gesteuert wird.

Die Interpretationen sprachlicher Ausdrücke gehören der konzeptuellen Ebene an.

Innerhalb dieses theoretischen Rahmens geht es bei der semantischen Analyse sprachlicher Ausdrücke nicht nur um die Struktur der semantischen Repräsentationen, sondern diese ist zu fundieren durch die Erarbeitung der entsprechenden Strukturen auf der konzeptuellen Ebene, auf die die semantische Repräsentation zugreift und mit denen sie verarbeitet wird. Sie ist weiter zu fundieren durch die Erarbeitung der Prinzipien, die die verschiedenen möglichen kontextuellen Interpretationen erzeugen. Das Ziel ist, den gesamten Interpretationsspielraum zu erfassen und zu erklären.

Zu den zentralen Fragen gehören also u.a. auch die folgenden:

Welche Strukturen der konzeptuellen Ebene spielen für die Verarbeitung der sprachlichen Bedeutung eine Rolle und welche generellen Prinzipien steuern diese Verarbeitungsprozesse. Um diese beiden Fragen wird es in dieser Arbeit vor allem gehen, denn ohne die genaue Untersuchung der Strukturen der konzeptuellen Ebene und der auf ihnen operierenden Verarbeitungsprozesse scheint gerade in der Präpositionensemantik kein Fortschritt mehr möglich zu sein.

---

1 S. vor allem M. Bierwisch / E. Lang 1987.

Die folgende Untersuchung beschränkt sich aus pragmatischen Gründen auf die lokalen Verwendungen von *dans*, einerseits, weil sich schon hier eine große Verwendungsvielfalt zeigt, andererseits, weil der lokale Verwendungsbereich der zentrale Verwendungsbereich und die Basis für die begriffliche Strukturierung anderer kognitiver Bereiche ist. Es erscheint daher sinnvoll, die Untersuchung der nicht lokalen, übertragenen Verwendungen in einem späteren Schritt an die Ergebnisse der Untersuchung der lokalen Verwendungen anzuschließen.

Die lokalen Verwendungen der französischen Präposition *dans* sind ebenso wie die der deutschen oder der englischen Präposition *in* in der neueren linguistischen Literatur relativ häufig behandelt worden. Keine der bisherigen semantischen Analysen hat aber den Interpretationsspielraum dieser im lokalen Bereich sehr weitgehend identischen Präpositionen befriedigend erfassen und erklären können.[2]

Es werden im folgenden die verschiedenen Verwendungsvarianten von *dans* im lokalen Bereich sowie die Beziehungen, die zwischen ihnen bestehen, systematisch analysiert.

Die Verwendungsvariation der Präposition *dans* kommt in erster Linie durch die Verarbeitung der semantischen Repräsentation mit den unterschiedlichen Gestalteigenschaften der verschiedenen möglichen Referenzobjekte zustande, wie im folgenden gezeigt wird. Alle anderen Kontextfaktoren, die Einfluß auf die Interpretation der durch die Präposition ausgedrückten Relation haben, operieren erst auf dem Ergebnis dieser Verarbeitung.

Auf der Basis der Analyse des Interpretationsspielraums von *dans* im lokalen Bereich wird ein informeller Vorschlag bezüglich der Informationen gemacht, die in der semantischen Repräsentation der Präposition kodiert sind, und es werden die Prinzipien erarbeitet, die die Verarbeitung dieser Informationen mit den Strukturen der konzeptuellen Ebene steuern und die verschiedenen Einzelinterpretationen erzeugen.

Eine zentrale Annahme im vorgeschlagenen semantischen Modell besteht darin, daß die semantische Repräsentation von *dans* nicht eine Abstraktion über alle kontextuellen Verwendungsvarianten darstellt und damit nur die

---

2 Im Bereich der lokalen Verwendungen ergeben sich nur in relativ wenigen peripheren Fällen - meist aufgrund unterschiedlicher Objektkategorisierungen - Verwendungsunterschiede zwischen der französischen Präposition *dans* und der englischen oder deutschen Präposition *in*, sowie darüber hinaus noch dort, wo in phraseologisch fixierten Ausdrücken im Französischen *à* oder *en* statt *dans* verwendet wird.

Bedingungen enthält, die für alle Verwendungen gelten, sondern daß sie spezifischer ist. Sie stellt eine Abstraktion über einen möglichst großen, intuitiv und statistisch zentralen Verwendungsbereich dar.

Die Prinzipien, die ihre Verarbeitung mit den verschiedenen Referenzobjekten auf der konzeptuellen Ebene steuern, machen die kontextuelle Einzelinterpretation der Präposition gegenüber den in der semantischen Repräsentation fixierten Bedingungen nicht nur spezifischer, sondern sie können sie auch abändern. Dadurch kommen Verwendungsvarianten zustande, deren Eigenschaften von den in der semantischen Repräsentation kodierten Eigenschaften abweichen können.

Das Hauptziel der Analyse ist es zu zeigen, daß und vor allem in welcher Weise an diesem Verarbeitungsprozeß bestimmte generelle Prinzipien der Objektwahrnehmung bzw. der Objektkonzeptualisierung und -kategorisierung beteiligt sind, sowie bestimmte Subsumptionsstrategien, d.h. Prinzipien der Ähnlichkeitszuordnung, wie sie im Prozeß der Objektkategorisierung wirksam sind.

Im Fall von *dans* sind es im wesentlichen Prinzipien des Umgangs mit Objektgrenzen und mit Dimensionalität auf der konzeptuellen Ebene, aber auch generelle Mechanismen der Übertragung bestimmter konzeptueller Strukturierungen oder Schemata auf andere ähnliche.

Es ist das Ziel zu zeigen, welche Rolle diese generellen Prinzipien bei der Verarbeitung der semantischen Repräsentation und der Erzeugung der verschiedenen Einzelinterpretationen spielen.

1.2. Verhältnis zur Prototypensemantik

Durch die Annahme einer Präpositionenbedeutung, die nicht Abstraktion aus allen Einzelverwendungen ist, d.h. die nicht alle und nur die Bedingungen enthält, die für alle Einzelverwendungen gelten, sondern die spezifischer ist, und von der die kontextuellen Einzelinterpretationen abweichen können, steht die vorliegende Analyse den prototypensemantischen Arbeiten über lokale Präpositionen nahe. Sie schließt in gewisser Weise, was die Beschreibung der Verwendungsvarianten von *dans* angeht, an sie an, unterscheidet sich aber von ihnen grundlegend bezüglich wesentlicher theoretischer Annahmen und geht in der Zielsetzung über die strukturierte Erfassung und Beschreibung der Verwendungsvarianten hinaus.

Die prototypensemantischen Arbeiten, die im Umfeld der Cognitive Grammar von R. Langacker entstanden sind, wie die von Herskovits 1986,

Hawkins 1984, Vandeloise 1986 u.a. sind die bisher detailliertesten Analysen der Verwendungsvielfalt lokaler Präpositionen. Sie zeigen die prototypische Struktur der verschiedenen möglichen lokalen Verwendungen der einzelnen Präpositionen auf und versuchen, in dem untersuchten Bereich den gesamten Interpretationsspielraum zu erfassen.

Ihr Hauptverdienst liegt m.E. darin, daß sie die Beziehungen zwischen den verschiedenen möglichen Interpretationen der einzelnen Präpositionen sichtbar machen. Allerdings sind sie eher deskriptiv als theoretisch orientiert und steuern relativ wenig zu der theoretischen Frage bei, welche Konsequenzen sich für eine Theorie des Lexikons aus diesen Befunden ergeben.

Als bloßer Polysemieansatz wäre dieser Ansatz aus verschiedenen Gründen theoretisch unbefriedigend.

Tatsächlich wird aber in den meisten dieser Arbeiten als weiterführendes Ziel anvisiert, auf der Basis der deskriptiven Ergebnisse die Prinzipien zu erarbeiten, die z.B. im Verstehensprozeß von der prototypischen Bedeutung zu der gemeinten, davon abweichenden Einzelinterpretation führen können, und es werden solche Prinzipien zumindest ansatzweise dargestellt.

In meiner eigenen prototypensemantischen Arbeit über die Präposition *dans*[3] habe ich versucht, über die bisherigen prototypensemantischen Analysen lokaler Präpositionen dadurch hinauszugehen, daß ich die Erarbeitung solcher Prinzipien zum eigentlichen Ziel der Untersuchung gemacht habe. Die detaillierte, systematische Beschreibung des Interpretationsspielraums von *dans* und seiner prototypischen Struktur ist nur die notwendige Vorarbeit dafür.

Ein zweistufiges semantisches Modell wie das hier zugrundegelegte bietet m.E. einen geeigneten theoretischen Rahmen für die Integration und Erklärung der Befunde der prototypensemantischen Arbeiten.

Zunächst eröffnet es einen geeigneten Rahmen für die Isolierung der semantischen Repräsentation von den Kontexteinflüssen einerseits und der systematischen Untersuchung der Interaktion mit dem Kontext andererseits.

Die prototypische Struktur des Verwendungsspielraums betrifft in diesem Modell nicht die semantische, sondern die konzeptuelle Ebene, was theoretisch wünschenswert ist. D.h. nicht die Bedeutung der Präposition ist prototypisch, sondern es gibt typische und weniger typische kontextuelle Verwendungen.

Die prototypische Struktur des Verwendungsspielraums ergibt sich erst aus der Verarbeitung der semantischen Repräsentation mit den jeweiligen unter-

---

3 S. P.-M. Hottenroth 1986.

schiedlichen Argumentobjekten, speziell den Referenzobjekten auf der konzeptuellen Ebene. Zu erarbeiten sind die generellen, kognitiv fundierten Prinzipien, die den Verarbeitungsprozeß lenken und die prototypische Struktur des Interpretationsspielraums erklären.

2. Die semantische Analyse von lokalem *dans*

2.1. Die generelle Struktur der semantischen Repräsentation der lokalen Präpositionen

Die Analyse der Oppositionsbeziehungen zwischen *dans* und anderen lokalen Präpositionen wie *sous*, *sur*, *devant*, *derrire* etc. ergibt, daß diese Präpositionen sich dadurch voneinander unterscheiden, daß sie sich jeweils auf eine andere charakteristische Region an ihrem Referenzobjekt beziehen:[4]

In neueren Arbeiten zur Präpositionensemantik wird daher von der folgenden generellen Struktur der semantischen Repräsentation lokaler Präpositionen ausgegangen:

(1) $\lambda y\ \lambda x$ (LOK (x,PRÄP* (y)))[5]

D.h. die Bedeutung lokaler Präpositionen ist eine Lokalisierungsrelation zwischen dem externen Argument der Präposition, d.h. dem lokalisierten Objekt, und einer spezifischen Region bezüglich des internen Arguments, d.h. des Referenzobjekts. Der Kern der Präpositionenbedeutung ist eine regionskonstituierende Funktion Präp*, eine Variable, die für jede Präposition geeignet zu spezifizieren ist. Es ist der Baustein, der für jede lokale Präposition die Identifizierung der für sie charakteristischen Region bezüglich der jeweiligen Referenzobjekte steuert, d.h. er muß die Identifizierungsbedingungen für diese charakteristische Region enthalten.

Dagegen enthält die Präpositionenbedeutung, zumindest im Falle der oben erwähnten Präpositionen und auch bei *dans*, keine spezifischen Anforderungen bezüglich bestimmter Gestalteigenschaften des ersten Arguments, also des zu lokalisierenden Objekts.

---

4 S. D. Wunderlich 1982.

5 S. M. Herweg 1988 im Anschluß an die Arbeiten von D. Wunderlich.

Das Ziel für die folgende semantische Analyse läßt sich jetzt präziser so bestimmen: die zentrale Frage ist, wie dieser Baustein der semantischen Repräsentation bei der Präposition *dans* zu spezifizieren ist und wie seine Verarbeitung auf der konzeptuellen Ebene zu denken ist.

2.2. Die Rolle der Eigenschaften des lokalisierten Objekts und weiterer Kontextfaktoren bei der Erzeugung der Verwendungsvarianten von *dans*[6]

Eigenschaften des lokalisierten Objekts, die die einzelne kontextuelle Interpretation von *dans* determinieren, gehören nach dieser Konzeption zu den Kontextfaktoren, die erst auf dem Ergebnis der Verarbeitung des Bausteins Präp* mit den verschiedenen möglichen Referenzobjekten operieren. Vergl. z.B.:

(2) a. les poires dans le bol
(die Birnen in der Schale)
b. la fissure dans le bol
(der Riß in der Schale)

(3) a. la clef dans l'armoire
(der Schlüssel im Schrank)
b. le trou dans l'armoire
(das Loch im Schrank)
c. les robes dans l'armoire
(die Kleider im Schrank)

(4) a. *l'oiseau dans l'arbre*
(der Vogel im Baum)
b. *la hachette dans l'arbre*
(die Axt im Baum)

u.ä.

---

6 Die folgende Analyse ist das Resultat der Untersuchung eines sehr großen Corpus von mehr als 2000 Beispielen, die aus modernen geschriebenen Texten aller Art, aus gesprochener Sprache und aus der linguistischen Literatur zusammengestellt wurden. Die ursprünglichen Beispielsätze wurden aus pragmatischen Gründen sämtlich auf die Form LO Präp RO reduziert.

Die Verarbeitung von *dans* mit den verschiedenen Referenzobjekten liefert oft mehrere mögliche Bezugsregionen am Referenzobjekt. Die Eigenschaften des lokalisierten Objekts, das Wissen um die normale oder typische Beziehung zwischen den Objekten und evtl. weitere Kontextfaktoren steuern die Auswahl der jeweils gemeinten Bezugsregion.

Auch nach der Verarbeitung mit dem lokalisierten Objekt können Konstruktionen mit *dans* noch ambig sein. Die Auswahl der gemeinten Bezugsregion erfolgt dann erst durch weitere Kontextfaktoren:

(5) le clou dans la caisse
(der Nagel in der Kiste)
(1.Lesart: im Hohlraum der Kiste
2.Lesart: in der Wand der Kiste)

(6) l' éclat de verre dans la main
(der Glassplitter in der Hand)
(1. Lesart: in die Hand eingedrungen
2. Lesart: in der Hand gehalten)

Das mit dem lokalisierten Objekt verbundene Wissen über die normalen oder typischen Beziehungen zwischen ihm und dem jeweiligen Referenzobjekt steuert weiter, ob das lokalisierte Objekt ganz oder teilweise in der Bezugsregion lokalisiert ist, ob es diese ausfüllt, kompakt, verteilt oder sogar durchmischt mit RO gegeben ist und welche eventuellen anderen Eigenschaften der Relation vorliegen. Vergl. z.B.:

(7) a. la pipe dans la bouche
(die Pfeife im Mund)
b. le bonbon dans la bouche
(das Bonbon im Mund)

(8) a. le paquebot dans l'eau
(das Boot im Wasser)
b. le poisson dans l'eau
(der Fisch im Wasser)

(9) a. l'eau dans le vase
(das Wasser in der Vase)
b. les fleurs dans le vase
(die Blumen in der Vase)

(10) a. le lait dans le café
(die Milch im Kaffee)
b. la cuillière dans le café
(der Löffel im Kaffee)

Wie die Beispiele zeigen, handelt es sich hier aber um sekundäre Operationen. Vorausgehen muß die Identifizierung der möglichen Bezugsregionen für *dans* am jeweiligen Referenzobjekt; welche Regionen als Bezugsregionen in Frage kommen und welche Eigenschaften sie haben, ergibt sich aus den unterschiedlichen Gestalteigenschaften der Referenzobjekte. Sie sind daher primär für die verschiedenen Verwendungsvarianten verantwortlich.

Im folgenden wird es daher ausschließlich um die Verwendungsvariationen gehen, die durch die unterschiedlichen Gestalteigenschaften der möglichen Referenzobjekte zustandekommen.

2.3. Die Verwendungsvarianten von *dans* in Abhängigkeit von den unterschiedlichen Gestalteigenschaften der Referenzobjekte

Referenzobjekte von *dans* können sehr vielfältige Gestalteigenschaften haben. Sie können dreidimensional, zweidimensional und sogar eindimensional sein. Sie können allseitig begrenzte Objekte oder auch teilbegrenzte oder unbegrenzte Entitäten sein, Objekte mit oder ohne Hohlraum, Materialien oder Entitäten, die etwas umhüllen, Substanzen oder selbst Hohlräume, Konkavitäten, Löcher u.v.a.

Das Bild ist zunächst mehr als verwirrend; es scheinen alle Arten von Objekten und Entitäten als Bezugsobjekte möglich zu sein. Die einzige Beschränkung scheint gegenüber nulldimensionalen Bezugsobjekten zu bestehen. *Point* kann nicht als Bezugsobjekt von *dans* erscheinen.

Die unterschiedlichen möglichen Referenzobjekte für *dans* bieten natürlich Bezugsregionen mit sehr unterschiedlichen Eigenschaften. Mit anderen Worten, die Beleginstanzen des Bausteins Präp* der semantischen Repräsentation haben sehr unterschiedliche Eigenschaften.

Gerade das macht es schwierig, diesen Baustein zu spezifizieren, d.h. die abstrakten Identifizierungsbedingungen für alle und nur diese Beleginstanzen anzugeben.

Nach bestimmten, für den Gebrauch von *dans* und die Oppositionsbeziehungen zu anderen Präpositionen wie *sur*, *sous* und *entre* relevanten Eigenschaften lassen sich aber die vielfältigen Verwendungsvarianten von *dans* in die folgenden neun Verwendungstypen klassifizieren:

Verwendungstyp 1: Die Bezugsregion von *dans* ist
-dreidimensional,
-"leer"
-materiell ganz umschlossen.

Die für diesen Verwendungstyp typischsten Beispiele sind die, bei denen das Referenzobjekt (im folgenden abgekürzt RO) ein geschlossener Behälter ist und das lokalisierte Objekt (im folgenden LO) sich im Hohlraum dieses Behälters befindet wie z.B. in:

(11) la lettre dans la boîte
(der Brief im Briefkasten)

(12) les robes dans l'armoire
(die Kleider im Schrank)

(13) le livre dans la serviette
(das Buch in der Aktentasche)

(14) le vin dans la bouteille
(der Wein in der Flasche)

(15) la farine dans le sac
(das Mehl im Sack)

(16) la lettre dans l'enveloppe
(der Brief im Umschlag)

u.v.a.

Es handelt sich bei diesen Bezugsregionen von *dans* nicht um physikalisch wirklich leere Räume, sondern um Hohlräume bzw. Räume, die "leer" sind in dem Sinne, daß sie nicht von RO selbst materiell besetzt sind. Es kommt dabei nicht darauf an, ob und wieweit das in ihnen Lokalisierte sie ausfüllt.

Dieselben Eigenschaften wie die oben angegebenen haben die Bezugsregionen von *dans* auch in Konstruktionen mit Gebäuden, Teilen von Gebäuden, Fahrzeugen, Kapseln oder Gehäusen, Körperhohlorganen u.ä. als Referenzobjekten:

(17) les gens dans la maison
(die Leute im Haus)

(18) le vin dans la cave
(der Wein im Keller)

(19) les enfants dans l'autobus
(die Kinder im Autobus)

(20) le cosmonaute dans la capsule spatiale
(der Kosmonaut in der Weltraumkapsel)

(21) le sang dans le coeur
(das Blut im Herzen)

u.v.a.

In den bisher angeführten Beispielen war das Vorhandensein eines Hohlraums konstituierende Eigenschaft der Objektkategorie, zu der das Referenzobjekt zählt. Eine Bezugsregion mit den für diesen Verwendungstyp charakteristischen Eigenschaften kann aber auch kontextuell induziert sein. Das ist z.B. der Fall bei Referenzobjekten, die verformbare Materialien sind und die typischerweise oder im aktuellen Kontext als Verpackungen und Umhüllungen dienen:

(22) les fleurs dans le papier jaune
(die Blumen in dem gelben Papier)

aber auch z.B. bei Händen, die ja eine verschiedene Haltung einnehmen können:

(23) les jetons dans sa main
(die Spielsteine in seiner Hand)

Ebenfalls eine Bezugsregion, die materiell nicht von RO besetzt, aber von RO umschlossen ist, bieten auch Bücher, Zeitschriften u.ä.:

(24) les fleurs séchées dans le livre
(die getrockneten Blumen in dem Buch)

(25) la lettre dans le journal
(der Brief in der Zeitschrift)
(in der Lesart: zwischen den Blättern der Zeitschrift)

sowie auch Rinden, Schalen, Häute u.ä.:

(26) la noix dans sa coquille
(die Nuß in ihrer Schale)

(27) le tronc d'arbre dans son écorce
(der Baumstamm in seiner Rinde)

(28) la pêche dans sa peau
(der Pfirsich in seiner Haut)

Obwohl hier eine Teil-von-Beziehung vorliegt, werden beide Entitäten konzeptualisiert und sprachlich behandelt, als handelte es sich um zwei unabhängige Objekte.

Eine weitere, relativ kleine Sondergruppe innerhalb dieses Verwendungstyps bilden Beispiele wie:

(29) qqn. dans l'escalier
(jemand auf der Treppe)

(30) la monnaie dans le tablier
(das Geld in der Schürze)

(31) le livre dans le bureau
(das Buch im Schreibtisch)

Im Beispiel (29) ist der RO umgebende Raum als zum Objektkonzept gehörig konzeptualisiert, und dieser ist Bezugsregion für *dans*.

In den Beispielen (30) und (31) bezieht sich *dans* dagegen auf einen Behälterteil, der nicht immer, aber häufig zum Referenzobjekt gehört. In beiden Fällen ist die Region, die *dans* identifiziert, nicht konstitutiv für die Kategorie der Referenzobjekte, aber aufgrund des Objektwissens kontextuell induzierbar.

Ziel der ausführlichen Darstellung in diesem Abschnitt war es, zu zeigen, daß bei den bisher angeführten Beispielen - die recht unterschiedlich sind, wenn man wie gewohnt, in Objektkategorien denkt - doch in allen Fällen die angegebenen Eigenschaften der Region, auf die *dans* sich bezieht, gleich sind, und es sich insofern um den gleichen Verwendungstyp handelt.

Verwendungstyp 2: Die Bezugsregion von *dans* ist
- dreidimensional,
- "leer", d.h. materiell von RO nicht besetzt,
- nur z.T. von RO umschlossen.

Die für diesen Verwendungstyp typischsten Beispiele sind Konstruktionen, in denen das Referenzobjekt ein offener Behälter ist und somit das lokalisierte Objekt in einer Region lokalisiert ist, die nur teilweise materiell von RO umschlossen ist:

(32) les pêches dans le bol
(die Pfirsiche in der Schale)

(33) le vin dans le verre
(der Wein in dem Glas)

(34) l'eau chaude dans la baignoire
(das Wasser in der Badewanne)

Von den physischen Gegebenheiten her liegt die Bezugsregion von *dans* hier außerhalb der Objektgrenzen von RO.

Die Verwendung von *dans* setzt aber voraus, daß die Bezugsregion, die teilweise von RO umschlossene Region mental als zu RO gehörig behandelt wird, d.h. als Teil der Region, die innerhalb der Objektgrenzen liegt, konzeptualisiert wird.

Diese An- oder besser Eingliederung eines Bereichs, der eigentlich rein physisch betrachtet außerhalb der Objektgrenzen liegt, beinhaltet die mentale Ergänzung der oberen Abschlußfläche, d.h. eine Art Gestaltschließungsprozeß.

Diese mentale Manipulation des Objektkonzepts und damit die Verfügbarkeit der teilweise umschlossenen Region als Bezugsregion für *dans* scheint kontextuell an bestimmte zusätzliche Bedingungen gebunden zu sein, z.B. an die Behälterfunktion des RO und die dafür notwendige kanonische Position u.ä., worauf ich in diesem Rahmen nicht näher eingehen kann.[7]

In diesem Verwendungstyp finden sich als Referenzobjekte alle die Objektkategorien wieder, die unter Verwendungstyp 1 angeführt waren, wenn sie im gegebenen Kontext offen sind, also eine nur teilweise materiell begrenzte Bezugsregion für *dans* bereitstellen, also z.B. neben offenen Behältern, Kapseln, Gehäusen aller Art auch offene Fahrzeuge wie Boote, Lastwagen etc.

(35) la vieille femme dans une petite barque à rames
(die alte Frau in dem kleinen Ruderboot)

---

7 Eine ausführliche Analyse findet sich in C. Vandeloise 1986.

sowie auch z.B. nicht ganz geschlossene Hände, Verpackungen, die nur z.T. umhüllen etc.

Eine nur teilweise materiell umschlossene und mental zu ergänzende Bezugsregion für *dans* bieten auch bestimmte Sitzmöbel wie Sessel (Rücken- und Seitenlehne umschließen die "leere" funktionale Region partiell):

(36) un vieil homme dans son fauteuil
(ein alter Mann in seinem Sessel)

sowie aber auch Lampen, Lampenfassungen u.v.a.

(37) l'ampoule dans la douille
(die Birne in der Fassung)

(38) la mouche dans la lampe
(die Fliege in der Lampe)

Eine Bezugsregion mit den für diesen Verwendungstyp angegebenen Eigenschaften liegt auch in Konstruktionen vor, bei denen RO nicht als ein Objekt mit Hohlraum (bzw. partiell begrenzten, mental eingegliedertem, "leerem" Raum) kategorisiert ist wie im Falle der Behälter, sondern wo umgekehrt RO selbst als Hohlraum mit materiellen Grenzen, die ihn partiell umschließen, kategorisiert ist.

(39) l'eau dans le trou
(das Wasser im Loch)

(40) le sable dans la fissure
(der Sand in der Felsspalte)

Die mentale Gestaltschließung und damit die Eingliederung der teilumschlossenen Region ist sehr oft schon mit der Kategorie des Referenzobjekts gegeben und konstitutiv für die Kategorie wie z.B. bei den zuletzt genannten Referenzobjekten, aber auch bei offenen Behältern, Fahrzeugen, Sesseln etc. Sie kann auch kontextuell induziert sein wie bei Händen, Armen:

(41) l'oiseau dans la main
(der Vogel in der Hand)

(42) le bébé dans les bras de son père
(das Baby im Arm seines Vaters)

Die materielle Teilbegrenzung der Bezugsregion von *dans* muß nicht immer konkav gegeben sein wie in den meisten der obigen Beispiele, sondern sie kann auf unterschiedlichste Weise reduziert sein. Es ergeben sich dabei verschiedene Kontinua, z.B. nach dem unterschiedlichen Öffnungsgrad ein Kontinuum von Schüsseln oder schüsselartigen Behältern bis hin zu Tellern:

(43) la viande dans l'assiette
(das Fleisch auf dem Teller)

Die Begrenzung kann beliebig oft durchbrochen sein wie bei Körben, Sieben, Käfigen u.ä. als Bezugsobjekten:

(44) les oranges dans la corbeille
(die Orangen in dem Korb)

(45) l'oiseau dans sa cage
(der Vogel in seinem Käfig)

Sie kann an zwei Seiten offen sein wie bei Rohren oder nach drei Seiten wie bei Rinnen oder Gräben u.ä.:

(46) le gaz dans le tuyeau
(das Gas im Rohr)

(47) l'eau dans la tranchée
(das Wasser im Graben)

(48) les voitures dans la rue
(die Autos (in) auf der Straße)

Die schrittweise Verkürzung der Rohre ergibt schließlich Rahmen, Ringe u.ä.:

(49) la vis dans l'écrou
(die Schraube in der Mutter)

(50) la serviette dans l'anneau
(die Serviette in dem Ring)

(51) l'homme dans l'encadrement de la porte
(der Mann im Türrahmen)

(52) la photo dans son modeste cadre
(das Foto in seinem bescheidenen Rahmen)[8]

---

8 Ich lasse hier die Frage offen, ob nicht im letzten Fall nur noch zwei Dimensionen eine Rolle spielen.

Es gibt verschiedenste weitere Kontinua der Reduktion der materiellen Begrenzung bis hin zu extremen Fällen, wo evtl. nur noch zwei punktartige Teile des Referenzobjekts die Bezugsregion begrenzen:

(53) la grosse tabatière dans ses doigts
(die große Tabakdose in seinen Fingern)

(54) l'insecte dans les pincettes
(das Insekt in der Pinzette)[9]

Rein materiell gesehen ist die Bezugsregion von *dans* hier eine Region außerhalb der materiellen Objektgrenzen von RO. Erst durch die mentale Manipulation der Ergänzung der sehr reduzierten Objektgrenzen und damit der Eingliederung dieser Region in RO ergibt sich eine mögliche Bezugsregion für *dans*.

Regionen, die "leer" und nur teilweise von RO materiell umschlossen sind, sind auch Zwischenräume bei stark zergliederten Objekten oder Objektmengen.

(55) l'homme dans la foule
(der Mann in der Menge)

(56) les castors dans la tremblaie
(die Biber im Espenwäldchen)

(57) l'oiseau dans l'arbre
(der Vogel im Baum)

Die Voraussetzung für den Gebrauch von *dans* ist auch hier eine Gestaltschließung, i.e. die mentale Ergänzung der Grenzen, und zwar hier nicht aus funktionalen Gründen wie bei den offenen Behältern u.ä., sondern aus perzeptuellen Gründen. Die Objektmenge wird als eine Entität, i.e. als Kollektiv nicht als Plural konzeptualisiert. Andernfalls würde nicht *dans*, sondern *entre* verwendet werden.

---

9 Diese Beispiele werden nicht von allen Informanten akzeptiert, fanden sich aber in unserem Corpus.

Verwendungstyp 3: Die Bezugsregion von *dans* ist
-dreidimensional,
-materiell von RO besetzt,
-allseitig begrenzt (durch den Objektrand).

Bezugsregionen dieser Art liegen bei allen Referenzobjekten vor, die keinen Hohlraum haben.

(58) le clou dans la planche
(der Nagel im Brett)

(59) la hachette dans le tronc d'arbre
(die Axt im Baumstamm)

(60) le couteau dans le pain
(das Messer im Brot)

Auch bei sehr flachen Objekten, die wir tendenziell als Flächen betrachten, kann sich *dans* nur auf die dreidimensionale, materiell von RO selbst besetzte Region beziehen - es sei denn, sie umhüllen LO:

(61) un trou dans le papier
(Loch im Papier)

(62) une aiguille dans le drap
(eine Nadel im Tuch)

(63) un éclat de verre dans la peau
(ein Glassplitter in der Haut)

(64) une tache dans le tissu
(ein Fleck im Stoff)

Bei Behältern und anderen Objekten mit Hohlraum kann sich *dans* außer auf den Hohlraum auch auf die Wand, also die materiell von RO besetzte Region beziehen, und solche Verwendungen gehören zum Verwendungstyp 3:

(65) la fissure dans le bol
(der Sprung in der Schale)

(66) le trou dans la caisse
(das Loch in der Kiste)

(67) un éclat de verre dans la main
(ein Glassplitter in der Hand)
(in der Lesart: 'eingedrungen`)

Die für diesen Verwendungstyp charakteristischen Eigenschaften der Bezugsregion liegen auch vor bei Substanzen als RO, wenn begrenzte Quantitäten gemeint sind:

(68) un insecte fossilisé dans l'ambre jaune
(ein erstarrtes Insekt im Bernstein)

(69) la hachette dans le bois
(die Axt im Holz)

(70) le couteau dans la viande
(das Messer im Fleisch)

(71) le sucre dans le café
(der Zucker im Kaffee)

Wenn Substanzen, die nicht auf begrenzte Quantitäten referieren, als RO von *dans* auftreten, gehören diese Verwendungen zum nächsten Verwendungstyp.

Verwendungstyp 4: Die Bezugsregion von *dans* ist
-dreidimensional,
und ganz oder z.T. vage begrenzt oder unbegrenzt.

In den folgenden Beispielen ist die Bezugsregion nur nach einer Seite, und zwar nach der allein zugänglichen Oberseite hin begrenzt. Diese Grenzfläche ist auch die für die Opposition zwischen *dans* und *hors de* allein relevante. Nach allen anderen Seiten ist sie unbegrenzt bzw. eventuelle Grenzen sind in dem Objektkonzept defokussiert.

(72) le pied dans la neige
(der Fuß im Schnee)

(73) la main dans l'eau
(die Hand im Wasser)

(74) Il est dans la vase jusqu'aux genoux
(Er ist im Sumpf bis zu den Knien) u.ä.

Unbegrenzt sind die Bezugsregionen für *dans* z.B. bei unbegrenzten RO wie *espace*, *l'infini*, *l'univers* u.ä. und bei Substanzen, die nicht als begrenzte Quantitäten konzeptualisiert sind:

(75) les galaxies dans l'espace
(die Galaxien im Weltraum)

(76) le ballon dans l'air
(der Ballon in der Luft)

(77) de l'oxyde de carbone dans l'air
(Kohlenoxyd in der Luft)

Auf der konzeptuellen Ebene scheinen jedoch auch hier mental Grenzen gesetzt zu werden allein dadurch, daß Unbegrenztes offensichtlich nicht vorstellbar ist und eine Konzeptualisierung als Entität vorliegt. Anders als bei offenen Behältern, Bäumen, Menschenmengen etc. sind diese mental gesetzten Grenzen jedoch im Objektkonzept nicht verfügbar; es kann weder *hors de*, noch *dedans*, noch *entrer* oder *sortir* angewandt werden, was bei den sonst mental geschlossenen Objekten selbstverständlich möglich ist.

Verwendungstyp 5: Die Bezugsregion von *dans* ist
-zweidimensional und
-allseitig begrenzt.

Zu diesem Verwendungstyp findet sich nur eine relativ kleine Menge von Beispielen, denn es gibt in der Sprache nicht viele Ausdrücke für zweidimensionale Entitäten. Solche Entitäten sind die geometrischen Flächen, wie Kreise, Ellipsen, Dreiecke u.ä. Die meisten dieser Ausdrücke sind ambig: Sie können die Linie, die eine Fläche umgrenzt, oder die Fläche selbst bezeichnen.

(78) le point dans le cercle
(der Punkt im Kreis)

(79) la boule dans le carré
(die Kugel im Viereck)

(80) les pylônes dans ce carré
(die Masten in diesem Geviert)

Dreidimensionale LO erfordern eine dreidimensionale Region, die entweder auf oder möglicherweise auch unter der Fläche zu suchen ist. Man könnte daher auf den Gedanken kommen, daß unter dem Einfluß von *dans* ein dreidimensionaler Raum über oder unter der Fläche in der Vorstellung konstruiert wird, d.h. daß eine mentale Angliederung einer solchen Region ähnlich wie etwa bei offenen Behältern auch hier anzunehmen ist.

Dafür spricht jedoch m.E. nicht viel. Denn anders als bei offenen Behältern wäre eine solche mentale Gestaltschließung nach oben oder unten für die Opposition zwischen *dans* und *hors de* irrelevant. Diese Opposition betrifft hier ausschließlich die Abgrenzung der Fläche auf der zweidimensionalen Ebene.

Nicht zweidimensional, sondern dreidimensional ist dagegen die Bezugsregion für *dans* bei RO wie z.B. *plafond*, *plancher*, *mur*, *façade* etc., und diese Beispiele gehören daher zum Verwendungstyp 3:

(81) la fissure dans la façade
(der Riß in der Fassade)

(82) le crochet dans le mur
(der Haken in der Mauer)

(83) une fissure dans le plafond
(ein Sprung in der Decke)

Façade, *mur*, *plafond*, *plancher* u.ä. sind ambig: sie können auf die dreidimensionale Entität oder nur auf die zugängliche Oberfläche dieser Entität referieren. Wenn sie als Referenzobjekte von *dans* auftreten, sind sie immer dreidimensional. *Dans* kann sich bei ihnen nicht nur auf ihre zugängliche Fläche beziehen, d.h. wenn dreidimensionale LO etwa auf dieser Fläche sind, kann hier - anders als bei geometrischen Flächen - nicht *dans* verwendet werden. Die Opposition zwischen *drinnen* und *draußen* betrifft nicht nur die Grenzen der Fläche in Bezug auf ihre zwei Dimensionen, sondern die Beleginstanz ist dreidimensional und gehört insofern zum obigen Verwendungstyp 3.

Das gleiche gilt für *surface* und *sol*, wenn sie als Referenzobjekte von *dans* auftreten. LO kann nur unter der Fläche lokalisiert sein, nicht auf ihr wie bei geometrischen Flächen; *sol* und *surface* werden dabei konzeptualisiert wie eine dünne Schicht, d.h. die Bezugsregion von *dans* ist nicht zweidimensional, sondern dreidimensional. Verwendungen mit diesen RO gehören daher ebenfalls zum Verwendungstyp 3 und nicht zu diesem Verwendungstyp 5.

(84) une fissure dans la surface d'un objet
(ein Sprung in der Oberfläche eines Objekts)

(85) la crevasse dans le sol
(die Spalte im Boden) u.ä.

Verwendungstyp 6: Die Bezugsregion von *dans* ist
- zweidimensional und
- nur z.T. umschlossen.

(86) *le point dans l'angle*
(der Punkt in dem Winkel)
(zweidimensionale Lesart)

Dieser Verwendungstyp entspricht, übertragen auf zwei Dimensionen, dem Verwendungstyp 2: Die Voraussetzung für den Gebrauch von *dans* ist hier ähnlich wie bei offenen Behältern, eine mentale Gestaltschließung der partiell begrenzten Region. Diese Gestaltschließung ist - wie bei offenen Behältern - hier in der Kategorie des RO bereits vorgegeben.

Verwendungstyp 7: Die Bezugsregion von *dans* ist
-dreidimensional,
-begrenzt;
-nur zwei Dimensionen sind relevant.

Zu diesem Verwendungstyp gehört eine sehr große Gruppe von lokalen *dans*-Verwendungen, nämlich die meisten der Konstruktionen, bei denen das Referenzobjekt ein geographisches Gebiet, ein Territorium gleich welcher Größe ist.[10]

(87) les usines de Ford dans la France d'aujourd'hui
(die Fabriken von Ford im heutigen Frankreich)

(88) les caravanes dans le désert
(die Karawanen in der Wüste)

(89) les saboteurs dans ce même territoire
(die Saboteure in demselben Territorium)

(90) les chalets dans les Alpes
(die Chalets in den Alpen)

---

10 Vor allem in diesem Bereich steht *dans* in Konkurrenz mit *en* und *à*, die aber in vielen Fällen durch *dans* ersetzt werden, wenn eine Attribution zur regierten NP hinzutritt.

Hierzu gehören auch Konstruktionen mit Bezugsobjekten wie *forêt*, *ville*, *village*, *banlieu*, *jardin*, *parc*, *champ*, *pré* u.v.a.

(91) les maisons dans les grandes villes
(die Häuser in den großen Städten)

(92) les moutons dans le pré
(die Schafe auf (in) der Wiese)

(93) les fleurs dans le jardin
(die Blumen im Garten)

(94) les animaux dans la forêt
(die Tiere im Wald)

Obwohl bei den Referenzobjekten in diesen Fällen die dritte Dimension eine z.T. sogar ausgeprägte Rolle spielt, sind, da es um territoriale Abgrenzungen geht, doch in den meisten Kontexten nur Ausdehnung und Grenzen auf der horizontalen Ebene für den Gebrauch von *dans* und die Opposition zu *hors de* relevant. Es liegen daher ähnliche Verhältnisse vor wie in Verwendungstyp 5 bei den geometrischen Flächen als RO von *dans*.

Eine *dans*-Region, wie sie für diesen Verwendungstyp charakteristisch ist, kann nicht nur durch ein RO, das ein Territorium ist, gegeben sein, sondern auch durch ein RO, das ein Territorium umschließt wie z.B. Umzäunungen, umgebende Mauern oder Grenzen.

(95) le monastère dans l'enceinte de fossés
(das Kloster innerhalb seiner Festungsgräben)

(96) la ville dans ses murailles
(die Stadt in ihren Mauern)

Verwendungstyp 8: Die Bezugsregion von *dans* ist
-dreidimensional;
-nur zwei Dimensionen sind relevant;
-sie ist vage oder nicht begrenzt.

Vage oder gar nicht begrenzte Territorien als Bezugsregionen von *dans* sind gegeben in:

(97) les maisons dans le voisinage
(die Häuser in der Nachbarschaft)

(98) cette petite tente dans l'immense étendue
(dieses kleine Zelt in der unendlichen Weite)

Dieser Verwendungstyp entspricht dem Verwendungstyp 4, übertragen auf Bezugsobjekte, bei denen nur zwei Dimensionen relevant sind.

Verwendungstyp 9: Die Bezugsregion von *dans* ist
-eindimensional.

Verwendungen dieses Typs sind eher peripher. Es gibt nur wenige Beispiele und selbst die sind nicht von allen Sprechern akzeptiert:

(99) l' intervalle dans la ligne
(die Unterbrechung in der Linie)

(100) l' astigmatisme dans l'axe
(die Verkrümmung in der Achse)

Möglich scheint die Konstruktion mit *dans* überhaupt nur zu sein, wenn LO ein fehlender Teil oder eine Verformung von RO sind, die konzeptualisiert und sprachlich behandelt werden wie eigenständige von RO getrennte Objekte. Selbst wenn LO ein Punkt und Teil einer Linie ist, kann nicht *dans*, sondern nur *sur* verwendet werden.

(101)*le point dans la ligne

sondern:

le point sur la ligne
(der Punkt auf der Linie)

Erst recht kann bei dreidimensionalem LO nur *sur*, nicht *dans* verwendet werden:

(102) un objet dans une ligne
(ein Objekt auf einer Linie)

Mit den angeführten Verwendungstypen sind die möglichen Beleginstanzen für *dans*, d.h. die möglichen Bezugsregionen und ihre Eigenschaften, erfaßt und klassifiziert. Es ist damit aufgezeigt worden, auf welche Strukturen der konzeptuellen Ebene *dans* zugreift.

2.4. Ein zweistufiges semantisches Modell für *dans*

2.4.1. Informeller Vorschlag für die in der semantischen Repräsentation von dans zu speichernden Informationen über die möglichen Bezugsregionen

Angesichts der Unterschiedlichkeit der möglichen Bezugsregionen, auf die *dans* zugreifen kann, ist es schwierig, wenn nicht unmöglich, Identifizierungsbedingungen anzugeben, die für alle und nur diese möglichen Bezugsregionen gelten, d.h. diesen Baustein der semantischen Repräsentation in einer Form zu spezifizieren, die einer Abstraktion über alle möglichen Beleginstanzen entspricht.

Häufig findet sich in der neueren Literatur der Vorschlag, diesen Baustein etwa als INTERIOR (RO), INNENRAUM (RO) o.ä. zu spezifizieren. Diese Spezifizierung ist m.E. nicht nur wegen der Zirkularität bezüglich *dans* unbefriedigend. Sie erfaßt nicht mehr als die grobe Intuition, daß es bei der Opposition zwischen *dans* und *hors de*, *sur*, *sous* etc. um den Kontrast zwischen der Region innerhalb der Objektgrenzen im Unterschied zur Objektumgebung geht. Sie ist aber zu wenig explizit darüber, welche Eigenschaften eine Region bei den verschiedenen RO haben muß, damit *dans* auf sie bezogen werden kann.

Was heißt z.B. INNENRAUM bei Linien? Diese Spezifizierung erklärt nicht, warum **le point dans la ligne* nicht möglich ist, während *l'intervalle dans la ligne* möglich ist. Bei offenen Behältern, Bäumen und Menschenmengen, Fingern, die etwas halten, u.ä. ist INNENRAUM etwas anderes als bei geschlossenen Behältern und bei diesen etwas anderes als bei Objekten ohne Hohlraum und Substanzen. Das Konzept erklärt nicht, warum *dans* sich in anderer Weise auf geometrische Flächen und Territorien bezieht als auf Flächen, die Oberflächen von Objekten sind. Bei unbegrenzten Entitäten schließlich entfällt die Opposition zur Objektumgebung, d.h. zur Region jenseits des Objektrandes.

Ein semantischer Baustein INNENRAUM definiert somit ganz und gar nicht Eigenschaften, die bei allen Beleginstanzen dieselben sind. Er ist unpräzise, noch dehnbarer als der umgangssprachliche Begriff und nicht eindeutig explizierbar.

Das gilt auch für einen neueren Vorschlag, nach dem Präp* als PLACE (RO) zu spezifizieren ist.[11] Dieser Vorschlag ist zwar in mancher Hinsicht

---

[11] S. Herweg 1988, S. 74.

dem oben angeführten überlegen, z.B. bei unbegrenzten Entitäten als RO, ist aber bezüglich aller anderen RO nicht erklärungsstärker. Er erklärt z.B. ebenfalls nicht, warum **le point dans la ligne* nicht möglich ist, sowie auch nicht, warum *dans* bei nulldimensionalen RO nicht verwendet werden kann:

(103) *qqc. dans le point

Ein weiteres Problem ergibt sich bei Zäunen, Umfriedungen, Verpackungen etc. als RO von *dans*; denn hier ist die Bezugsregion gerade nicht der Ort, den RO selbst einnimmt.

Angesichts der Schwierigkeiten, den Baustein *dans* mittels eines abstrakten Konzepts zu spezifizieren, das die Identifizierungsbedingungen repräsentiert, die für alle und nur die möglichen Beleginstanzen gelten, wird im folgenden davon ausgegangen, daß das in diesem Baustein der semantischen Repräsentation kodierte Wissen spezifischer ist. Es wird angenommen, daß dieses Wissen, das den Zugriff auf alle möglichen Beleginstanzen auf der konzeptuellen Ebene steuert, nicht eine Abstraktion über alle möglichen Verwendungen ist, sondern nur eine Abstraktion aus einem möglichst großen, zentralen Verwendungsbereich. Durch spezielle Verarbeitungsmechanismen auf der konzeptuellen Ebene kann auch auf Beleginstanzen mit abweichenden Eigenschaften zugegriffen werden.

Der Verwendungsbereich, der intuitiv und statistisch der zentralste ist, ist der Bereich des oben beschriebenen Verwendungstyps 1. Es sind die Verwendungen, bei denen die Bezugsregion von *dans* dreidimensional, "leer" und allseitig materiell begrenzt ist. Die typischsten Beispiele sind die, bei denen LO im Hohlraum eines Behälters lokalisiert ist, also z.B. in

(103) le vin dans la bouteille
(der Wein in der Flasche);

Verwendungen, bei denen die Bezugsregion die genannten Eigenschaften hat, sind die im Corpus bei weitem die häufigsten; es sind die Verwendungen, die Informanten zuerst einfallen, die in der sprachwissenschaftlichen Literatur durchweg an erster Stelle, wenn nicht überhaupt ausschließlich behandelt werden, und die offensichtlich im Primärspracherwerb zuerst gelernt werden. Dieser Verwendungstyp stellt damit den prototypischen Verwendungsbereich von *dans* dar; hier liegen auch im Gegensatz zu den anderen Verwendungstypen klare Oppositionsbeziehungen zu den Präpositionen *hors de*, *sur* u.a. vor.

Es wird daher angenommen, daß die in der semantischen Repräsentation kodierten Eigenschaften, die die Identifizierung der möglichen Bezugsregionen steuern, die Eigenschaften der für den Verwendungstyp 1 charakteristischen Bezugsregion sind: Sie ist dreidimensional, "leer" und allseitig materiell begrenzt.

Das bedeutet, daß im Interpretationsprozeß bei RO, die eine Region mit diesen Eigenschaften bieten wie z.B. geschlossene Behälter, diese unmittelbar als mögliche Bezugsregion für *dans* identifiziert wird.

Wenn *dans* bei einem RO-Konzept auf keine Region mit diesen Eigenschaften trifft, steuern generelle, konzeptuelle Prinzipien, daß Regionen mit bestimmten abweichenden Eigenschaften als ähnlich zugeordnet und damit als mögliche Bezugsregionen für *dans* identifiziert werden können.

Für die Annahme, daß *dans** in der obigen Weise zu spezifizieren ist, nämlich daß die Eigenschaften der für den Verwendungstyp 1 charakteristischen Region in diesem Baustein gespeichert sind, spricht vor allem die Tatsache, daß sich alle anderen, vom Verwendungstyp 1 abweichenden Verwendungen mittels relativ weniger, genereller Prinzipien von dieser Startbedeutung aus generieren lassen.

2.4.2. *Die Verarbeitungsprinzipien*

Im einzelnen wird die Identifizierung der möglichen, vom Verwendungstyp 1 abweichenden Bezugsregionen für *dans* von den folgenden Prinzipien gesteuert:

(1) Regionen, wie sie beim Verwendungstyp 2 vorliegen, d.h. dreidimensionale, nur z.T. von RO materiell umschlossene "leere" Regionen (wie die "leere" Bezugsregion bei offenen Behältern), werden durch das Prinzip der Gestaltschließung, d.h. die Ergänzung einer mentalen Grenzfläche, RO eingegliedert. Diese Gestaltschließung, die oft schon mit der Objektkategorisierung gegeben ist, ist die Voraussetzung, daß Regionen dieser Art, die eigentlich außerhalb der materiellen Objektgrenzen von RO liegen, als Bezugsregion für *dans* in Frage kommen. Durch die mentale Gestaltschließung werden diese Regionen erst denen ähnlich, die allseitig materiell von RO umschlossen sind, d.h. sie bekommen ähnliche Eigenschaften wie die in der Präpositionenbedeutung kodierten und werden damit als Bezugsregion für *dans* identifizierbar.

(2) Um Regionen, wie sie im Verwendungstyp 3 vorliegen, d.h. dreidimensionale, materiell von RO selbst besetzte und durch den Objektrand begrenzte Regionen (wie in *le clou dans la planche*) als mögliche Bezugsregion für *dans* zu identifizieren, ist ein Prinzip notwendig, das das

Schema "leere" Region/materieller Rand auf die Gegebenheiten materiell besetzte Region/Objektrand überträgt. Erst durch diese Übertragung werden letztere als ähnliche Regionen und damit als mögliche Bezugsregionen für *dans* identifizierbar.

(3) Für die Identifizierung unbegrenzter, dreidimensionaler Regionen - wie sie in Verwendungstyp 4 vorliegen - als mögliche Bezugsregionen für *dans* ist die mentale Setzung von Grenzen Voraussetzung. Dieses Prinzip der mentalen Grenzsetzung steht dem unter (1) genannten Prinzip der Gestaltschließung nahe, ist aber nicht mit ihm identisch.

(4) Die Identifizierung von zwei- und eindimensionalen Regionen - wie sie in Verwendungstyp 5 und 9 vorliegen - als mögliche Bezugsregionen für *dans* setzt ein Prinzip der Übertragung des dreidimensionalen Schemas auf zwei- bzw. eindimensionale RO voraus. Zwei- und eindimensionale Regionen werden durch dieses Prinzip als ähnliche Regionen und damit als Bezugsregionen für *dans* identifizierbar.

(5) Die Konstituierung von Bezugsregionen, wie sie für den Verwendungstyp 7 charakteristisch sind, nämlich von zweidimensionalen Regionen an eigentlich dreidimensionalen Entitäten, setzt ein Prinzip voraus, daß tatsächlich gegebene Dimensionalität auf die einzig verhaltensrelevanten, beiden horizontalen Dimensionen reduziert. Hier liegt eine Anwendung des unter (4) genannten Prinzips auf eigentlich dreidimensionale Entitäten vor.

Die Identifizierung der für die Verwendungstypen 6 und 8 charakteristischen Bezugsregionen ergibt sich aus der Kombination von jeweils zwei der genannten Prinzipien.

Die Kombination des unter (4) genannten Prinzips der Übertragung des dreidimensionalen Schemas auf zweidimensionale Regionen mit dem unter (1) genannten Prinzip der Gestaltschließung führt zu den für den Verwendungstyp 6 charakteristischen Bezugsregionen, d.h. Regionen, die zweidimensional und nicht allseitig begrenzt sind wie in *le point dans l'angle*.

Die Kombination des unter (5) genannten Prinzips der Reduzierung der tatsächlich gegebenen Dreidimensionalität auf die zwei verhaltensrelevanten horizontalen Dimensionen mit dem Prinzip der mentalen Grenzsetzung (3) führt schließlich zu den für den Verwendungstyp 8 charakteristischen Regionen wie in *la maison dans cette immense étendue*.

Im Anhang wird ein schematischer Überblick über die Verwendungstypen von *dans* und die Prinzipien, die sie generieren, gegeben.

Wie gezeigt wurde, können die Prinzipien, die die Verarbeitung von *dans* mit den verschiedenen möglichen Referenzobjekten auf der konzeptuellen

Ebene steuern und in diesem Prozeß die verschiedenen möglichen Bezugsregionen von *dans* identifizieren, auf nur vier generelle, konzeptuelle Prinzipien zurückgeführt werden.

Wenn im Konzept eines Referenzobjekts keine Region mit den in der semantischen Repräsentation spezifizierten Eigenschaften gegeben ist, wird entweder wie im Falle des Gestaltschließungsprinzips oder des Prinzips der mentalen Grenzsetzung auf der Basis bestimmter Objekteigenschaften eine Region geschaffen, die den zentralen Beleginstanzen ähnlich ist und damit als Beleginstanz für *dans** in Frage kommt, oder es kommen bestimmte generelle Übertragungsmechanismen zur Anwendung. Dies sind Mechanismen, die das Schema der in *dans** kodifizierten Regioneneigenschaften auf Regionen mit bestimmten anderen Eigenschaften übertragen und sie dadurch als ähnlich und damit als mögliche *dans*-Regionen identifizieren.

Das bedeutet, daß es sich hier um Prinzipien handelt, wie sie bei den Prozessen der Objektwahrnehmung bzw. Objektkonzeptualisierung und der Objektkategorisierung wirksam sind.

Diese Prinzipien determinieren eindeutig, in welcher Weise Bezugsregionen für *dans* von den in der semantischen Repräsentation spezifizierten Eigenschaften abweichen können. Anders ausgedrückt: sie determinieren den Bereich der Regionen, die als den zentralen Beleginstanzen ähnlich zu gelten haben und damit eben falls als Beleginstanzen für *dans** identifizierbar sind.

Die Prozesse, die diese Prinzipien in Gang setzen, entsprechen daher Ähnlichkeitszuordnungen, wie sie im Prozeß der Objektkategorisierung wirksam sind. Der Unterschied besteht darin, daß *dans* nicht Referenzobjekte kategorisiert, sondern daß die Verarbeitung von *dans* mit den Referenzobjekten und die Identifizierung der möglichen Bezugsregionen sich nach demselben Muster vollzieht, wie es den Prozessen der Objektkategorisierung zugrunde liegt. Sie basiert auf Ähnlichkeitszuordnungen, die von den beschriebenen Prinzipien gesteuert werden.

Literatur

Bierwisch, Manfred. 1986. On the Nature of Semantic Form in Natural Language. In Klix F./Hagendorf H. (eds.). 1986. *Human Memory and Cognitive Capabilities. Mechanisms and Performances.* Amsterdam: North-Holland.

Bierwisch, Manfred und Ewald Lang. 1987. *Grammatische und konzeptuelle Aspekte von Dimensionsadjektiven.* Berlin: Akademie-Verlag.

Hawkins, Bruce W. 1984. *The Semantics of English Spatial Prepositions*. San Diego, Cal. Ph.D. Diss. Univ. of Cal.

Herskovits, Anette. 1986. *Language and Spatial Cognition*. Cambridge: Cambridge University Press.

Herweg, Michael. 1988. Zur Semantik einiger lokaler Präpositionen des Deutschen. Überlegungen zur Theorie der lexikalischen Semantik am Beispiel von *in*, *an*, *bei* und *auf*. LILOG-Report 21. Stuttgart: IBM.

Hottenroth, Priska-Monika. 1986. Die Semantik lokaler Präpositionen. Ein prototypensemantisches Modell für die französische Präposition *dans* mit einer Analyse der Beziehungen zwischen der Präposition und den Objektbezeichnungen in den Präpositionalsyntagmen. Habilitationsschrift, Universität Konstanz, September 1986.

Jackendoff, Ray. 1983. *Semantics and Cognition*. Cambridge, Mass.: MIT-Press.

Lang, Ewald. 1987. Semantik der Dimensionsauszeichnung räumlicher Objekte. In Bierwisch M./Lang E. (eds.) 1987. *Grammatische und konzeptuelle Aspekte von Dimensionsadjektiven*. Berlin: Akademie-Verlag.

Lang, Ewald. 1988. Gestalt und Lage räumlicher Objekte: Semantische Struktur und kontextuelle Interpretation von Dimensionsadjektiven. In Bayer, J. (ed.). *Grammatik und Kognition. Psycholinguistische Untersuchungen*. Opladen: Westdeutscher Verlag. 163-191.

Lang, Ewald. 1989. Primärer Orientierungsraum und inhärentes Proportionsschema. In Habel, C., Herweg, M. and Rehkämper, K. (eds.). *Raumkonzepte in Verstehensprozessen. Interdisziplinäre Beiträge zu Sprache und Raum*. Tübingen: Niemeyer. 150-173

Vandeloise, Claude. 1986. *L'Espace en Français. Sémantique des Prépositions Spatiales*. Paris: Editions du Seuil.

Wunderlich, Dieter. 1982. Sprache und Raum. Studium Linguistik 12; 13: 1-19 und 37-59.

Mögliche Beleginstanzen für DANS*

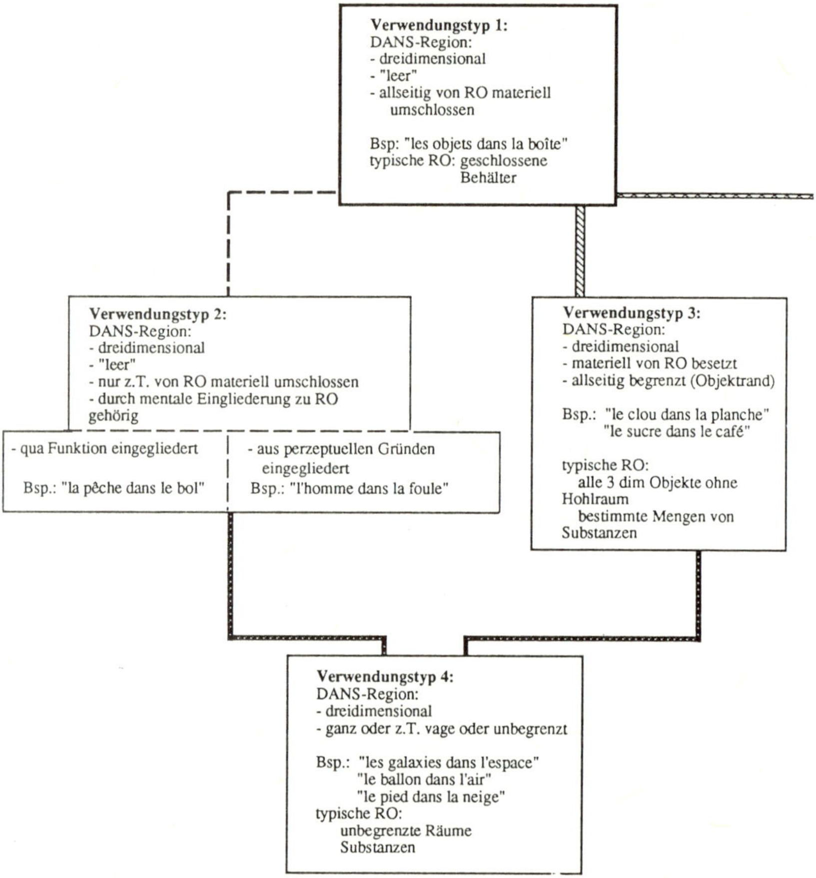

(1) Subsumption auf der Basis von Gestaltschließungsprozessen
(2) Subsumption auf der Basis mentaler Grenzsetzung bei unbegrenzten RO
(3) Subsumption auf der Basis der Übertragung des Schemas von Verwendungstyp 1 auf Objekte ohne Hohlraum (materiell besetzte Zone und Objektrand)
(4) Subsumption auf der Basis der Übertragung des zweidimensionalen Schemas von Verwendungstyp 1 auf zwei dimensionale und eindimensionale RO
(5) Subsumption durch Rückübertragung des zweidimensionalen Schemas (Ergebnis von (4)) auf drei - dimensionale Entitäten, wenn Ausdehnung und Grenzen nur in Bezug auf zwei Dimensionen relevant.

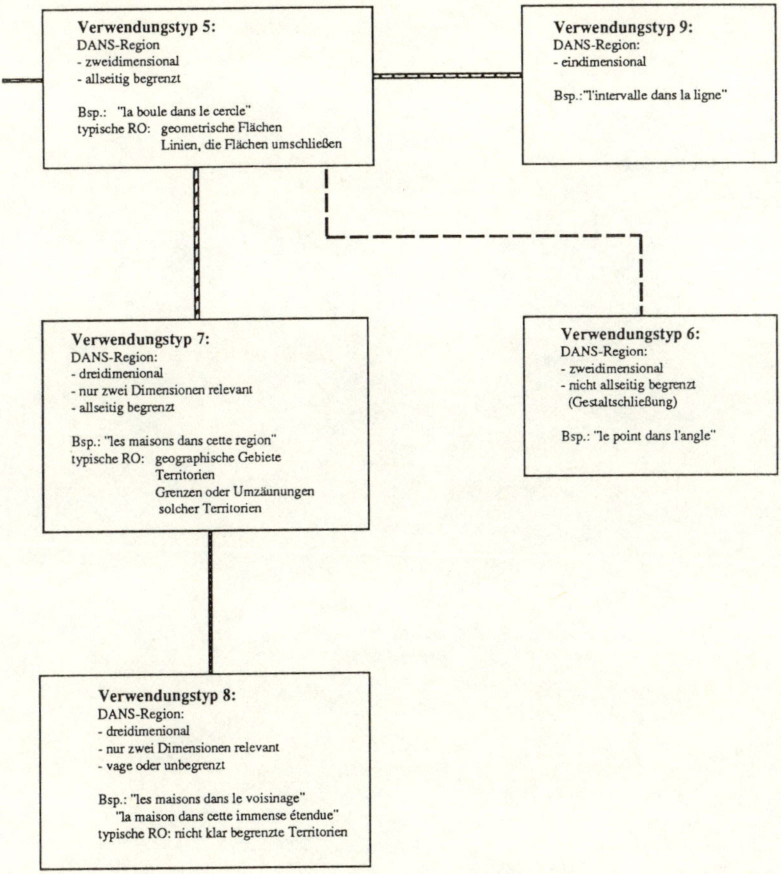
Verwendungstyp 5:
DANS-Region
- zweidimensional
- allseitig begrenzt
Bsp.: "la boule dans le cercle"
typische RO: geometrische Flächen
Linien, die Flächen umschließen
Verwendungstyp 9:
DANS-Region:
- eindimensional
Bsp.:"l'intervalle dans la ligne"
Verwendungstyp 7:
DANS-Region:
- dreidimenional
- nur zwei Dimensionen relevant
- allseitig begrenzt
Bsp.: "les maisons dans cette region"
typische RO: geographische Gebiete
Territorien
Grenzen oder Umzäunungen
solcher Territorien
Verwendungstyp 6:
DANS-Region:
- zweidimensional
- nicht allseitig begrenzt
(Gestaltschließung)
Bsp.: "le point dans l'angle"
Verwendungstyp 8:
DANS-Region:
- dreidimenional
- nur zwei Dimensionen relevant
- vage oder unbegrenzt
Bsp.: "les maisons dans le voisinage"
"la maison dans cette immense étendue"
typische RO: nicht klar begrenzte Territorien

On the reanalysis of verbs as prepositions[1]

Ekkehard König & Bernd Kortmann
(Berlin)

0. Introduction

It is a well-known fact that the inventory of prepositions in English and other languages is only a very limited one. The tags in the Lancaster/Oslo/Bergen (LOB) Corpus of British English identify 134 expressions as prepositions and a similar, though slightly smaller number is assigned to that class in the BROWN Corpus. Mindt & Weber 1989 list 94 prepositions as central members of the class both for American and British English, but if all complex or phrasal prepositions are included into the count, one ends up with a list of about 180-190 items (cf. Quirk et al. 1985: 665-671).

It is equally well-known that the class of prepositions is by no means a closed class, but admits of new additions and in fact constantly changes its extension in the course of the history of a language (cf. Dill 1986; Vestergaard 1973, etc.). All major lexical categories seem to have provided suitable sources for the development of prepositions in the history of English and other European languages: The monosyllabic and many disyllabic prepositions of English and German are generally assumed to derive from adverbs. That adjectives may develop into prepositions is shown by German examples such as *fern, unweit, längs, entlang, frei* and English examples such as *along, near, worth, subsequent to, precious to*, etc. The most important sources for the development of new prepositions in English and apparently all languages, however, are relational nouns and certain groups of verbs. Most complex or phrasal prepositions, which according to frequency counts are somewhat marginal in English (cf. Mindt & Weber 1989), derive from relational nouns. In contrast to German where uninflected forms of

1 Thanks are due to E. Lang, G. Rauh and D. Wunderlich for helpful comments on an earlier version of this paper.

nouns (e.g. *kraft, zeit, trotz, statt, laut*) and inflected forms of nouns (e.g. *seitens, zwecks, mittels, angesichts, ausgangs, mangels*) have developed into prepositions, denominal prepositions in English are always accompanied by one (e.g. *thanks to, contrary to, (by) courtesy of*) or two monosyllabic prepositions (*in front of, in spite of, by means of, on behalf of, in exchange for, with respect to, in addition to,* etc.). Such complex or phrasal prepositions may later be condensed into single words, as a result of a process frequently called 'univerbation' (e.g. *be sidan > beside(s), on top > atop, in steede > instead, on gemang > among, on middan > amid(st)).* In addition to such complex prepositions all grammars of English and other European languages list a number of cases among this class that clearly derive from verbs, but behave in many ways like prepositions (e.g. *barring, concerning, during, except, excepting, considering, pending, notwithstanding, given, granted, come*).

It is the latter historical process that our paper is concerned with. Whereas the development of relational nouns and verbs containing these nouns to complex prepositions has been analyzed in some detail for several European languages (cf. Eisenberg 1979; Quirk & Mulholland 1964) and whereas the criteria for distinguishing between such complex prepositions and ordinary prepositional phrases seem to be fairly clear (cf. Quirk et al. 1985: 671f.), the process through which verbs may develop into prepositions has received very little attention as far as European languages are concerned. Compared with these, much more is known about reanalyses of verbs as prepositions in languages with serial verb constructions, such as Chinese or the large group of African languages normally assigned to the Niger-Congo family (cf. Li & Thompson 1973; Lord 1973; Givón 1975).

In our analysis of this process we will discuss and try to answer the following questions:

- What are the major sources of this process of reanalysis? Do the verbs that tend to develop into prepositions belong to a restricted number of semantic domains?
- What are the exact steps, i.e. the phonological, syntactic and semantic changes, involved in this process? Are the preposition-like properties acquired gradually or does this process lead to a clear differentiation between verbal and prepositional expressions?
- How does this process interact with other properties of a language? What are the similarities and differences between a reanalysis of serial verbs as prepositions and the process of reanalyzing participles and finite verb

forms in European languages? How do the differences with regard to this process in English and German relate to other differences between the two languages?
- What do these processes tell us about the relationship between the major lexical categories: nouns, verbs, adjectives and prepositions?

1. Layers of prepositions

Prepositions provide a particularly good illustration of the principles and laws formulated by G.K. Zipf (1949), notably of the Law of Abbreviation, which establishes an inverse relationship between the length of words and their frequency of occurrence, and the Principle of Economic Versatility, which establishes a direct correlation between the semantic versatility (number of different meanings) of a word and its relative frequency. Frequency counts (cf. Mindt & Weber 1989; Mindt 1989) have shown that the following 13 expressions, listed in the order of their frequency, are the most frequent prepositions in both the BROWN and the LOB corpus and that the distribution of these prepositions covers nearly 90% of all occurrences of this word class in the two corpora:

(1) of, in, to, for, with, on, by, at, from, as, into, about, than;

Of these 13 core cases, the first two are by far the most frequent ones and make up nearly 45% of all occurrences.

These figures show that the most frequent prepositions in English are nearly all monosyllabic. It is not until we get to position 11 and 12 that we find a disyllabic expression. So Zipf's Law of Abbreviation is nicely confirmed. Moreover, it is also intuitively obvious that the most frequent prepositions are also the most versatile ones semantically. This intuition is confirmed by a brief look into a dictionary. The entries for *of, in, to, for*, etc. are by far the longest and certainly much longer than that given for *about*, which in turn is slightly longer than that given for the less frequent preposition *above*. Prepositions with a very low frequency of occurrence like *alongside, underneath, amongst, opposite, amidst* tend to have a very specific meaning and use.

Prepositions (or adpositions) as markers of thematic (Θ-) roles are sometimes ranked together with case affixes on a scale of grammaticalization.[2] On the basis of criteria such as morphological complexity and the nature of meaning expressed (concrete/objective vs. abstract/grammatical meaning) C. Lehmann (1985,1986) distinguishes primary adpositions (morphologically simplex, elementary objective or grammatical meaning, e.g. E. *of, to*), secondary adpositions (morphologically complex, objective/concrete meaning) and relational nouns (phrasal or complex prepositions) as focal points on a scale that also includes fusional and agglutinative case affixes.

If we use the criteria discussed above (morphological complexity, mode of meaning, frequency of occurrence and semantic versatility), which, of course, coincide only very roughly, several layers of prepositions can be distinguished in English: (i) a group of very frequent, typically monosyllabic prepositions, with a broad range of meanings that includes very abstract, 'grammatical' meanings and uses, (ii) a group of less frequent, typically disyllabic and morphologically complex prepositions with a narrow range of more specific meanings and uses, (iii) a group of phrasal or complex prepositions, which tend to be very rare and are composed of relational nouns and prepositions of the first group. In between these focal points further subgroups could be distinguished on the basis of the criteria mentioned and on the basis of such syntactic criteria as the use as part of phrasal verbs (*get in, get out, get along, get up, get by,* etc.), the use in combination with prepositional objects (*laugh at sb., refer to sth., blame sth. on sb., look after sb.,* etc.) and the permissibility of Preposition Stranding. The use of prepositions as parts of phrasal verbs is restricted to the most frequent monosyllabic and disyllabic ones. The prepositions that may occur as part of a prepositional object also belong to a very restricted set. And Preposition Stranding as in sentences like (2) is generally confined to the primary, more frequent members of the class:

---

2 The reason why we avoided the term *grammaticalization* and use the more neutral term *reanalysis* is that prepositions are regarded as major lexical categories like nouns, verbs and adjectives in X-bar theory. Many syntacticians would therefore reject the view that the development of prepositions from verbs or nouns can be seen as a change from lexemes to grammatical formatives or from less grammatical to more grammatical elements. However, it is noteworthy that even a proponent of X-bar theory like Joseph Emonds does not recognize prepositions as a major lexical category, but only as a "grammatical category which is also a 'head of a phrase'" (1985:13).

(2) a. Who are you looking for?
b. That's the man I work with.
c. She is an interesting woman to talk to.

The class of prepositions is thus not a very homogeneous one, but includes a core group and several layers of more and more peripheral members. One of the questions we will also raise and try to answer in this paper concerns the place that deverbal prepositions occupy with respect to the other layers. More specifically, we need to ask whether deverbal prepositions form a homogeneous subgroup or whether they exhibit varying degrees of integration into the class of prepositions.

2. Steps to reanalysis

A necessary condition for reanalysis is that two different analyses (bracketing, assignment of categorial labels) must be possible for a sequence of expressions, such that the same overall interpretation is arrived at through different composition or projection. Participles and other untensed, uninflected verbal forms combining with nominal arguments bear a striking similarity to adpositional (i.e. prepositional or postpositional) phrases and are in fact used in the same functions as the latter, viz. as adverbials (cf. (3)) and as post-nominal modifiers (cf. (4)):[3]

(3) a. Considering his age, he works extremely hard.
b. In many respects the new version is worse than the old one.

(4) a. The book containing all this information
b. The book with the green cover ...

Given these similarities in the possible functions of participial verb phrases and prepositional phrases and given the similarity in their formal make-up it is quite plausible that reanalysis may take place in these cases.

---

3 For PPs headed by *of*, the most frequent preposition in Present-Day English, it should be noted that they do not display the prototypical behaviour of PPs anymore. They are largely confined to a function as postnominal modifier or part of a prepositional object, thus suggesting that *of* is on the way of developing into an inflectional morpheme.

2.1. Change in word order

One factor that clearly shows that such a reanalysis has taken place or is taking place is a change of word order in such structures where the preposition derives from an absolute construction with a participle serving as head of the predicate. Sources of this kind can be assumed to underlie deverbal prepositions like *during, pending, failing, notwithstanding, excepted, given, granted,* or *ago*. The change makes itself felt as a restriction of the variation in word order, i.e. either SV or VS order, that was formerly possible in these constructions (cf. also Curme 1931: 155f.):

(5) a. þei bene heyest in grece in August alle the moneth during. (1410; Visser 1966: 1219)
b. Durynge that persecucioun Silvester ... flig out of the citee. (1387; *MED*, s.v. *during)*

(6) a. The same dissuasion, and, that failing, the same kind exer tions in my behalf I met with at Manchester. (1817; Visser 1966: 1219)
b. He undertakes to show A fouler than himself, - but, failing that, Return with him. (1841; Visser 1966: 1219)

(7) a. His father the king excepted there is none whose honor I more tender and love. (1568; *OED*, s.v. *except*)
b. The bluddy tyrant brought them all to ende Excepted me. (1559; *OED*, s.v. *except*)

In Present-Day English almost all of these prepositions allow only for either pre-nominal or post-nominal position. The majority, e.g. *during, except* (in contrast to *excepted*), *pending, failing* or *given*, always precede their complement; *ago* and *excepted* occur exclusively in post-nominal position and thus function as postpositions. *Notwithstanding*, on the other hand, just like German *entsprechend* still admits of both word orders:[4]

[4] The optional or even obligatory post-nominal position of what are undeniably deverbal pre- or adpositions can be observed to cause problems for the assignment of the respective items to this lexical category. Thus in a number of traditional grammars or even in a standard dictionary like the *Dictionary of Contemporary English ago* or *excepted* are classified as adjectives, *notwithstanding* following its complement as an adverb (cf. also Huddleston 1984:337).

(8) a. We did it, his objections notwithstanding.
b. We did it notwithstanding his objections.

2.2. Change of grammatical relations, Θ-role assignment and control properties

A change of word order exemplified by (5)a. or (6)a. to that exhibited by the respective b.-sentences is, of course, accompanied by other changes: a change in grammatical relations, a change in the pattern of Θ-role assignment and a change in the control properties associated with the relevant lexical item.

In the reanalysis of absolute constructions like (5)a. or (6)a. as prepositional phrases, the subjects (external arguments) of the relevant verbs are reanalyzed as complements (internal arguments) of prepositions. This process may be supported, on the one hand, by an (oblique) case marking of the argument. Thus the objective case of the pronominal argument of *failing* in (9)a., which can be traced back to the case marking of the subject of a so-called Absolute Accusative, as in (9)b., with SV-inversion, may be viewed as the typical case of the internal argument of English prepositions:[5]

(9) a. In default of these, the heritage goes to the son of the...aunt. Or, failing him, it passes... (Visser 1966: 1219)
b. ...without th'advis of my lord of Bedford, him being in England,... (Visser 1966: 1147)

On the other hand, reanalysis of a preposed participle as a preposition gains support if the former no longer exhibits agreement with a following argument. In Modern French this is often even obligatorily so, e.g. for *attendu* or *vu*:

(10) Vu sa charge énorme, la voiture marchait très lentement.

Now, if a former subject comes to function as a complement, this naturally has repercussions on the Θ-grid of the reanalyzed item. For instance, it raises

---

5 In Middle English, the normal situation for absolute constructions with pronominal subjects was that the pronoun received objective case marking only in VS-position (Visser 1966: 1147). Examples like (9) b. are therefore exceptional in this respect in this early period; they alone, but not "Absolute Accusatives" with SV-inversion, can still be found in informal and regional varieties of English.

the question what, if anything, is then the external argument of the derived preposition? Whether prepositions can always be assumed to have an external argument is a controversial question. It does seem, however, that in many cases the part of the sentence a prepositional phrase combines with can be considered as such an external argument. This view is supported by contrasting pairs like the following, where the subject of the sentence can be taken as understood subject (controller) of the verbal *-ing*-form (and, correspondingly, of the German *-end*-form) in one case, and the whole main clause in the other:

(11) a. Following the instructions of his boss, John examined each part carefully.
b. Following a sharp decline last year, prices rose again this year.

(12) a. Excluding the American pair, Becker acknowledges five le gitimate grass-court challengers.
b. Since September, $ 22 billion in deposits, excluding inter est, have been withdrawn.

(13) a. Den Wünschen meiner Frau entsprechend, werde ich auf Lametta ganz verzichten.
b. Den Wünschen meiner Frau entsprechend, wird auf Lametta ganz verzichtet.

In contrasting pairs like these we are much more inclined to analyze the participial form in (11)b.-(13)b. as a preposition than the corresponding form in the a.-examples, i.e. those instances seem to be more like prepositions where a whole clause rather than a part of a clause functions as external argument. A criterion of this kind is also used in Quirk et al. (1985: 660), where only *considering* in (14)b. is analyzed as a preposition (cf. similarly (4)a.):

(14) a. Considering the conditions in the office, she thought it wise not to apply for the job.
b. Considering his age, he has made excellent progress in his studies.

In (14)a. it is the subject of the main clause that controls the participle, i.e. functions as its understood subject.

2.3. Phonological and morphological criteria

In some cases, the reanalysis of verbs as prepositions is also advanced by phonological changes, i.e. phonological attrition or erosion and orthographic reanalysis. In English this concerns exclusively past participial forms. Thus *ago* and *past*, and similarly *except*, have undergone such phonological changes, as the examples in (15) show:

(15) a. Three dayes agone I fell sicke.(1611; *OED*, s.v. *ago*)
b. It was passed 8 of the clokke. (1391; Visser 1966: 1292)

One of the main differences between verbs and prepositions is that the former may inflect for tense, mood, person, number, etc. Prepositions never inflect and it is therefore not surprising that reanalysis of verbs as prepositions is particularly common in isolating languages like Chinese, Thai or members of the Niger-Congo phylum. In English, a few imperative or subjunctive forms of verbs, which are identical in form to the base forms, have also provided the source for the development of prepositions (cf. *bar, come*). In those cases where prepositions do derive from inflectional forms (e.g. Fr. *il y a un an* 'a year ago' or It. *un anno fa* 'a year ago') the relevant expressions have become frozen expressions that do not inflect anymore. Moreover, for languages with a high degree of inflection an example like (10) should be recalled, which illustrates how the formal invariability resulting from a loss of agreement supports the development from participles to prepositions.

In addition to the changes discussed so far as formal indicators of a process of reanalysis, the following less important ones should also be mentioned very briefly. Condensation of several expressions into one word (univerbation) has taken place in connection with the expression *notwithstanding*. In some cases (e.g. *touching, barring*) reanalysis was accompanied by semantic depletion or bleaching (including the loosening of selection restrictions). The retention of primary prepositions as second elements of participial forms (e.g. *according to, relating to*; cf. Poutsma 1929: 711) and the loss of the underlying verb (e.g. *during* < **dure, pending* < **pend*; Lat. *trans* < **trare*) can be seen as further factors contributing to the process of reanalysis.

The preceding discussion has shown that the deverbal prepositions are by no means a homogeneous group. The relevant expressions have been affected by reanalysis to varying degrees. Some expressions (*concerning, during, pending, come, except, past*) have been integrated fairly well into the class of prepositions, whereas others may still exhibit participial syntax (e.g. *notwithstanding*) and still others (e.g. *following*) can only be regarded as prepositions in some of their occurrences at best. Furthermore, even the clearest instances of a group of deverbal prepositions can only be considered as peripheral or marginal members of this class (cf. Quirk et al. 1985: 667). A further point revealed by the preceding discussion is that a clear demarcation between verbal participles and deverbal prepositions is not possible. Finally, we should also note that only some, but by no means all changes observable in connection with the process of reanalysis discussed above are part of the criteria formulated by Lehmann and others for grammaticalization. This concerns, for instance, what Lehmann (1986: 7) labels *paradigmaticization* (from a rather loose participation in a semantic field of a weakly grammaticalized item to its tight integration into a small, homogeneous morphological paradigm) and *obligatorification*, i.e. the loss of paradigmatic variability (from a largely optional to a grammatically constrained, obligatory choice (i) of the whole category expressed by the paradigm and (ii) between the members of the paradigm).

3. Interaction with other properties of a language

In the following section we will try to throw additional light on the historical process through which prepositions may be derived from verbs by comparing our findings with those discussed in a variety of studies on languages with serial verb constructions (cf. Chao 1986; Li & Thompson 1973; Lord 1973; Givón 1975 and references given there). Moreover, we will also briefly compare the process of reinterpreting verbs as prepositions in English and German. Although these two languages seem to have a comparable number of deverbal prepositions and although similar domains seem to be involved - which may partly be the result of loan translation - there also seem to be subtle, but significant differences with regard to the relevant historical process which are worth mentioning. Through these comparisons we hope to be able to distinguish general tendencies from language-specific facts and to find out how the reanalysis of verbs interacts with other properties of a language.

Serial verb constructions are generally defined as combinations of two verb phrases with one subject, i.e. as structures of the form [NP VP VP]:

(16) a. Wǒ jiè qián gěi nǐ. (Mandarin)
(I lend money give you
'I'll lend you some money.')
b. di man tek di tIk bit di bobo. (Krio)
(the man take the stick beat the boy
'The man beat the boy with the stick.')

If verbs in serial constructions are marked for tense, aspect, mood or polarity they generally agree in their marking. Whether serial verb constructions derive diachronically from coordination or subordination is not clear. Nor do linguists agree whether these constructions can be analyzed synchronically as instances of coordination or subordination. There seems to be general agreement, however, with respect to the following semantic criterion: Serial verb constructions describe different aspects or parts of a larger, comprehensive event or at least events which are related in some way, such that one verb phrase may often stand for the whole construction.

Serial verb constructions are found in Chinese, Thai, in the Benue-Kwa branch of the Niger-Congo family (e.g. Gwe, Twi) and in a variety of creoles (e.g. Krio). These examples show that serial verb constructions typically occur in languages with isolating morphological structure and SVO order.

One of two verbs in a serial construction may lose its verbal properties and be reinterpreted as a preposition. A clear indication of such a reanalysis is the loss of the ability to take the usual verb affixes (aspect, tense, mood, negation) and the loss of the ability to form the centre of a predication, i.e. to occur as the only verb in a sentence. Moreover, verbs tend to lose some semantic substance in the course of such a change, which is generally assumed to be a gradual one (cf. Givón 1975: 80-89). It is precisely this gradual character of the reanalysis which makes the synchronic analysis of these constructions so complicated. There are many expressions that can be analyzed as verbs by some criteria and as prepositions by others. Special terms like *verbid* or *coverb* have been introduced to characterize these intermediate cases. The correlations between sources and targets in this diachronic process show a surprising degree of consistency across languages. On the basis of data taken from Chinese and Niger-Congo, generalizations about possible paths of semantic change are formulated in Givón (1975: 93). A striking fact about the verbs that provide the sources for such changes (e.g. 'take', 'get', 'hold', 'do', 'go', 'come', 'give', 'beat', 'join', 'accompany', 'use') is that they are rather unspecific in their meaning so that it does not take much bleaching for them to develop into even less specific expressions.

One of the questions also raised in several studies on serial verbs in transition is about the functional motivation of such changes from verbs to prepositions. Essentially, two answers are given to this question: On the one hand, this reanalysis provides one path - in addition to relational nouns or genitive-noun syntax - a language whose system of case marking has been eroded may take to restabilize its system of expressing thematic roles (cf. Givón 1975). On the other hand, the reanalysis of verbs is seen as a consequence of the relationship between the meanings of the two verb phrases in a serial construction: The less prominent of the two verbs, i.e. the one denoting the less significant part of the comprehensive event, will generally be reanalyzed (cf. Lord 1973).

The preceding summary of some studies on serial verb constructions in transition reveals a number of striking similarities between the reanalysis of serial verbs and the changes described for English and other European languages above. There is specifically the gradual nature of this change. As pointed out above, those deverbal forms that can be analyzed as (marginal) prepositions in English or German still exhibit some verbal properties to varying degrees. There is also a great deal of similarity in the exact morphological, syntactic and semantic criteria regarded as crucial for reanalysis. There are, however, also clear differences. There is no evidence, for example, that reanalysis of verbs as prepositions restabilizes an eroded system of case distinctions in European languages, and there also seems to be a difference with regard to the semantic domains involved in this change. Deverbal prepositions in English seem to be derived from three major semantic domains:

(17) a. "time/motion": during, pending, following, (enduring, last ing, continuing)[6], ago, come, past;
b. "exception": bar, barring, except, excepted, excepting, ex cluded, excluding, omitting, save, saving, not counting, (outnomen, outtaken, bating, abating);
c. "topic/perspective": concerning, considering, pertaining to, regarding, respecting, touching;

6 Some older expressions that are no longer used in Present-Day English are given in brackets.

What these three groups, the last two in particular, show is that deverbal prepositions tend to develop where primary prepositions are not available. In English there are no primary prepositions available that express a restriction on a quantifier or a perspective of a statement. So, if there is a functional motivation behind the development of deverbal prepositions in English, it could be seen in problem-solving, i.e. in conceptualization by expressing one thing in terms of another.[7]

It has often been noted (e.g. Friederich 1969: 89) that a participle in English may frequently correspond to a preposition in German. Given that participial constructions are much rarer in German than in English in adverbial function and even totally impossible in attributive function, this should not really come as a surprise. However, the use of participles as parts of post-nominal modifiers is not only a matter of stylistic variation in English, but often the normal and preferred option (cf. (18)-(21)) or even only possibility (cf. (22)-(23)) in structures where German uses prepositions:

(18) a. Für Reisende *mit* DB Tourist-Karte.
b. For travellers *holding* DB Tourist-Karte.

(19) a. The mystery *surrounding* the ship Marie-Celeste has never been satisfactorily explained.
b. Das Geheimnis *um* die Marie-Celeste ist nie völlig geklärt worden.

(20) a. A film *starring* Bruce Lee.
b. Ein Film *mit* Bruce Lee.

(21) a. Wenn er so tief liegt, wird es ein Schwede *mit* Eisenerz sein, schätzte Oskar.
b. Must be a Swede *carrying* iron ore to draw so much water, Oskar reflected.

(22) a. Die Texte *zu* den abgebildeten Pflanzen ...
b. The texts *accompanying* the photographs ...

(23) a. The answer to the question *facing* modern man ...
b. Die Antwort auf die Frage *an* den Menschen von heute ...

---

7 Heine et al. (to appear) regard grammaticalization largely as "... the result of a process which has *problem-solving* as its main goal".

Rohdenburg 1990, who investigated such correspondences in some detail and provided the preceding examples, lists 56 verbs as frequent translational equivalents of 21 prepositions in German. The participles in the examples (18)-(23) are certainly not prepositions. A comparison of such sentences with the translational equivalents in German shows, however, that participles in English are increasingly used in functions reserved for prepositions in German. Given the similarity between prepositional phrases and participial verb phrases in adverbial and attributive function and given the impossibility of strict delimitation between the two categories, there is always the potential for reanalyses in these cases. In view of the contrasts illustrated by (18)-(23) and those described in more detail by Rohdenburg 1990, it seems justified to say that the tendency for non-finite verb phrases to be reanalyzed as prepositions is stronger and more pervasive in English than in German. The English examples listed above may well provide the starting point for such reanalyses. And, although this is again somewhat speculative, one reason for this difference between English and German could well be seen in the isolating character of the former.

4. Concluding remarks

Within more recent versions of generative grammar, prepositions are counted among the major lexical categories, together with nouns, verbs and adjectives. These major categories, however, are treated as further analyzable and decomposable by means of a feature system that postulates [±N] and [±V] as basic features (cf. Chomsky 1970; Stowell 1981, etc.). The distinction between 'nominal' and 'verbal' is assumed to be a universal one and the four categories are defined in terms of these basic features as follows:

(24) a. N: [+N,-V]
b. V: [-N,+V]
c. A: [+N,+V]
d. P: [-N,-V]

This decomposition makes it possible to define natural classes like [-N] or [+N] and to state syntactic generalizations like the following:

(25) a. Categories with the feature [+N] do not take bare NP objects.
b. Categories with the feature [-N] are case assigners.
c. Categories with the feature [+V] can be modified by adverbs.
d. Categories with the feature [-V] form phrases that may be focused in cleft constructions in English.

To round off our discussion, we will briefly examine whether the decomposition of prepositions as [-N,-V] is supported in any way by the historical change discussed in this paper and whether this specification throws any light on this reanalysis.

In terms of the feature specifications given above the historical process discussed in this paper can be seen as a change from [-N,+V] to [-N,-V]. Although such a notation does not capture the gradual nature of the relevant change, it does throw some light on this process and does receive some justification from the facts presented above. As is shown by the specifications given in (24), prepositions have a feature in common and may thus form a natural class with both nouns and verbs. It is therefore to be expected that both nouns and verbs, but not adjectives, provide the major sources for the development of new prepositions. And that is indeed the case. In each case the change can be seen as a loss of specific (nominal or verbal) properties: Nouns lose their articles and thus their potential for reference (*in* (**the*) *spite of the rain* vs. *in the still of the night*). Verbs lose the ability to inflect for tense, aspect and mood or to combine with the relevant affixes. Furthermore, verbs lose their ability to occur as the only predicate in a sentence. The negative specification of prepositions also captures nicely the fact that a development from nouns or verbs to prepositions is much more common than the reverse. Grammaticalization, which to a certain extent the reanalysis of verbs as prepositions is, generally involves a loss of features: Constraints on word order variability, loss of agreement, phonological and morphoerosion as well as semantic bleaching.

References

Chao, Yuen Ren. 1968. *A Grammar of Spoken Chinese*. Berkeley: University of California Press.

Chomsky, Noam. 1970. Remarks on Nominalization. In Jacobs, Roderick A. and Peter S. Rosenbaum (eds.). *Readings in English Transformational Grammar*. Waltham, Mass.: Ginn and Company. 184-221.

Curme, George O. 1931, repr. 1983. *A Grammar of the English Language*, Vol. II: *Syntax*. Essex, Conn.: Verbatim.

Dill, Lesa B. 1986. *English Prepositions: The History of a Word Class*. Unpubl. Diss., Athens, Georgia.

Eisenberg, Peter. 1979. Syntax und Semantik denominaler Präpositionen des Deutschen. In Weydt, Harald (ed.). *Die Partikeln der deutschen Sprache*. Berlin: de Gruyter. 518-527.

Emonds, Joseph E. 1985. *A Unified Theory of Syntactic Categories*. Dordrecht: Foris.

Friederich, Wolf. 1969. *Technik des Übersetzens*. München: Hueber.

Givón, Talmy. 1975. Serial Verbs and Syntactic Change: Niger-Congo. In Li, Charles N. (ed.). *Word Order and Word Order Change*. Austin: University of Texas Press. 47-112.

Heine, Bernd et al. to appear. From Cognition to Grammar: Evidence from African Languages. In Traugott, Elizabeth C. and Bernd Heine (eds.). *Approaches to Grammaticalization*, Vol.I. Amsterdam: Benjamins.

Huddleston, Rodney. 1984. *Introduction to the Grammar of English*. Cambridge: C.U.P.

Lehmann, Christian. 1985. Grammaticalization: Synchronic Variation and Diachronic Change. *Lingua e Stile* XX:303-318.

- - -. 1986. Grammaticalization and Linguistic Typology. *General Linguistics* 26:3-22.

- - -. 1982. *Thoughts on Grammaticalization - A Programmatic Sketch*, Vol.I (akup 48). Köln: Institut für Sprachwissenschaft der Universität.

Li, Charles N. and Sandra Thompson. 1973. Serial verb constructions in Mandarin Chinese: Subordination or coordination? In Corum, Claudia et al. (eds.). *You Take the High Node and I'll Take the Low Node. Papers from the Comparative Syntax Festival*. Chicago: Chicago Linguistic Society. 96-103.

Lord, Carol. 1973. Serial Verbs in Transition. *Studies in African Linguistics* 4:269-296.

Middle English Dictionary. 1956 ff. Kurath, Hans and Sherman M.Kuhn (eds.). Ann Arbor: University of Michigan Press.

Mindt, Dieter. 1989. Prepositions in LOB and BROWN. *ICAME Journal* 13:67-70.

- - - and Christel Weber. 1989. Prepositions in American and British English. *World Englishes* 8:229-238.

The Oxford English Dictionary. 1933. Murray, James A.H. et al. (eds.). Oxford: The Clarendon Press.

Poutsma, Hendrik. 1926. *A Grammar of Late Modern English*, Part II/2: *The Verb and the Particles*. Groningen: Noordhoff.

Quirk, Randolph and Joan Mulholland. 1964. Complex Prepositions and Related Sequences. *English Studies* 45, Suppl.:64-73.
- - - et al. 1985. *A Comprehensive Grammar of the English Language*. London: Longman.

Rohdenburg, Günter. 1990. Aspekte einer vergleichenden Typologie des Englischen und Deutschen. In Gnutzmann, Claus (ed.). *Kontrastive Linguistik*. Frankfurt/M./Bern: Lang.

Stowell, Timothy A. 1981. *Origins of Phrase Structure*. Unpubl. Diss., MIT.

Vestergaard, Torben. 1973. On the Open-Endedness of the Form-Class 'Preposition' in English. *English Studies* 54:148-163.
Visser, F. Th. 1966. *An Historical Syntax of the English Language*, Part II/2: *Syntactical Units with One Verb*. Leiden: Brill.

Zipf, George K. 1949. *Human Behavior and the Principle of Least Effort*. Cambridge, Mass.: Addison-Wesley Press.

A two-level approach to projective prepositions

(German *über-unter*, *vor-hinter*, *rechts-links*)

Ewald Lang
(Wuppertal/Stuttgart)

1. Introduction

1.1. Scope of the data

German locative expressions include a subset of projective[1] prepositionals, the inventory of which is formed by six basic prepositions

(1) a. *über - unter;*
b. *vor - hinter;*
c. *rechts - links*

and a somewhat idiosyncratic set of adverbials somehow derived from them:[2]

---

1 The term is due to Herskovits (1986:156 ff.), who calls "these prepositions 'projective', because all fundamentally involve the experience of viewing and the idea of a point of observation." Though I do not fully agree with this definition, I shall stick to the term as it has become a familiar label in the literature.

2 In comparison to German, the inventory of projective prepositions in English is (a) richer and (b) patterns across simple and complex expressions. Thus, the equivalents of (1) include at least the following items (for completion see Herskovits (1986), Boers (1987)):
(i)*above/below, over/under, on top of ...*
in front/at the back of, before/behind ...
right/left of, at/on/in/to/by the right/left (hand) side of ...
Though I will not delve into details, two points should be noted. First, in explicitly making reference to designated sides (or parts) of objects, the complex expressions in (i) reveal what the semantics of projective prepositions is about - it is a device to locate an object in relation to a reference object by specifying a side-based neighbourhood-region of the latter. Second, there is a wide range of uses where simple and complex projective expressions are interchangeable, but there are also

(2) a. *darüber - darunter, oben - unten, oberhalb - unterhalb*
b. *davor - dahinter, vorn - hinten*
c. *rechts-links davon, zur Rechten - Linken von, rechterhand-linkerhand*

Needless to say, it remains a major task to elucidate the interplay of morphosyntactic and semantic properties in this field. However, as I will be concerned with semantic aspects of these expressions that seem to be constant across categorial distinctions, I will confine the analysis to the core prepositions in (1). Moreover, I will deal only with the locational meanings of these prepositions, restrict the data to attributive constructions or simple copula sentences as in (3), and neglect the distinction between local vs. directional interpretation.[3]

1.2. Undisputed preliminaries

1.2.1.The general structure of local prepositions

Semantically, phrasal or sentential expressions of the form

(3) x (ist) *bei/an/auf/über/vor/rechts von ....* y
[x (is) near/at/on/above/in front of/to the right of y]

all involve the localization of x (the entity to be located, for short: LE) with respect to a spatial region surrounding y (the reference object, for short: RO). This much is common sense among all students of local prepositions and we will adopt this view by assuming (4) as a first approximation to representing the lexical meaning of local prepositions. Leaving out controversial details of competing recent proposals (Herweg 1988; Wunderlich/Herweg 1986/89; Bierwisch 1988; Kaufmann 1988, Habel 1989), the

---

differences, e.g. the puzzling fact that *in front of, on top of* etc.hardly combine with measure phrases, whereas the German adverbials in (2) do.

3 But note the following asymmetry in (1). While for a. and b., as with other prepositions, local vs. directional uses correlate with dative vs. accusative, the pair in c. is different in requiring genitive for local use and in lacking directional use altogether. I take this as evidence in support of the claim that the three axes involved (viz. Vertical, Observer Axis, Horizontal) differ significantly as to their role in the conceptualization of space and hence as to the way they figure in the semantic structure of spatial expressions (see sections 2 - 4).

general format to represent the lexical meaning of spatial prepositions is supposed to be this:

(4) ^y ^x (LOC (x, REG*(y)) ...)

In this schema, 'x' and 'y' are variables to be replaced with appropriate representations of (object-)individuals; 'LOC (x, R)' is a localization relation to be read as "the place of x is locally included in some region R"; 'R' in turn is determined by a set of functions REG*, the elements of which assign a prepositionspecific region to the object represented by 'y'. The '...' mark the place for the possible addition of further constraining conditions.

1.2.2. Theta-roles

Mediated by the notion of theta-roles, the semantic distinction of RO and LE correlates with the syntactic distinction of internal vs. external arguments associated with the preposition at issue. Thus, in terms of syntactic-semantic composition, the argument y occupying the governed position (= the one assigned case by the prepositional head governing it) is assigned an internal theta-role ^y to be saturated by a constituent naming the reference object RO. The argument x is assigned the external theta-role ^x, which is discharged depending on whether the given PP syntactically functions as an argument, a predicate, or a modificational adjunct (cf. Bierwisch (1988)). In our sample of data, the external theta-role is eventually saturated by a constituent naming the located object LE. Consideration of the syntactic roots of the distinction RO vs. LE is relevant in deciding on transitivity and conversion relations with projective prepositions.

1.2.3. Delimitation of Meaning

What is specific to each of the prepositions in (1) and (3) is the way it determines a particular neighbourhood region of y. Thus, as a first step in specifying REG* in (4), it makes sense to distinguish a BEI-region, an AUF-region, an ÜBER-region etc. Given this, the next step is to establish which of these particular regions surrounding y are disjoint and which possibly overlap. Being determined by the putative prime **proximity** solely, the BEI-region can be considered to be the least specific of all preposition-based neighbourhood regions (which is obviously somehow related to the fact that *bei,* in contrast to the items in (1), neither has a lexical opposite nor takes measure phrases).

Now, in a sense, the projective prepositions in (1), which come in three pairs of lexical polar opposites, seem to divide the BEI-region into six (partially overlapping) subregions. This much is *opinio communis* among students of prepositions, but there is much debate on the conceptual basis as well as on the proper semantic ingredients by means of which the prepositions can be accounted for. Instead of reviewing all the relevant literature (for a useful survey see Retz-Schmidt 1988), in the section to follow I will give an outline of my own proposal. Put in a nutshell, the claims I am going to discuss amount to the following:

(5a) For the prepositions in (1), the component REG* in (4) can be specified by a set of **semantic parameters** that determine the pertinent neighbourhood regions by making reference to conceptually available axis-based sides ("top", "bottom","front", "back" etc.) of the RO.

(5b) The parameters for side-assignment are derived from the three axes that form man's primary perceptual space, viz. the Vertical, the Observer Axis, and the Horizontal. It is in relation to these axes that objects are assigned dimensions, positions, and locations in space and it is the properties of these axes that govern the semantics of projective prepositions.

(5c) The relevant spatial properties of objects are to be represented on a level distinct from that of (4) by means of **Object Schemata** that reflect our everyday knowledge of spatial objects (which is compatible with, but distinct from, our linguistic knowledge needed to use object names properly).

(5d) The need to account for the various **intrinsic** vs. **extrinsic uses** of these prepositions as well as for relations like **transitivity** and **conversion**, is what calls for a two-level approach as proposed here.

2. Basic assumptions

2.0. Background

The two-level approach to the semantics of projective prepositions outlined below is an extension of a framework which was originally developed in a comprehensive analysis of dimensional expressions (see Bierwisch/Lang 1987, 1989; Lang 1988, 1989 a, b) and which has since been adopted and modified by other researchers in a series of studies on prepositions (Herweg 1988; Wunderlich/Herweg 1986/89; Bierwisch 1988; Kaufmann 1989, Habel 1989) or position verbs (Maienborn 1989 a, b). The move from dimensional terms to prepositions involves two aspects of continuity worth being noted. The first, discussed in 2.1, concerns the shared spatial knowledge forming the conceptual domain which both groups of lexical items refer to. The second, discussed in section 3, relates to the fact that, to a certain extent, projective prepositions and dimension expressions pose the same types of semantic problems.

2.1. The framework of spatial knowledge

2.1.0. What are the basics?

It is intuitively obvious that there is an inherent affinity between spatial expressions designating the height, width or depth of objects and prepositions locating objects in relation to the top-bottom, front-back etc. axis of other objects. We stay within the same domain, so the extension suggests itself. But it makes a difference where you start from. Thus, an approach that draws on basic concepts that proved adequate for the analysis of dimensional terms, verbs of position and other spatial vocabulary should be preferred to an account which draws solely on concepts and rules that are specifically devised for the analysis of spatial prepositions (as holds for e.g. Herskovits' work).

As regards the source of spatial knowledge and the inventory of conceptual elements that are made use of in the descriptive framework, the 'experiential' approach adopted by Herskovits and others is, roughly speaking, **observer-centered** and **situation-based**. That is, the primary concepts for approaching the meaning of locative expressions are defined in terms of prototypical **situation types** which involve a human being in "canonical position" (standing upright on horizontal ground) as the central source for orientation cues (among them the six halfline axes relevant for the description of projective prepositions (see Herskovits 1986:156 ff.)).

In contrast, the two-level approach I am advocating may be called **object-centered** and **axes-based**, as it primarily draws on an inventory of categorized **object concepts** (see section 4) and the categorization grids that define their constitutive spatial properties. In this approach, then, spatial knowledge is basically organized by what I call the **Primary Perceptual Space (PPS)**, that is, a system of axes that form our internal model of the external space. (Though it is difficult to compare the ontologies of both approaches, I dare say the latter is more general and comprehensive, as it seems to obey Occam's razor more clearly than Herskovits' system.)

Presupposing the details discussed at length in Lang 1987, 1989, Lang & Carstensen 1990, we will take a brief look at these axes by examining briefly how they are involved in the semantics of dimensional terms and projective prepositions.

2.1.1. The Vertical

Originating from the effects of gravitation as perceived by the human body, the Vertical is an orientation cue which is **ubiquitous and constant**, that is, available everywhere in our terrestrial habitat and with the same effect at all times. This makes verticality a primary cue of spatial perception to the effect that, within Primary Perceptual Space, the Vertical is granted the status of an **independent** axis.

Man's upright posture assigns the Vertical a natural **foot** on the earth's surface (or on a parallel plane that serves as ground level) and a **fixed direction** which is determined as **geofugal** by the top-bottom asymmetry of the human body. In geometrical terms, the Vertical thus has the attributes of a ray or directed segment. The foot serves as a zero-point F such that any points F', F"(distinct from F) on the Vertical define directed segments that increase unidirectionally. The direction defined by F, F', F"... etc. corresponds to the direction of the height scale whose intervals are construed as increasing degrees of height assigned to the objects in question.

Due to these features, the Vertical is physically as well as conceptually the most salient and also the dominant axis of Primary Perceptual Space; the other axes are defined in relation to the Vertical. In other words, the Vertical is the backbone of spatial orientation.

2.1.2. Linguistic reference to the Vertical

Consider the sample of spatial expressions in (6) showing the inherent relationship of dimension adjectives (in dimensional as well as in distance or positional interpretation) and projective prepositions.

(6) a. *Das Fenster ist 2m hoch*
(dimension and distance interpretation)
[The window is 2 metres high]
b. *Das Fenster ist 2m höher als der Tisch*
(distance interpretation)
[The window is 2 metres higher than the table]
c. *Das Fenster ist 2m über dem Tisch*
(projective preposition)
[The window is 2 metres above the table]

Fig. 1 Interpretations of *Das Fenster ist 2m hoch*

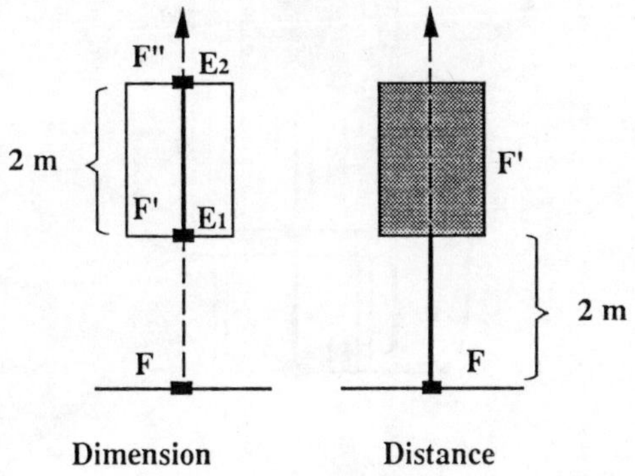

The semantic differences to be correlated with the morphosyntactic distinctions between dimension adjective, distance adjective[4], and projective preposition emerge from the different ways in which the points F, F', F" of the Vertical are instantiated by an object said to be *high* (in itself) or to be located in a *higher place* (compared to another object) or to be located in the region determined by the *highest part* (= the top side of) the reference object. In a way, the distance adjective forms the bridge between dimension term and projective preposition. Fig. 1 above illustrates the two interpretations of (6) a., Fig. 2 indicates those elements that the interpretations of (6) b. and c. have in common, their differences will be commented on.

Fig. 2 Spatial configuration referred to by (6)(b) and (c)

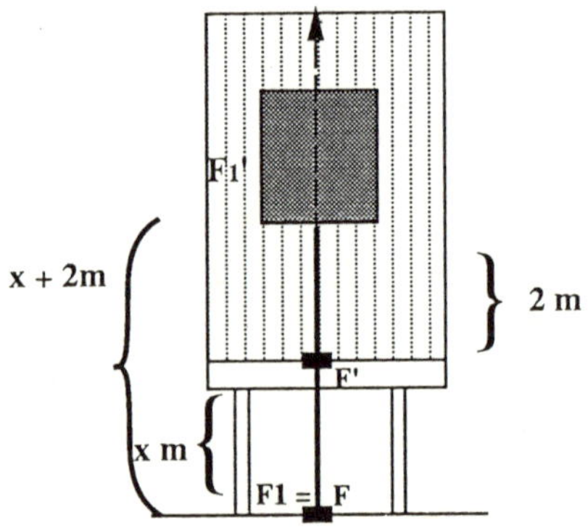

4 Based on evidence from e.g. French or Spanish, where the translation of (6) a. would yield two morphologically distinct constructions, I assume two separate lexical entries for *hoch* (or *high)* corresponding to dimension and distance interpretation, respectively. Cf. (7)(a, b).

The **Dimension** Interpretation of *hoch/high* in (6) a. involves the projection of two axis endpoints E_1 and E_2 onto the Vertical such that the segment formed by $\overline{E_1E_2}$ is transformed into a directed segment defined by the points $\overrightarrow{F'F''}$ of the Vertical. The deciding condition of this interpretation is that the relevant points of the Vertical, i.e. F', F'', are instantiated by axial endpoints of one and the same object *x*. Given this, it it these endpoints that define the **object's bottom and top**, respectively.

In contrast, the **Distance** Interpretation of *hoch /high* in (6) a. is based on the condition that the points F', F''of the Vertical are instantiated by distinct objects. In the example given it is the window as a whole which is projected onto F', thereby defining the directed segment $\overrightarrow{\mathbf{F'F''}}$ of the Vertical as a distance between ground level (the default value of F) and window (instantiating F'). So the comparative construction in (6) b. involves two distances to be compared, the directed segments marked as $\overrightarrow{FF'}$ and $\overrightarrow{F_1F_1'}$ in Fig. 2, which have the foot F in common ($F = F_1$).

In short, the Dimension Interpretation is based on a directed segment **defined within one object**, which entails the object being assigned bottom and top; whereas the Distance Interpretation is based on a directed segment **defined between objects** that are conceived as mere points, which entails that the objects' sides (including top, bottom, front and rear) are disregarded.

The interpretation of the projective preposition in (6) c. involves aspects of both dimension and distance interpretation plus something special. The dimension aspect is involved indirectly in establishing the top of the table, which, in turn, determines the relevant ÜBER-region (dotted area in Fig. 2). The distance aspect is involved inasmuch as the local relation between the located object and the reference object is conceived as a measurable distance - this is the basis for the near-equivalence of (6) b. and (6) c.

To sum up, the lexical meanings of *2m hoch, 2m höher* and *2m über* all involve the Vertical to localize objects in space; but while the adjectives operate **on geometric concepts** like axes, directed segments, (end-)points, sides etc., the projective preposition *über* (or any other item of (1) or (2)) involves a **topological concept** of neighbourhood region as indicated by the dummy REG* in (4). Semantically, the projective prepositions (unlike the spatial adjectives, on the one hand, and unlike the pure topological prepositions such as *bei* or *an,* on the other hand) thus form a field of structure formation where geometry and topology intersect and interact.

The different though obviously related ways in which reference to the Vertical is involved in (6) a.-c. are rooted in the internal semantic structure and the morphosyntactic features of the spatial expressions at issue. What we are looking for, then, is a representational format capable of capturing both the common reference to the Vertical and the different ways in which this reference is grammatically coded. With this end in view I will assume lexical entries for *hoch* and *über* as shown in (7) that associate the morphosyntactic features of these lexical items with semantic representations (designed as Semantic Forms along the lines of Bierwisch & Lang 1987, 1989 and Bierwisch 1988 - see 3.2 below) that account for dimension adjectives (7) a., distance adjectives (7) b., and projective prepositions (7) c. respectively:

(7) a. /hoch/; [+N,+V]; ^c^x [[QUANT **VERT** x] ⊇ [v + c]]
/niedrig/; [+N,+V]; ^c^x [[QUANT **VERT** x] ⊆ [v - c]]
b. /hoch/; [+N,+V]; ^c^x [[QUANT **VERT** [**DIST y** x]] ⊇ [v + c]]
c. /über/; [-N, -V]; ^y^x [Loc x ⊆ [Loc [**VERT*F'** y]]]
/unter/; [-N, -V]; ^y^x [Loc x ⊆ [Loc [**VERT*F** y]]]

The central point is how the semantic parameters that refer to the Vertical (indicated by **bold type**) are integrated into complex units that differ as to argument structure and syntactic categorization. I cannot repeat here the details that support the design of the representations given above, so let me note just three points that are of immediate interest to our topic.

First, note that compared to the dimension adjectives in (7) a., the distance adjective *hoch* in (7) b. embodies an additional component **DIST**, which induces a third argument place y, where y figures as a parameter to be replaced with an appropriate value from the context. Thus, in the interpretations of (6) a. and b., this parameter y will assume the value "ground level", that is, the default value to instantiate F (see Fig. 1), where F is brought in by the semantic component **VERT**. But y can also be replaced with a value available from the structural context as in e.g. *das Fenster ist vom Fußboden aus 2m höher als der Tisch* .

Second, note that there are differences in antonymy relations. The polar antonymy of the dimension terms *hoch* - *niedrig* draws on scaling operations (represented by '⊇... +' and '⊆... - ' in (7) a.) that are reversals of each other but operate on the same scale determined by **VERT.** In other words, the Vertical yields the common scale basis on which opposite operations underlying *hoch* [high] and *niedrig* [low] are carried out. This is reflected in (7) a. by according the parameter **VERT** the same place in the semantic form of both adjectives.

The distance adjective *hoch* in (7) b. does not have an antonymous counterpart *niedrig* (note that e.g. *Der Tisch ist 2m niedriger als das Fenster* is not a converse of (6) b.). In some cases, this gap can be filled by using the distance adjective *tief* as in *Davos ist höher gelegen als Zürich = Zürich ist tiefer gelegen als Davos* [D is higher-lying than Z = Z is lower-lying than D].[5] However, despite the fact that, in certain contextual frames, *hoch* and *tief* may denote opposite directions, they are not lexical antonyms (for details cf. Lang 1989). These observations are accounted for in (7) b. by assuming a parameter **DIST** (a component shared by all distance terms like *hoch*, *tief*, *weit* and their derivatives) such that the particular representations of *hoch* or *tief* are obtained by combining **DIST** with a specificatory component **VERT** or **OBS**. Though the so-called distance adjectives are poorly understood as yet, the representation suggested in (7) b. seems to capture some of their peculiarities.

At any rate, assuming a separate component **DIST** that induces the additional argument y will account for the fact that the items containing it refer to distances defined between objects, while allowing for **DIST** to be specified by **VERT** in the manner just outlined will account for the fact that the distance adjective *hoch* refers to the Vertical as the carrier axis of the distance it denotes.

The antonymy of the prepositions *über* - *unter* emerges from applying a relation of local inclusion (represented by 'Loc ... $\subseteq$ Loc ...y') to neighbourhood regions of the reference object y that are determined by opposite sides of y. These object sides are defined by coincidence with the designated points F,F' of the Vertical induced by **VERT.** In other words, the Vertical yields the orientation cue with reference to which an object y can be assigned opposite sides which, in turn, define correspondingly opposite neighbourhood regions of y. Thus, the antonymy of *über* - *unter* is due to their making reference to neighbourhood regions of y determined by opposite sides of y. This is reflected in (7) c. by assuming two correspondingly distinct parameters, viz. **VERT*F'** and **VERT*F**, which are taken to represent sets of conditions for identifying the respective regions. Note that **F**, **F'** are meta-variables ranging over the points F, F', F".of the Vertical induced by **VERT** in such a way that **F** refers to the object's bottom as defined by the actual foot F_a, whereas **F'** refers to the object's top as defined by the corresponding F'_a .

5 I refrain from discussing the details with respect to which German here differs from English or French.

I hasten to add that the labels used to symbolize the relevant parameters in (7) a.-c. are meant to give an idea of their internal composition. What really matters is the substantial interpretation these parameters are given as notional elements within a theory. As regards **VERT** and **DIST**, this has been done at length in the studies quoted above. Now, based on the assumption that the representations suggested in (7) c. can be shown to be a notational variant of the format used in (4), we will consider **VERT*F'** and **VERT*F** promising candidates to replace the place-holder REG* in (4), yielding

(8) a. *über*: ^y ^x (LOC (x, **VERT*F'**(y)) ...)
b. *unter*: ^y ^x (LOC (x, **VERT*F** (y)) ...)

Spelling out the full range of a semantic parameter is a thorny business to do, so we will focus on answering the simple question:
What's in a **VERT*F** ?

2.2.1. The Observer Axis

Originating in the visual organ, this axis is determined by the line of sight of a (potential or actual) observer. Because of this it is - in contrast to the Vertical's ubiquity and constancy - **flexible in two respects.** First, having a movable source (i.e. the observer), this axis does not have a fixed anchorage in the surrounding physical space but is induced by a moving human interpreter of physical space. Second, the Observer Axis has an anatomically determined pivot allowing for a 180° turn in either of two planes (vertically and horizontally). Being the axis of depth perception, the Observer Axis certainly provides another pillar of spatial perception. However, due to the fact that the Observer Axis is bound to human carriers whose normal position (upright posture) is defined as normal only in relation to the surrounding physical space, this axis is **not** as **independent** an axis within Primary Perceptual Space as is the Vertical.

Defined by a (real or imaginary) observer's gaze, the Observer Axis has a **direction** which is biologically fixed as **away from the observer**, and it has a **bounding point** O, which (disregarding disparity) is given by the anatomically determined origin of an observer's line of sight.

In geometrical terms, the Observer Axis can also be described as a ray or directed segment. It is defined by the bounding point O and has a direction in that any points O', O" determine unidirectionally increasing distances from O. Due to this, the Observer Axis provides the scale basis for **depth**

assignment. Originating in the visual organ of a human observer, however, the Observer Axis of Primary Perceptual Space simultaneously serves other purposes as well. It also forms the basis for perspectivizing spatial objects.

perspectivization consists of assigning objects observer-determined "fronts" and "backs" etc. and locating objects *x, y* relative to one another, as in *x is in front of y* or *y is behind x* etc. In short, the Observer Axis is the carrier of two major cognitive cues of spatial orientation: **depth assignment** and **perspectivization**. Coming from the same biological source, these two cognitive devices closely interact. Note, however, that **depth assignment** and **perspectivization** are partially independent in that they draw on distinct spatial structures; therefore, they have to be kept separately (cf. 2.2.2 below).

In the unmarked case, given by the position of the eyes of an observer in upright posture, the Observer Axis is orthogonal (at 90°) to the Vertical. In the other relevant configuration, the Vertical and the Observer Axis lie at an angle of 180° such that they run parallel but in diametrically opposed directions. The third case, where the Vertical and the Observer Axis run in the same direction (at 0°), is perceptually quite clear but, interestingly enough, does not constitute a conceptually relevant parameter (cf. Lang 1987, 1989).

2.2.2. *Linguistic reference to the Observer Axis*

The examples (9) a.-d. show, in a way quite parallel to those in (6), the inherent relationship of dimension terms, distance terms, and projective prepositions. But due to the two functions of the Observer Axis, i.e. **depth assignment** and **perspectivization,** we have to consider a wider range of possibilities.

(9) a. *Die Kiste ist 2m tief*
(dimension interpretation)
[The box is 2 metres deep/in depth]
b. *Die Kugel ist 2m tief im Mauerwerk*
(distance interpretation)
[The ball is 2 metres deep in the masonry]
c. *Die Kugel ist tiefer im Korb als das Dreieck*
(distance interpretation)
[The ball is deeper in the basket than the triangle]
d. *Im Korb ist das Dreieck vor der Kugel*
(projective prepositions)

Im Korb ist die Kugel hinter dem Dreieck
[In the basket, the triangle is in front/behind of the ball]

Fig. 3 illustrates spatial configurations to which the sentences in (9) may be applied. In these cases, the relevant points of the Observer Axis, that is the bounding point O and its successors O', O", can be furnished with the appropriate instantiations needed for **depth assignment.**

Fig. 3 Spatial configurations referred to by (9)(a) - (d)

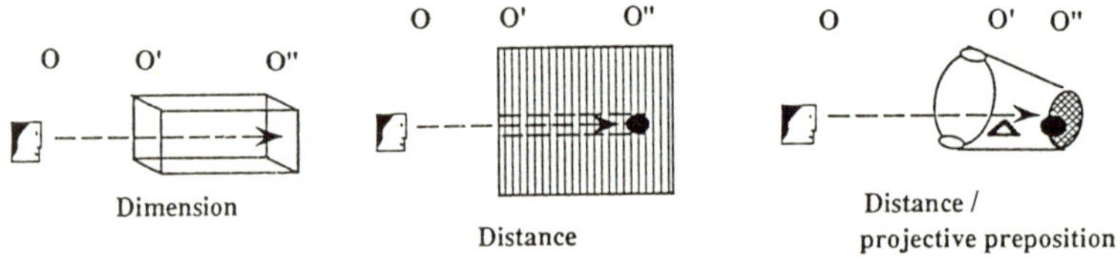

As regards the semantics of the prepositions *vor* - *hinter*, however, **depth assignment** is only part of the story. The close relationship between (9) c. and (9) d. rests on the availability of a hollow object (viz. the basket) forming the frame of reference with respect to which the triangle and the ball can be ordered on the depth axis. If you imagine the scene with the basket removed, you will immediately realize that the spatial relation between the triangle and the ball can no longer be described by *tief(er)*, but has to be referred to by means of the projective prepositions *vor* - *hinter*. This is the point where **perspectivization** takes over.

There are basically two strategies for assigning observer-related sides to an object which does not have any intrinsically fixed front-back distinction. Each of these strategies corresponds to a specific spatial situation defined by the observer's location with respect to the object(s) at issue. Following familiar terminology (e.g. Herskovits 1986: Chap.10), one is called the **encounter situation** - the observer faces the object from a distance; the other is called the **coincidence situation** - the observer transfers his own front-back distinction onto the object in question. Consider the situations according to which an object, say, a block, is assigned "front" (F) and "back" (B), and how, depending on that, a ball and a triangle are located in relation to the block. Fig. 4 shows the relevant spatial configurations of observer, objects, and observer-related object sides.

Fig. 4 Perspectivization and side assignment

ENCOUNTER SITUATION

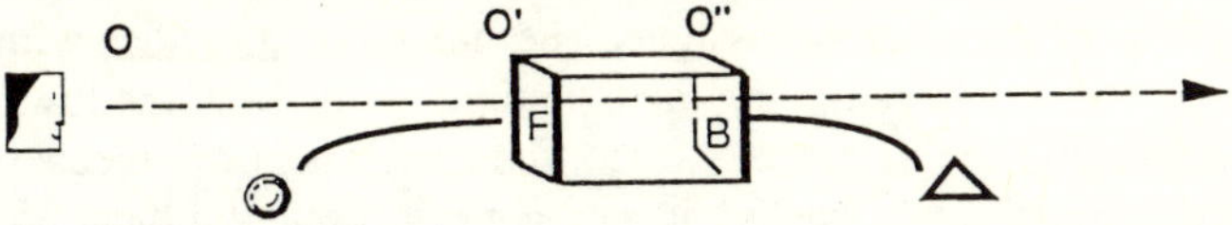

COINCIDENCE SITUATION

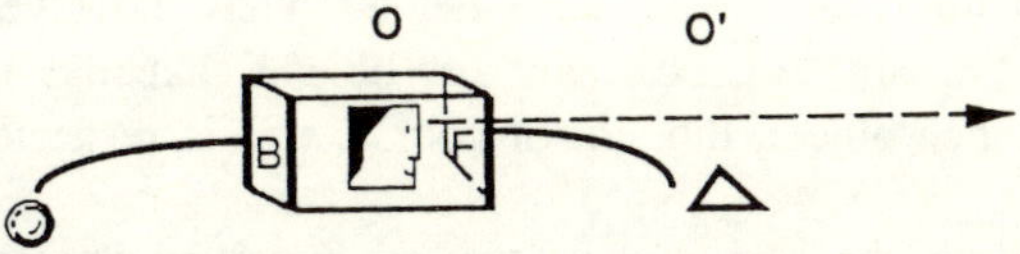

While the bounding point O of the Observer Axis is given by the observer in a like manner for both situations, there is an important difference between the two situations as to the role of the successor points O', O". Consider the interpretations of *x ist vor der Kiste / z ist hinter der Kiste* [x is in front of the box / z is behind the box], where die Kiste [the box] is the reference object with respect the to side-based neighbourhood regions of which the objects *x* and *z* are located.

In the encounter situation, point O' is instantiated by the less distant object face, which is then designated as "front" (F) or "accessible face"; O" is instantiated by the more distant object face, which is designated as "back" (B) or "remote face". Note the analogy to the Dimension Interpretation of *deep* in Fig. 3 above. According to this strategy, "front" and "back" are assigned to an object in terms of increasing distance from O on the Observer Axis. This is the source of the well-known mirror effect of assigning an object an observer-determined front.(i.e. the front of an object is the side which the observer faces or, which amounts to the same, the side which faces the observer).

Given this, we have the appropriate side-determined regions (surrounding the block) at our disposal, with reference to which the ball is said to be *vor* [in front of], and the triangle to be *hinter* [behind], the block. The crucial feature of this strategy of assigning observer-related sides and side-related locations to objects lies in the fact that the concepts "front" and "back" consistently correlate with less distant and more distant object faces, respectively.

In the **coincidence situation**, however, the crucial point is that the reference object to which sides are assigned (i.e. the box), coincides with the observer her/himself in instantiating the bounding point O (cf. the lower part of Fig. 4). According to this strategy, then, the assignment to objects of observer-related "fronts" and "backs" is not a projection of object sides onto points O', O" of the Observer Axis, but a transfer of the observer's intrinsic front and back onto the object in question - hence the altered distribution of "front" and "back" with respect to the block in Fig. 4. In fact, based on **coincidence** the triangle may be said to be *vor* [in front of] and the ball to be *hinter* [behind] the box. Even under this view, however, the Observer Axis remains available for localizing any objects that may instantiate O' outside the reference object, though, of course, this is restricted to front-based regions.

As regards the semantic parameters involved in *vor* and *hinter,* let me summarize the points made so far:

First, the observation that *vor* and *hinter,* with respect to the configuration of objects shown in Fig. 4, may assume the full range of interpretations assignable by either strategy (i.e. **encounter** and **coincidence**) is based on the fact that none of the objects involved (box, ball, triangle) has an intrinsic front or rear side. Hence, objects like these can be assigned fronts and backs only via projection from an external source.

Second, the observer, who forms the source of these projected assignments, has two orientation cues at her/his disposal, i.e. **depth assignment** and **perspectivization,** either of which may be used to assign fronts and backs to objects. Hence the range of possibilities illustrated in Fig. 4.

Third, despite the fact that **depth assignment** and **perspectivization** may produce the same effects (cf. the interpretations of *tief(er)* and *vor - hinter* in (9) c.-d.), their distinctness on the semantic level is linguistically overt in that e.g. *tief* embodies the former while *vor - hinter* embody the latter.

Fourth, on the conceptual level, **perspectivization** involves two assignment strategies, i.e. **encounter** and **coincidence situation**, which are to be considered as cognitively distinct devices. However, the fact that the interpretations of *vor* and *hinter* involve the availability of either strategy is not a sufficient reason for stipulating correspondingly distinct semantic representations of *vor* and *hinter*. In contrast with the case of dimension vs.

distances adjectives discussed above, there is no linguistic evidence available that would force us to assume separate lexical entries to represent, say, an "encounter - *vor* " and a "coincidence - *vor* ", and the same with *hinter*. In short, as regards the semantics of *vor* - *hinter*, I claim that the assignment strategies at issue do not figure as structural parameters on the level of semantic representation but are part of the procedures by means of which semantic parameters are processed on the language-independent level of conceptual representation.

Fifth, this leaves us with two things to be represented in the Semantic Form of the prepositions *vor* - *hinter* : a. establishing the VOR*-region and the HINTER*-region of a given reference object requires the object to be **perspectivized** on the basis of the Observer Axis; b. the **perspectivization** has to be spelled out in terms of assigning the reference object a front and a rear.

Thus, in analogy to the representations in (7)(a.-c.) and (8)(a.-b.), we may assume the following lexical entries:

(9) a./tief/; [+N,+V]; ^c^<u>x</u> [[QUANT **OBS** x] $\supseteq$ [v + c]] [6]
b. /tief/; [+N,+V]; ^c^<u>x</u> [[QUANT **OBS** [**DIST** **y** x]]$\supseteq$[v + c]]
c. /vor/; [-N, -V]; ^y^<u>x</u> [Loc x $\subseteq$ [Loc [**OBS*O** y]]]
/hinter/; [-N, -V]; ^y^<u>x</u> [Loc x $\subseteq$ [Loc [**OBS*O'** y]]]

(10)a. *vor*: ^y ^<u>x</u> (LOC (x, **OBS*O**(y)) ...)
b. *hinter* ^y ^<u>x</u> (LOC (x, **OBS*O'**(y)) ...)

OBS is a parameter identifying an axis by coincidence with the Observer Axis, **DIST** accounts for distances in the way outlined in section 2.1.2, the parameters **OBS*O** and **OBS*O'** are taken to represent sets of conditions for identifying the respective front-based and rear-based regions of the reference object y. In the spelling out these parameters we will focus on the question: Where do fronts and backs of objects come from?

2.3. The Horizontal

For reasons discussed elsewhere (cf. Lang 1987, 1989), the third axis of **PPS** is not an axis we are equipped to identify by primary perceptual infor-

6 The dimension adjective *tief* lacks a lexical antonym, for discussion cf. Lang 1987,1989.

mation, but is **derived from**, hence **dependent on**, the two others to fill the gap determined by the properties of the latter.

Based on this, the Horizontal does **not have any bounding points** or **directions**. Geometrically, it is reduced to the attributes of a simple line. This is the source of the well-known difficulties in distinguishing "left" from "right". When an object axis is assigned horizontality, its endpoints E and E' are left unspecified with respect to instantiations of "left" or "right". All that can be said about side assignment is that E and E' may not be assigned the same value. As a consequence, I do not have much to say about the semantics of the projective prepositionals *rechts - links (von).*

The distribution of "left" and "right" on the sides of an object, however, is (partially) dependent on the side assignments the object receives due to its verticality features and/or its intrinsic or observer-determined "front" - "back" features. (Which clearly reflects the dependency mentioned above).

Filling in the pertinent items, we get the pattern shown in (11) and (12). Spatial expressions that refer to the Horizontal all share a feature of inherent relativity, as reflected, inter alia, by the additional parameter d' induced by the parameter **ACROSS** in (11) a. - for details, see Lang 1987,1989; by the absence of any specificatory component in (11) b. such that *weit* refers to "distance pure" (in contrast with *hoch* and *tief* in (7) b. and (9) b.); and by making *rechts - links* in (11) c. inherit the type of dependency we observe in the meaning of *breit.*

(11) a. /breit/ [+N,+V]; ^c^$\underline{x}$ [[QUANT **ACROSS** d' x] ⊇ [v + c]]
/schmal/ [+N,+V]; ^c^$\underline{x}$ [[QUANT **ACROSS** d' x] ⊆ [v - c]]
b. /weit/ [+N,+V]; ^c^$\underline{x}$ [[QUANT [**DIST y** x] ⊇ [v + c]]
c. /rechts/ [-N, -V]; ^y^$\underline{x}$ [Loc x ⊆ [Loc [**ACROSS*R** y]]]
/links/ [-N, -V]; ^y^$\underline{x}$ [Loc x ⊆ [Loc [**ACROSS*L** y]]]

(12) a. *rechts* ^y ^$\underline{x}$ (LOC (x, **ACROSS*R**(y)) ...)
b. *links* ^y ^$\underline{x}$ (LOC (x, **ACROSS*L**(y)) ...)

While '**R**' and '**L**' in themselves might be assessed to be mere shibboleths, the structure of the representational framework in which they appear makes them nevertheless informative about the place they occupy within the system of spatial expressions.

Having thus narrowed down the basic set of semantic parameters that are specific to the projective prepositions in (1) and (2), the next step is to examine how these parameters receive the appropriate values in order to cover the wide range of interpretations they can assume. We will do this by taking up the second thread which links this approach to prepositions with the study of spatial dimension terms.

3. Polysemy problems

The second point in favour of extending the analysis of dimension terms to the analysis of projective prepositions is just this: the problems of polysemy raised by projective prepositions like *über, unter, vor, hinter* etc. are strikingly similar to the ones we face regarding the range of interpretations assignable to *high, deep, wide* .

Thus we would expect the representational means that account e.g. for the difference between primary designation (*high building, tall tower, deep hole, *high / *tall / *deep ball*) and contextual specification (*deep plot of ground, tall pole*) also to be appropriate to cope with the difference between intrinsic vs. extrinsic uses of projective prepositions (cf. *the poster above / in front of the building* vs. *the ball is above / in front of the pole*). In short, spatial prepositions make a rewarding test case of the framework that proved to be operative for dimension and distance adjectives and other spatial vocabulary.

As regards the treatment of polysemy, the two-level approach to the semantics of prepositions I propose in this paper differs markedly from the approach taken by Herkovits (or by related work within a prototype-semantics framework e.g. Vandeloise 1984, Langacker 1986, Hottenroth 1988, Lakoff 1987, 1988). A discussion in full detail would take us back to the very fundamentals of semantics. It will suffice to mention some of the major assumptions based on which my approach differs from the studies just mentioned.

3.1. Modularity

While other approaches are implicit in this respect, the two-level approach explicitly ascribes to the view that our cognitive behaviour is essentially based on structures and processes which are determined by the interaction of relatively autonomous systems and subsystems called 'modules'. This is the basic assumption which the two-level approach attempts to elaborate in tackling crucial problems of lexical semantics like the following:

(13) a.How to interrelate the lexical meanings of spatial terms with the morpho-syntactic category features assigned to them ?

b. How to draw a justified distinction between the linguisti cally coded semantic contents of a lexical item and the range of contextual specifications it may undergo ?

c. How to distinguish between, but at the same time allow for the interaction of, word meanings as part of linguistic knowledge and concepts as part of everyday or world knowledge ?

Evidently, these questions (touched on in 1.1 and 2.1 - 2.3 above) are aimed at specifying appropriate interfaces between different levels of mental representation, and it is along these lines that the two-level approach I am advocating has suggestions to give and solutions to offer. This takes us back to the problem of polysemy.

The problem raised by the theoretical need to assume abstract "ideal meanings" of spatial prepositions on the one hand, and by the empirical fact that we have to cope with complex contextual factors determining a wide range of actual interpretations of these prepositions on the other hand, is fully acknowledged but given a different status in the theory I propose.

The two-level approach accounts of various forms of polysemy by making it the result of the division of labour or interaction between two levels of knowledge representation that are differentiated from, and specifically mapped onto each other in the process of semantic interpretation. The characteristics given in 3.2 and 3.3 below may serve as "wanted" posters for the representation levels at issue (for details see Lang 1988, 1989 a, b).

3.2. Semantic Form

(SF-level) = level representing language-bound word meanings as grammatically determined sets of conditions for the identification of conceptual elements. The SF of a lexical item represents the internal structure of its lexical meaning as part of the item's entry in the lexicon and thus specifies what the given item can contribute to the compositional formation of complex structures. In fact, what was proposed in (7) - (12) above are SF-representations of adjectives and prepositions.

Let me briefly repeat: the SF of a lexical item is composed of categorized constants and variables representing grammatically coded parameters the values of which are available on the level of conceptual structure. As to their form, the SF-parameters are determined by compositionality conditions; as to substance, they have to be justified with respect to the domain-specific values they take on the conceptual level. In the case of dimensional designation this means that SF-level representations of object names like *tower, river, pole* etc. serve as addresses for access to (generic) object concepts to be represented on the level of conceptual structure - see (16), (21) and (23) in 4.4 below.

The SF-representations of the spatial terms proposed in (7) - (12) are composed of **semantic primes** that are construed to represent sets of conditions to identify an object extension (**VERT,OBS, ACROSS**), an axis-based distance between objects (**VERT**, **OBS** combined with **DIST**),or an object side-based neighbourhood region (**VERT*F, OBS*O** etc.). In technical terms, these components are parameters on the SF - level which are assigned values on the CS - level.

3.3. Conceptual Structure

(CS-level) = level representing language-independent, intermodally accessible elements and complexes of conceptual knowledge. CS-level is where (generic) concepts stored in longterm memory are processed to create contextually specified reference instances.

On CS-level, object concepts appear in the form of **object schemata (OS),** which represent the defining properties of a class of spatial objects. OS are thus representational units of the CS-level serving as location frames within which the parameters of the SF-level are instantiated, i.e. are assigned Dimension Assignment Values (DAV) or, in the case of projective prepositions, Side Assigment Values (SAV). We will come back to this in 4.5 below.

Given this, various phenomena subsumed under 'polysemy' can be accounted for by what I have called the division of labour between SF-level and CS-level. The claim is that each dimensional term has exactly one representation on SF-level, but a range of admissible interpretations on CS-level. This range of interpretations is provided by exactly that subset of object schemata which provide admissible values for the SF-representation at issue. Take for instance the putative polysemy of *tief* in view of the range of interpretations it is assigned in *tiefer Fluß, tiefe Nische, tiefe Wunde, tiefer Topf* [deep river, deep niche, deep wound, deep pan]. Within the two-level approach, there is one SF-representation for *tief* containing the relevant parameter **OBS** (cf. (9) a., but there are four distinct object schemata (for *river, niche, wound, pan* respectively, cf. Fig. 6) which determine four different ways of assigning the SF-parameter **OBS** a value on CS-level. Likewise, it is due to the differences in the object schemata that *vor* in e.g. *vor dem Fluß / der Nische / der Wunde / dem Topf* is assigned the range of distinct interpretations it covers.

3.4. Contextual determination

In the approach proposed here, the level of Semantic Form is considered to be the **interface** between grammatically determined linguistic knowledge and conceptually determined everyday or encyclopedic knowledge about the world, while Conceptual Structure is taken to provide a unified level of representation to which visual, auditory, motor, and, of course, linguistic information can be related and hence be interrelated among each other. Instead of retelling the whole story of contextually determined dimensional designation (cf. Lang 1988, 1989 a, b), I will just quote my paragon example of how object schemata on CS-level deal with contextual specification.

Note that the interpretation of a sentence like *Das Brett ist breit genug* [*the board is wide enough*] is highly context-dependent regarding the object extent to be identified by *breit* [*wide*]. Now, this sentence has the same range of interpretations when applied to the spatial situations shown in (14)(I-III), which form non-verbal contexts, as when embedded in the verbal contexts ... *und lang* or *und hoch* or *und tief genug, aber zu dünn* provided in (15)(1-3). Thus, either of the contextual sources produces the same effects on CS-level, that is, (14) and (15) result in the same set of specified object schemata (16) b. for *Das Brett ist breit*. Note that the generic concept "Brett" ["board"] is represented by the unspecified basic schema in (16) a., which may undergo the contextual specifications shown in (16) b.. For details of OS - see 4.4 below.

Technically speaking, non-verbal contexts like (14) and verbal contexts like (15) are equivalent as regards their role in determining the way in which the SF-parameter **ACROSS** of *breit* - cf. (11) a. - is assigned its appropriate value *across* in the specified object schemata in (16) b.

(14) *Das Brett ist breit genug* [*the board is wide enough*]

I II III

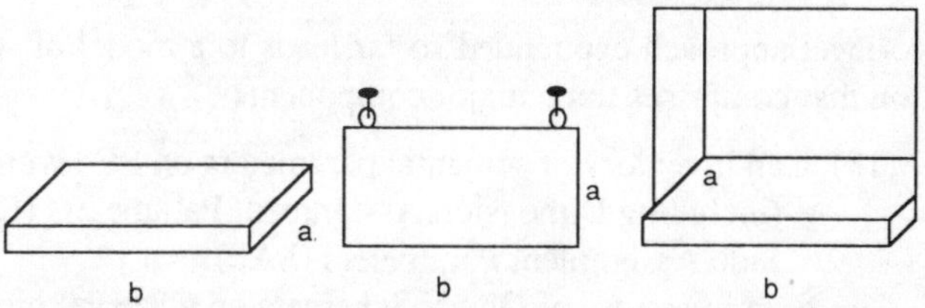

breit	= a	*breit*	= b	*breit*	= b
lang	= b	hoch	= a	tief	= a

(15) a. *Das Brett ist breit* und <u>lang</u> genug, aber zu dünn
(*breit* = a as in I)
b. *Das Brett ist breit* und <u>hoch</u> genug, aber zu dünn
(*breit* = b as in II)
c. *Das Brett ist breit* und <u>tief</u> genug, aber zu dünn
(*breit* = b as in III)
[*The board is wide* and <u>long/high/deep</u> *enough* but too thin]

(16)(a) "Brett" < a b c > (unspecified basic schema)
max ø sub

(b)(I/i)			(II/ii)			(III/iii)		
< a	b	c >	< a	b	c >	< a	b	c >
max	*ø*	*sub*	*max*	*ø*	*sub*	*max*	*ø*	*sub*
max	*across*	*sub*	*across*	*vert*	*sub*	*across*	*obs*	*sub*

The possible equivalence of verbal and non-verbal contexts for determining the interpretation of linguistic expressions such as *breit* [*wide*] provides strong evidence for the claim that the contextual restrictions involved must be accounted for and checked against each other on the intermodally accessible level of conceptual structure representation (CS-level).

As concerns projective prepositions, it is on the level of CS-representations of objects where intrinsic and deictic uses have to be accounted for, more precisely, it is the object schema of the reference object *y* that provides the relevant information determining whether or not expressions like *x ist vor / hinter y* [x is in front of/behind y] are assigned an intrinsic or a deictic reading. We will come back to this in section 4.4 and 4.5 below.

3.5. Interim Balance

The two-level approach expounded so far leads to a model of semantic interpretation that comprises three major components:

(18) a. an inventory of semantic parameters on SF-level (including Dimension Assignment Parameters (DAP) and Side Assignment Parameters (SAP))
b. an inventory of Object Schemata on CS-level providing sets of values for these SF-parameters
c. a suitable device for mapping the former onto the latter

At first sight, the model may look somewhat simple in view of the complexity of the phenomena it is devised to account for. However, the complexity is not abstracted away but anchored in the internal make-up of the components a.-c. The apparent simplicity of the model is not the starting point but the final result of detailed investigations into object categorization (as summarized in Fig. 5 and Fig. 6 below).

Having given an idea of what sort of elements the semantic parameters are taken to be, we will now turn to the internal structure of object concepts and take a look at the inventory of the Object Schemata.

4. Object concepts

Knowledge of an object embodies knowledge of the object's spatial dimensions, that is, the gradable characteristics of its typical, possible or actual, extension and position in space.

As regards the role of the Vertical and the Observer Axis in this respect, we will say an object y is given an **orientation** if one of of the object's axes coincides with the Vertical, and an object is given a **perspectivization** if one of the object's axes is identified by being aligned to the Observer Axis.

4.1. Orientation

There are various ways in which objects make reference to the surrounding space via **orientation**. Thus the distribution of *hoch* subdivides 3D objects into four subclasses of objects with respect to having

(19) a. fixed orientation
(mountain, river)
b. canonical orientation
(tower, desk)
c. inherent orientation
(book, picture), or
d. being unspecified as to orientation
(brick, pole)

Let me briefly comment on these properties by focussing on the interrelations between dimension, position, movability, and side assignment.

An object *o* is said to have a **fixed orientation** if *o* has an axis which **shares all of the properties of the Vertical**, specifically, if the foot **F** of the Vertical located on the earth's surface is instantiated as the "bottom" of *o,* without any shift or projection. This, of course, restricts the class of objects which *x* may be an element of to those objects which in a way form material shells or embodiments of the Vertical *per se*. Therefore, the objects that have a fixed orientation are designated parts of the earth's surface, folded upwards, which are either natural (mountain, hill, dune) or man-made (rampart, embankment). Being conceived of as material embodiments of the Vertical implies that these objects do have both a fixed position and a fixed location within Primary Perceptual Space, i.e., they cannot be moved or displaced or tilted etc. In short: **fixed orientation correlates with immobility**. Both are non-detachable features of the conceptual representation of the objects concerned.

An object *o* is said to have a **canonical orientation** if *o* has an axis which is assigned verticality on the basis of **transferring the properties of the Vertical** listed in 2.1.1 to an axis of the object at issue. The mapping is defined by a function C which takes the end-points E, E' of the object axis as arguments and yields the specified end-points B and T as values, where B and T are interpreted as **fixed projections** of the points F and F' of the Vertical. Thus, F projected onto E yields B, which is instantiated by "bottom"; while E' (which, due to the transfer of the geofugal direction of the Vertical, is a projection of F') is specified as T yielding "top". Verticality, thus assigned, implies that the objects concerned are simultaneously assigned a normal position which is defined in reference to the Vertical of the surrounding space. Objects having a canonical orientation may thus of course be moved, turned around, tilted etc. but any position of theirs not meeting the conditions of fixed projection has to be judged as marked (*e.g.* a desk standing upside down) or even deviant (e.g. a tower lying after having toppled down, as suggested by *long tower*). In short, having canonical orientation is part of the conceptual representation of the objects concerned.

An object *o* is said to have an **inherent orientation** if *o* has an axis which is assigned verticality in a way similar to the one described above, but with the crucial difference that "top" and "bottom" are instantiated in the object's own right, that is, that the inherent height of object *o* no longer has any links with the Vertical of the surrounding space. Thus a book, for instance, has an inherent height (and therefore an inherent "top", "bottom", "beginning", "end") due to the inscription it carries. Likewise, a photograph showing the Queen or a button showing Gorbi have an **inherent verticality** which is maintained absolutely **independently of the object's actual position** (standing, lying, hanging upside down etc.).

Inherent verticality of an object is thus to be conceived as a way of orientation which, though originally derived from the Vertical, has become independent of the axes of Primary Perceptual Space due to pragmatic conditions. This explains why a difference between the intrinsic and actual verticality of an object *o,* say, if *o* is tipped over, can produce quite distinct results as to conceptualization. To imagine a mountain as tipped over or standing on edge is almost impossible; to conceive a tower as long (i.e. as lying down) involves loosening the concept "tower"; whereas to see a book lying on the table or standing upside down does not at all affect our understanding of "book". At best, the difference between the inherent and the actual verticality of a book may be taken as an indicator of pragmatic deviation.

An object *o* is said to have a **contextually induced orientation** if *o* has an axis which is assigned verticality in such a way that the projection of F and F' onto the endpoints E and E' of an axis of o, and therefore the instantiation of "bottom" and "top", apply to the **actual position** of the object at issue. Verticality can be induced contextually with objects that in themselves are unspecified as to orientation (cf. a long pole specified as a *tall pole,* a brick specified as being *17 cm in height* etc.) or that have an inherent orientation. The latter case causes the multiple interpretation of *e.g. The tombstone is too high to fit into the trunk*, where *high* can either refer to the tombstone's inherent top - bottom extent or to its contextually specified thickness. With objects having a canonical orientation, contextually induced verticality makes sense only if the object at issue is not in normal position. Otherwise, the parameter **VERT** (cf. *tall tower, low table*) will always be instantiated by the canonically oriented object axis.

Contextually induced orientation thus amounts to specifying the **actual position of an object with reference to the Vertical**. Normally, this applies to freely movable objects which do not have an intrinsic (fixed or canonical) orientation. At the conceptual level, the difference between intrinsic and contextually induced orientation reappears in the way the parameter **VERT** is instantiated at CS-level: in the first case an intrinsic verticality feature of an object axis is **identified**, in the second case a suitable object axis is **specified** by inducing a verticality feature. The instantiation of a SF-parameter by either identification or specification of a value on CS-level is also of central import to the analysis of projective prepositions - cf. 4.5 below.

4.2. Perspectivization

Moving on to PERSPECTIVIZATION we find a very similar picture, except that there seems to be one type of assignment missing with **OBS**. The distribution of *tief* subdivides 3D objects into three subclasses of objects with respect to having

(20) a. canonical perspectivization
  (river, cupboard)
 b. inherent perspectivization
  (hole, wound), or
 c. being unspecified as to perspective
  (brick, board)

The first point to note is that here there is no analogue to fixed orientation in (19) a.. Unlike the Vertical, the Observer Axis is not constant and independent, but flexible in two respects. It has a pivot allowing for a 180° turn in the vertical and the horizontal plane, and it has a moving source which - taking upright posture as normal position - is at least partially determined by its relation to the Vertical. This has the consequence that there is no way of assigning an object a fixed perspective in exactly the same sense as an object may have a fixed orientation. It takes but a moment's reflection to see why.

In view of the flexibility of the Observer Axis, it holds that the position it assigns to an object is also determined by the position of the observer. Hence there cannot be any object *o* which embodies depth in such a way that this alone would suffice to locate *o* in the surrounding space and simultaneously determine its position. Note the rule: **Perspectivization is always linked with orientation.** So much for why the analogue of **fixed orientation** is absent with **depth assignment**.

An object *o* is said to have a **canonical perspectivization** with respect to the Observer if *o*, on account of its intrinsic orientation according to (19) a. or b., also has an axis that is designated as being aligned to the Observer's line of sight. Based on the fact that there are two relevant angles at which the Observer Axis may run to the Vertical, we have to distinguish two cases of canonical perspectivization.

The first case is exemplified by objects such as cupboard or doorway (cf. Fig. 6 below), where the depth axis is orthogonal to the canonically assigned vertical axis. These objects are movable but have a canonical position determined by their orientation and, depending on that, by their perspectivization. The mapping of O' and O" onto the endpoints E and E' of the axis concerned follows the **encounter** strategy (shown in Fig. 4) in such a way that O' is mapped onto E and instantiated as canonical "front"; O" is mapped onto E' and instantiated as canonical "back". These are sides which may be accessed by the parameters **OBS*O** and **OBS*O'** contained in *vor* and *hinter*.

The second case is exemplified by objects such as river, ditch or well (cf. Fig. 6 below), where the depth axis runs at an angle of 180° to the Vertical, that is, the object axis designated as depth axis continues the Vertical from F in the opposite direction ("downward"). The function D that maps the bounding point O of the Observer Axis onto the foot F of the Vertical and takes account of the opposite directions in an appropriate way is discussed at length in Lang 1987, 1989: Chap. 2. Note that the immobility of objects such as river or ditch is due to their having a fixed orientation in the sense of (19) a., that is, a fixed relation to the Vertical similar to objects such as mountain or rampart. Thus, mountain and river group together in being designated parts of the earth's surface, and therefore being immobile objects, but they differ in their relation to the Observer Axis.

The fact that the depth axis assigned to a river continues the Vertical in the opposite direction does have its consequences regarding the mapping of O and O' onto the end-points of the object axis at issue. In short: the mapping also follows the **encounter** strategy described above, but with the additional effect (induced by the Vertical) that O, when mapped onto E, is instantiated as "accessible surface" (which conflates "top" and "front"); while O', when mapped onto E', is instantiated as "ground" (which conflates "bottom" and "remote face"). In other words, this explains why a river or a ditch cannot be said to have front and rear sides or top and bottom sides.

This view of **canonical perspectivization** seems to match with the way depth is conceptualized, not least due to the fact that it reflects the dominant role of the Vertical and the subsidiary role of the Observer Axis.

An object *o* is said to have an **inherent perspectivization** if *y* has a disintegrated axis which can only be identified by being aligned to the Observer Axis. In other words, if there are **no other cues available** for assigning *o* a position property (by relating the axis at issue to the Vertical) or for assigning *x* a maximal or substance-determined axis, then precisely this object axis is designated as depth.

Note that, in line with **inherent orientation** in (19) b., the notion of **inherent Perspectivization** is basically defined as "assigning an axis of object *o* the properties of an axis of **PPS** without regard to the object's actual position in space". Regarding inherent depth, this is exactly the case with either immobile hollow objects, e.g. holes, or freely movable objects with an interior, e.g. cups, pots, bottles etc. A (non-perforated) hole, no matter whether it is in the floor, in the wall, or in the ceiling, is invariably assigned depth. As the example suggests, a hole or the interior of a cup is conceived as a designated (negative or missing) part of the solid object containing it. Therefore, a hole or the interior of a cup cannot move or change position by itself. Given this, it is due to the flexibility of the Observer Axis that such objects can be inherently assigned depth without regard to their location in the surrounding space.

The mapping of O and O' onto E and E' proceeds along the lines of the **encounter** strategy shownd in Fig. 4 above, that is, O is mapped onto E and instantiated as "front" or "accessible surface"; while O' is mapped onto E' and instantiated as "rear" or "remote face".

An object *o* is said to have a **contextually induced perspectivization** if *o* has an axis which is assigned depth due only to the **actual position** of the object at issue, that is, if neither (20) a. nor (20) b. apply. As was discussed above, there are two ways of mapping O and O' onto the end-points of the object axis that is designated as depth axis. This claim would predict that contextual perspectivization, when applied to objects that in themselves are unspecified as to perspectivization, should yield two different assignments of "front" (or "accessible face") and "back" (or "remote face"), resulting from either the **encounter situation** or the **coincidence situation.** And this is indeed the case - cf. the discussion in section 2.2 above.

The different ways of perspectivizing an object discussed so far are closely related to the familiar distinction of **intrinsic** vs. **deictic** assignment of sides to objects. As can be easily seen, objects that have a **canonical** or **inherent perspectivization** along the lines of (20) a. and b., have, in consequence, **intrinsically** determined "fronts" and "backs" (or, "accessible surfaces" and "remote faces"), construed as instantiations of the end-points of that object axis that is designated as being aligned to the Observer Axis. Given this, it is up to **contextually induced perspectivization** to account for **deictically** determined "fronts" and "backs".

4.3. Object categorization

We summarize the facts about **orientation** and **perspectivization** and their interrelations to an object's (im-)mobility by the following diagram shown in Fig. 5. To give an indication of what it really means, some brief comments seem to be in order.

First, for the purpose of transparency, the division of objects into immobile objects and movable objects is indicated by dotted and white backgrounding, respectively. Notice, however, that these mobility characteristics are not independent, but result from the values each object assumes with respect to boundedness, dimensionality, and relation to PPS-axes.

Second, the terminal nodes of the taxonomy, thus determined, are exemplified by illustrative samples of object concepts. They give an idea of what information is included in the Object Schemata (cf. section 4.4).

Third, the categorization of objects in Fig. 5 is designed to account for the range of conditions according to which the parameters **VERT** and **OBS** are instantiated by values at the CS - level. The division of spatial objects into four classes, that is, immobile objects on the one hand, and three classes of movable objects on the other, directly reflects the range of positional variation each of these classes of objects can be subjected to. Put in terms of, say, *lying*, *standing*, *tilted* etc., the following holds: immobile objects do not allow for any variation or change of their position; canonically oriented objects allow for certain changes in their verticality assignment (a tower can be said to *lie* - after having toppled down; roots can be said to *lie* - when they have been dug of the ground; a shelf can stand *upside down* etc.); inherently oriented objects allow for all changes of position (*lying, standing, upside down*); and so do contextually oriented and/or perspectivized objects.

Fourth, the parameter **ACROSS**, as will be remembered, is in any case assigned a contextually induced value (cf. the remarks in 2.3). Due to the fact, however, that **ACROSS** is a stop-gap, it is neutral with respect to mobility features and hence applies across movable and immobile objects (as indicated by dotted backgrounding in Fig. 5).

Fifth, Fig. 5 offers a complete categorization of objects with respect to intrinsically or/and deictically assigned sides. It is this information that is accessed by the parameters **VERT*F'**, **VERT*F** in *über* - *unter* and/or by **OBS*O**, **OBS*O'** in *vor* - *hinter* . The overlapping area marked by hatching at the bottom of Fig. 5 shows the range of objects that are available for both intrinsic and deictic assignment of sides.

4.4. Object Schemata

The most plausible way in which conceptual representations of spatial objects may be construed is to render them in the form of a matrix with 3 rows and 1, 2 or 3 columns (depending on the nature and number of the axes of the object represented). We call such a matrix an **Object Schema** (OS). An OS contains entries which represent the defining properties of a class of spatial objects. OS are thus representational units of the CS level serving as location frames within which the parameters of the SF level are instantiated. The structure of an object schema and the selection of entries it may contain are again entirely determined by the categorization shown in Fig. 5. Let me exemplify the make-up of OS by commenting on the OS that represents the object concept "cupboard":

(21)	"cupboard"	< a	b	c >
		vert	across	obs
		F', i-top	S , i-les	O', i-back
		F , i-bottom	S', i-ris	O , i-front
		---------------	---------------	---------------

Fig. 5 The interaction of dimension, position, and side-based region assignment to spatial objects

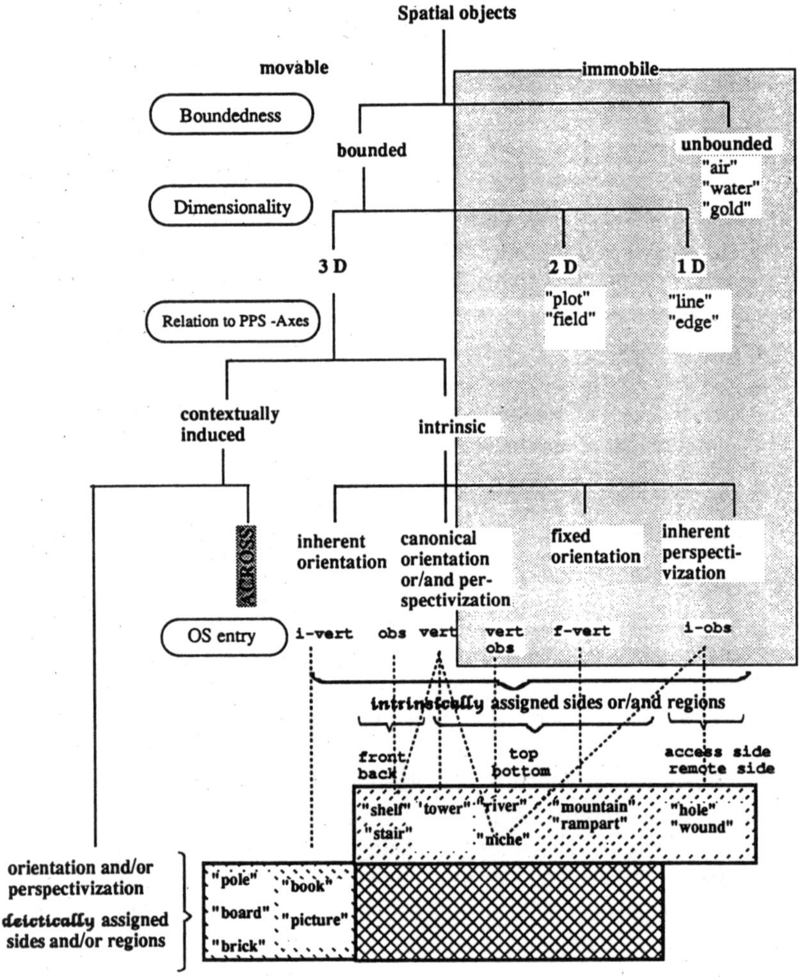

Fig. 6 Categorization of Spatial Objects at the Conceptual Level and Inventory of Object Schemata

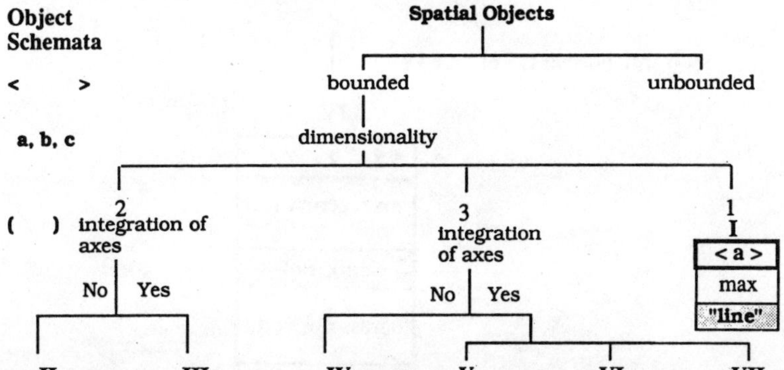

II	III	IV	V	VI	VII
<a b>	<(a b)>	<a b c>	<a (b c)>	<(a b) c>	<(a b c)>
max ø	dist	max vert sub	max sub	diam sub	diam
"yard"	"hole"	"wall"	"pole"	"disk"	"ball"
max across	diam	max i-vert sub	vert sub	diam vert	
"sidewalk"	"circle"	"ruler"	"cylinder"	"tart"	
max i-vert		max vert obs	max subvert	diam f-vert	
"banner"		"ledge"	"tower"	"hill"	
vert across		max vert across	max dist	dist sub	
"door"		"Great Wall"	"pipe"	"hoop"	
f-vert dist		max across vert obs	max distvert	dist vert	
"doorway"		"river"	"bottle"	"saucepan"	
ø vert		max ø vert	i-obs dist	dist i-obs	
"window"		"banquet table"	"bore hole"	"hole"	
ø i-vert		vert across i-obs	vert dist	dist vert obs	
"picture"		"niche"	"barrel"	"den"	
		vert across obs	vert dist obs		
		"cupboard"	"well"		

[Fig. 6'] Further OS of type IV

IV

<a	b	c>
max i-obs	across	vert
"mine hole"		
across	obs	vert
"stair"		
max vert obs	ø	ø
"elevator shaft"		
i-vert	ø	sub
"book"		
ø	vert	obs
"chest"		
obs	dist	vert
"doorway"		
ø	ø	sub
"brick"		
ø	ø	i-obs
"wound"		
ø	ø	vert
"coffin"		

Take the head row first. In containing one, two, or three variables for object axes (a, a b, a b c) it represents the dimensionality of the object at issue, the boundedness by angled brackets, the integration of axes by brackets. This yields exactly 7 types of OS as shown in Fig. 6.

The second row reflects defining gestalt and position properties of the given object, i.e. entries such as *vert*, *i-vert*, *obs*, *i-obs*, *max*, *sub* etc. Being part of an OS, these symbols now stand for conceptual values instantiating the parameters **VERT, OBS** etc. of the SF-level (note the typographic distinction). It is these entries which account for the different ways according to which an object is **oriented** or/and **perspectivized** (cf. 4.1 and 4.2 above). For instance, the entry *vert* in (21) indicates the object's canonical orientation, an entry *i-vert* inherent orientation (cf. "book" in Fig. 5), an entry *f-vert* fixed orientation (cf. "mountain" in Fig. 5); and similarly so for **perspectivization** by means of entries like *obs* or *i-obs*. For further objects the OS of which contains such entries see Fig. 5 and Fig 6.

Based on the entries, which specify the object's axes, the OS contain information on the end-points of the pertinent object-axes (cf. F', F; S, S'; O', O in (21)) and on the intrinsic sides of the object defined by these end-points. Thus, the canonical height-axis of the cupboard (indicated by *vert*) has the end-points F', F which, in turn, determine the cupboard's intrinsic **top** and **bottom sides**, indicated by 'i-top' and 'i-bottom', respectively. Similarly, the endpoints O, O' of the canonically perspectivized depth axis of a cupboard are used to determine the object's intrinsic **front** (i-front) and **rear** (i-back), respectively. The end-points of the third axis, which by themselves would not have designated values due to the specific nature of *across*, are - in the given context of the other OS-sections - marked as carriers of intrinsic **lefthand side** (i-les) and **righthand side** (i-ris), respectively.

The third row (below the line) of an unspecified generic OS contains slots with variables (omitted here for transparency's sake) to be replaced with contextual specifications induced by linguistic or situational contexts (Cf. the examples in (14) - (16) above). In the course of processing an OS, the third row is filled with appropriate values.

Fig. 6 (quoted from Lang/Carstensen 1990) presents a complete catalogue of those admissible object schemata for which we were able to find some empirical instances. Well, we would not argue about adding one or two further OS that might have escaped us. But if this is granted, we may claim that the catalogue of OS presented below is **exhaustive** as regards those spatial properties that are involved in dimensional designation, positional variation, and intrinsic **orientation** and **perspectivization** of objects.

Now, let me briefly outline how the meaning of the projective prepositions interacts with the information contained in the OS. To begin with, it is the entries on intrinsic sides in an OS which are accessed to by the SF-parameters contained in the projective prepositions *über - unter, vor - hinter, rechts - links* Thus the semantic interpretation of, say,

(22) *Der Tisch ist vor dem Schrank*
[The table is in front of the cupboard]

proceeds in the following way. Based on general rules of composition, the SF-representation of *vor*, i.e. ^y ^x (LOC (x, **OBS*O**(y)) ...), is linked to the SF-representation of the reference object denoted by *Schrank*. To avoid thorny problems of delimiting linguistic knowledge, I have not discussed the proper lexical meaning of object names like *Schrank*. (It might be conceived as a set of parameters that range over the properties encoded in the top two rows of the corresponding OS). At any rate, the compositional amalgamation of the SF-representations of *vor* and *dem Schrank* makes the OS associated with the latter available to the SF-parameter **OBS*O** of *vor* such that the OS shown in (21) provides a proper subset of the range of values that instantiate **OBS*O.**

In the given case, the first choice to evaluate **OBS*O** is to assign it the value 'i-front' from the OS in (21). The result is that (22) is given an interpretation of *vor* that corresponds to the so-called intrinsic use, that is, an interpretation that involves a VOR*-region which is determined by the intrinsic front of the reference object. Due to the *nullo obstante* - principle, this way of evaluating the parameter **OBS*O** would yield the default interpretation of (22), that is, if there is no indication that the cupboard is not in its normal position as encoded in the top two rows of the OS. The default evaluation results in a specified OS containing a second entry 'd-front', which is inserted in the third row, third column under 'i-front' to indicate that intrinsic front and actual front of the given reference object are matching (cf. (23) a.).

But (22) is open also for other interpretations. Suppose a situation where a cupboard is laid down and tilted to the back and the table is now facing the intrinsic bottom side of the cupboard. Given these situational framework, the evaluation of the parameter **OBS*O** in *vor* would lead to a different result. In fact, the OS of cupboard will notify in the third row the contextually induced changes with respect to the entries contained in the top two rows. What we get is a specified OS of *Schrank* that shows all the differences between intrinsic and actual side assignments of the given object - cf. (23) b.. For transparency I indicate only the relevant entries in the third row.

(23) (a) *vor dem Schrank* (default interpretation)

<a	b	c >
vert	*across*	*obs*
F', i-top	S, i-les	O', i-back
F , i-bottom	S',i-ris	O , i-front
		d-front

(23) (b) *vor dem Schrank* (with cupboard laid down and tilted to the back)

<a	b	c >
vert	*across*	*obs*
F', i-top	S, i-les	O', i-back
F , i-bottom	S',i-ris	O , i-front
d-back,	i-les,	d-bottom,
.d-front	i-ris	d-top

Note that the specified OS in (23) b. contains all and only the relevant values that determine the interpretation of (22) under the assumed situational setting.

Along the same lines we obtain any other contextually determined interpretation that (22) can assume. In other words, by allowing for the parameter **OBS*O** to take both values that match with intrinsic OS-entries (cf. (23) a. and values that differ from, but are compatible with, intrinsic OS-entries (cf. (23) b., we are able to account of the full range of interpretations which *vor* can assume in localizing a given object x in the VOR*-region of the reference object y.

Moreover, the interpretation of *hinter, über, unter* proceeds along the same lines. The reader is invited to examine the complete list of Object Schemata given in Fig. 6 in order to check himself which objects provide which intrinsic sides that may serve to determine object-based neighbourhood regions. This much as to structure and inventory of OS, which form, as claimed in (18), the second component of the two-level approach I am advocating. We will now turn to the third component.

4.5. The mapping device

Needless to say that the evaluation of SF-parameters like **VERT, OBS, VERT*F, VERT*F', OBS*O, OBS*O'** etc. is to be construed as a restricted mapping from elements on the SF-level onto elements of the OS on the CS-level.

The mapping device comprises two basic operations called **identification and specification** of semantic parameters (DAP and SAP) with respect to the set of values (DAV and SAV) they may assume on the CS-level. I will refrain from retelling the story of how it works with dimension terms (cf. Lang 1987, 1989 and Lang /Carstensen 1989 a, b), though this forms the background, but instead move directly to the projective prepositions.

Suppose the set of semantic parameters needed to account for the projective prepositions in (1) is given by **SAP** = { **VERT*F, VERT*F', OBS*O, OBS*O', R, L**}, while the set of side assignment values is given by the set **SAV** = {<*vert,* F', i-top>, <*vert,* F', d-top>, <*vert*, F, i-bottom>, ...<*obs*, O, i-front>, ...} - see (23). Now, an element P of **SAP** is mapped onto an element p of **SAV** by way of identification iff P matches the first chunk of p. Somewhat simplified we get:

(24) **Identification:** P $\Rightarrow$ p,
where P $\in$ { VERT*F, VERT*F', OBS*O, OBS*O'},
p $\in$ {< *vert*, F, i-top>, ..<*obs*, O, i-front>... } and
p $\notin$ {<i-vert,...>, < i-obs, ...> }

In contrast, an element P of **SAP** is mapped onto an element q of **SAV** by way of **specification** iff P attaches p to q in an OS-section. Attachment is restricted by suitable conditions determining possible specifications (see below). Somewhat simplified we get:

(25) **Specification:** P $\Rightarrow$ q,
where P $\in$ { VERT*F, VERT*F', OBS*O, OBS*O' },
q $\in$ { <*max*, _,_>, <ø, _,_ >, ...} and
q $\notin$ {< *vert*, F, i-top>, ..<*obs*, O, i-front>,... } and
q is licensed as a landing site for P in OS

Two remarks on the conditions constraining the mapping might be in order. The second condition in (25) excludes OS-entries for fixed and canonic orientation from being specified vacuously with identical or contradictorily with incompatible values. The third condition refers to general compatibility conditions among spatial parameters - for details see Lang/Carstensen 1990.

The second condition in (24), however, prevents inherent verticality or perspectivization values from automatically instantiating **VERT*F** or **OBS*O**. This accounts for the fact that e.g. inherent top or front sides (as with books) do not define proper subregions of the reference object of a projective preposition. This can be illustrated by the follwing example:

(26) *Das Dreieck ist über dem Buch, der Ball ist vor dem Buch*
[The triangle is *above* the book, the ball is *in front of* the book]

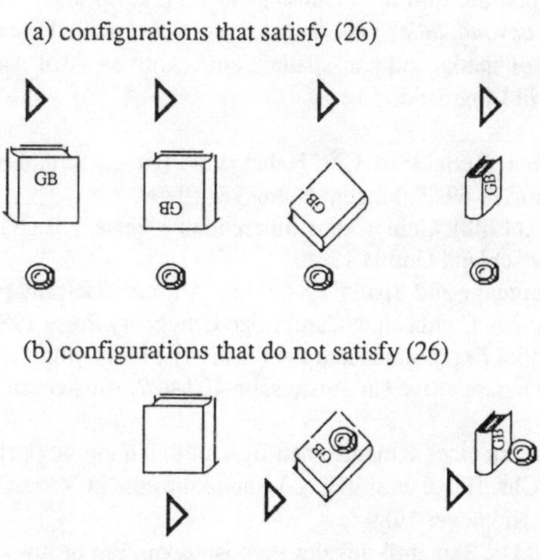

Moreover, the restricted range of interpretations (26) may assume is indicative of the following rule: if intrinsic and extrinsic verticality assignments are at variane, the extrinsic way of assigning top and bottom prevails. This rule, in turn, is but another piece of evidence for the claim that the Vertical is the dominant axis. There is an order of preference also among the various ways of assigning objects fronts and rears - but the discussion of this issue should better be reserved for my next paper on projective prepositions.

"The purpose of science", says Paul Valéry, "is to give us a completely different idea of the things we know best." The object-centered and axis-based approach to prepositions outlined in this paper seems to serve this purpose almost literally.*

References

Bierwisch, M. (1988): On the Grammar of Local Prepositions. In: M. Bierwisch, W. Motsch, I. Zimmermann (eds.) Syntax, Semantik und Lexikon. pp. 1-65. Berlin: Akademie-Verlag 1988.

Bierwisch, M./Lang, E., (Hrsg). Grammatische und konzeptuelle Aspekte von Dimensionsadjektiven. Berlin: Akademie-Verlag 1987

Bierwisch, M./Lang, E. (eds.). Dimensional Adjectives: Grammatical Structure and Conceptual Interpretation. Berlin-Heidelberg-New York: Springer-Verlag 1989

Boers, F. (1987): *Behind, beyond,under,underneath,beneath,below:* A Descriptive and Explanatory Study of spatial and non-spatial Senses.University of Antwerp.1987 (=Antwerp Papers in Linguistics 53)

Habel, Chr.(1989): *zwischen-* Bericht. In: Chr. Habel et al . (Hrsg.) Raumkonzepte in Verstehensprozessen.37-69. Tübingen: Niemeyer 1989

Habel, Chr. /Pribbenow, S.(1988): Gebietskonstituierende Prozesse. LILOG-Report 18. Stuttgart: IBM Deutschland GmbH 1988

Herskovits, A. (1986): Language and Spatial Cognition. An Interdisciplinary study of the prepositions in English. Cambridge: Cambridge University Press 1986.

Herskovits, A.(1988): Spatial Expressions and the Plasticity of Meaning. In: B. Rudzka-Ostyn (ed.) Topics in Cognitive Linguistics. pp.403-427. Amsterdam: Benjamins 1988.

Herweg,M.(1989): Ansätze zu einer semantischen Beschreibung topologischer Präpositionen. In: Chr. Habel et al. (Hrsg.) Raumkonzepte in Verstehensprozessen. 99-127. Tübingen: Niemeyer 1989

Hottenroth, P.-M. (1988) : Die Semantik lokaler Präpositionen. Ein prototypensemantisches Modell für die französische Präposition *dans* mit einer Analyse der Beziehungen zwischen der Präposition und den Objektbezeichnungen in den Präpositionalsyntagmen. Habilitationsschrift, Universität Konstanz 1988

Kaufmann, I. (1989): Direktionale Präpositionen.In: Chr. Habel *et al* . (Hrsg.) Raumkonzepte in Verstehensprozessen. 128-149. Tübingen: Niemeyer 1989

Lakoff, G. (1987): Women, Fire, and Dangerous Things. What Categories Reveal about the Mind.Chicago: The University of Chicago Press 1987

---

* I am grateful to Gisa Rauh and Martin Othmar for their patience and scrutiny in preparing this volume, and to Colin J. Foskett for correcting my English.

Lakoff, George, (1988).Cognitive Semantics. In U. Eco et al. (eds): Meaning and Mental Representations. 119-154. Bloomington : IUP

Lang, E. (1988): Object Schemata and Räumliche Konfigurationen.Papier zum Projekt "Räumliche Lokalisierung". Düsseldorf 1988.

Lang, E. (1989 a): The Semantics of Dimensional Designation of Spatial Objects. In: M. Bierwisch/ E. Lang (eds.) (1989). pp. 263-417.

Lang, E. / Carstensen, K.-U. (1989 a): OSKAR - ein Prolog-Programm zur Modellierung der Struktur und Verarbeitung räumlichen Wissens. GWAI '89. pp. 234-243. Berlin-Heidelberg-New York: Springer Verlag 1989.

Lang, E. / Carstensen, K.-U. (1990): OSKAR - a Prolog program for modelling dimensional designation and positional variation of objects in space. LILOG-Report 109. Stuttgart: IBM Deutschland GmbH 1990 [to appear in Lecture Notes on Artificial Intelligence, Berlin-Heidelberg-New York: Springer Verlag]

Langacker, R. W. (1987): Foundations of cognitive grammar. vol. I. Theoretical Prerequisites.Stanford, CA: Stanford University Press 1987

Levelt, W.J. M.(1984): Some perceptual limitations on talking about space. In A.J. van Doorn et al. (eds) Limits in Perception. 323-358.Utrecht:VNU Science Press 1984

Maienborn, C. (1989 a): Zur Semantik von Bewegungs- und Positionsverben - Perspektiven der kognitiven Linguistik. LILOG Report 64. Stuttgart: IBM Deutschland GmbH 1989.

Maienborn, C. (1989 b): Semantische und Konzeptuelle Analyse der Bedeutungskonstitution: Verbalphrasen der Bewegung und Lage. Magisterarbeit. Universität Hamburg 1989.

Retz-Schmidt, G. (1988): Various Views on Spatial Prepositions. AI Magazine 9.2, 95-105

Vandeloise, C. (1986): L'Espace en français. Sémantique des prépositions spatiales. Paris: Éditions du Seuil 1986

Wunderlich, D. /Herweg, M. (1986/88): Lokale und Direktionale. [To appear in A.v. Stechow /D. Wunderlich (eds.) Handbuch der Semantik.]

Prepositional forms in the lexicon: problems and suggestions

Gisa Rauh
(Wuppertal)

1. Introduction

It is a well-known fact that prepositions which belong to the basic inventory of the category, such as *in*, *on*, *at*, *to*, *for*, *by*, etc. in English not only allow a wide range of uses semantically, but also syntactically. Thus, for example, *on* may be used to mark a prepositional predicate,

(1) a. The book is on the table.
b. Mary on drugs is terrible news.

disjuncts or conjuncts in the sense of Greenbaum 1969,

(2) On second thoughts, he was unsuccessful.

(3) On the other hand, he likes music.

adjuncts in the context of verbs, nouns, adjectives or adverbs,

(4) He read the book on the boat.

(5) He wanted the book on the table.

(6) Scientific instruments were now available on a large scale.

(7) He waited outside on the pavement.

complements with adverbial function in the context of verbs or nouns,

(8) a. He stayed on the hill for an hour.
b. He jumped on the table.

(9) a. His stay on the hill lasted an hour.
b. His jumping on the table caused problems.

or complements as prepositional objects in the context of verbs, nouns or adjectives:

(10) He insisted on his reward.

(11) They made a special broadcast on the subject.

(12) He is dependent on his salary.

In addition, the same form *on* may occur in the context of so-called "phrasal verbs":

(13) a. He put on his hat.
b. He switched on the light.

It is - according to the classification of Traditional Grammar - also used as an adverb:

(14) He talked on and on.

Finally, *on* may occur as a constituent part of compounds or derivations, such as *upon* or *onto*, *hanger-on* or *put-on*, *onset*, *onlooker* or *ongoing*.

With respect to their semantic diversity, prepositions will be considered here only as far as different semantic domains or dimensions are involved, excluding domain internal variability which - as far as the spatial domain is concerned - has been the topic of various recent publications.[1] Thus, for example, *on*, originally a spatial preposition, may be used to express temporal relations,

(15) a. Her eyes are blue as the sea on a cloudless day.
b. Shakespeare was born on 23 April 1616.
c. It was on 2 January.

or causal relations,

(16) a. She was brought before court on a charge of child neglect.
b. He read the book on my suggestion.
c. His speech on behalf of the scientist was praised.

or relations of manner:

---

1 See, for example, Wunderlich 1982; Hawkins 1984; Herskovits 1986; Vandeloise 1986; Herweg 1988; Hottenroth (this volume).

(17) a. Discussions on a higher level are useful.
b. They are at once on a far better footing.
c. Janet spoke on a rising tone.
d. They flew on one engine.

Even more domains may be involved. An investigation of the transfered meanings of English prepositions is presented by Radden 1982; 1985.

In view of the diversity of the syntactic and semantic uses of prepositions it must be asked how - during the process of language acquisition - a child acquires the necessary knowledge about phonologically identical, yet syntactically and/or semantically divergent prepositional forms and how this knowledge is finally stored in the mental lexicon of the adult speaker. The linguist is faced with the question of how to represent such knowledge in a lexicon which is designed as a model of the mental lexicon. It is the aim of this paper to approach a solution to this question.

In the following (section 2) the role of the lexicon with respect to other parts of the grammar will be discussed. In addition, it will be pointed out what kinds of problems arise given the above assumed situation that a single phonological form is related to more than one syntactic and/or semantic representation. Section 3 is devoted to the question of what has been considered a preposition in previous approaches. It will be shown that different answers are provided by different approaches and that this is due to the fact that different sets of uses of prepositions have been investigated. This is taken as an indication of the fact that the class of prepositions is heterogeneous. In section 4 selected syntactic variants of prepositional forms are identified on the basis of syntactic tests. It will be shown that the same prepositional forms may differ with respect to some properties of projection, substitution and coordination, while sharing others. Section 5 presents an attempt to develop lexical representations for prepositional forms which reflect the analytic results achieved in section 4. Wherever possible, the prepositional form *on* will be used as an example.

2. The role of the lexicon

If a grammar is viewed as a model of the linguistic competence of a native speaker, then the lexicon should be a model of all the knowledge a native speaker has about individual linguistic items of his language such as words or constituents of words, as well as about the relations holding between these. This knowledge about "lexical items" includes knowledge about their connection with conceptual units. In this sense the lexicon forms an interface with respect to the conceptual system.[2] This knowledge about lexical items also includes everything necessary as a prerequisite to produce and understand grammatically well-formed sentences, starting out with lexical units. In this sense the lexicon is a part of the grammar, and a central one which provides prerequisites for the functioning of other parts with which it interacts. The information in the lexicon which represents lexical units as lexical entries is composed of bits of information which correspond to and are compatible with information provided by other parts of the grammar. Thus, for example, if it is assumed - as is the case within the framework of the Theory of Principles and Parameters (cf. Chomsky 1981) - that a grammar provides syntactic and semantic as well as phonological representations of sentences then lexical entries must provide representations of lexical items on these very levels. If, in addition, it is assumed that a grammar is modular, organized on the basis of principles and parameters and furthermore constituting a marked periphery, then this same form of oranization also holds for the lexicon, for isolated lexical entries as well as possibly for the architecture of the lexicon as a whole. Given these assumptions about a concept of a grammar, the following characterization of the lexicon and its role can be developed.

The lexicon contains a collection of lexical entries. Each lexical entry contains syntactic, semantic and phonological information about lexical items, i.e. about words, constituents of words or fixed phrases. This information includes a representation of the lexical item itself as well as contextual information about the conditions under which a lexical item may be inserted into a given context. The contextual syntactic information includes specification of strict subcategorization, or "C-selection", as well as the

---

2 According to this view, words are labels for experiences a speaker has made with the objects the labels represent. A word provides access to stored visual, accoustic, tactile or motor experience, for example. Just imagine the words "frog" and "hedgehog", or "feather" and "lead" and the experiences they evoke. A word also provides access to knowledge about the organization of a society, for example, "school", "parliament" or "government". The puzzling problem of how to determine the meaning of a word which differs in different contexts mainly has to do with the fact that the same word may provide access to very different domains of experience which all together represent what is called the "knowledge of the world".

range of possible specifiers. Properties of government also belong here, concerning, for example, case assignment, especially assignment of inherent case. Theta properties form the interface between contextual syntactic and semantic properties. The theta grid - or "S-selection" - indicates which theta role is assigned to the entity under consideration. Contextual semantic properties include information about the number of - explicit and implicit - arguments as well as information related to their inherent semantic properties.

Information of this kind may be idiosyncratic for a given lexical item and thus marked. In this case it will be explicitly represented within a lexical entry. It may, however, be derived from general or modular principles and parameters. In this case it is implicit and need not be mentioned. If, for example, a parameter for the English language determines that verbs assign objective case or the accusative case to noun phrases under government and adjacency (cf. Chomsky 1981:172 or van Riemsdijk & Williams 1986:299) then this type of case assignment is unmarked, implicit in the feature combination [-N,+V], and no additional information is needed. If, however, case properties deviate from this unmarked situation because, for example, adjacency is not given - as is the case with ditransitive verbs - then this "inherent" type of case assignment is marked and has to be captured somehow within the lexical representation (cf. Chomsky 1981:170ff). We will see later on in what way this is relevant for the lexical representation of prepositional forms.

The distinction between marked and unmarked information here demonstrated with respect to case assignment is also relevant for other properties, for example the relation between strict subcategorization and theta properties on the one hand and case assignment on the other. We will not go into this here but rather refer to Chomsky 1986:86ff and the references given there.

The lexicon may thus be characterized as a set of lexical entries which represent marked and unmarked syntactic, semantic and phonological information about lexical items. The identity and individuality of a lexical item is determined - amongst other things - by the way the various levels of representation are mapped onto one another. It is thus the role of the lexicon to provide this information for the other parts of the grammar. In language production and perception this information is accessed in order to produce or understand complex linguistic units such as sentences, starting from single lexical items. It should be noted that, depending on production or perception, the address of access is different. With respect to perception the address of access is the phonological matrix. The lexical mapping onto syntactic and semantic information allows analysis of the syntactic and the semantic structure to be performed. With respect to production the address is either the syntactic or the semantic representation.[3] Again the lexical mapping gives access from the address to the other levels of representation.

Access from one level of representation to another is unproblematic even if different addresses are involved, as long as the mapping is bi-unique, i.e. as long as exactly one phonological representation is mapped onto exactly one syntactic and semantic representation, and conversely. No matter which level serves as the address, the result will always be the same. But what happens if one phonological representation is related to more than one semantic and/or syntactic representation, as is assumed to be the case with respect to prepositional forms? The situation is comparable to that of homonyms such as *bank*, denoting the land along the side of a river on the one hand and a monetary institution on the other. The semantic distance between these two denotations, however, suggests that the phonological identity is mere chance in this case. That is, the mapping of the phonological and the semantic representations onto each other - the syntactic representation may be ignored - arrives at alternatives which are independent of each other. During the process of language acquisition they must be learned independently and they are stored independent of each other in the mental lexicon of an adult speaker. This solution seems inadequate with respect to prepositional forms. It is counterintuitive to assume that each syntactic and/or semantic variant of a prepositional form, for example *on*, must be learned like a new word and is finally stored separately in the mental lexicon. But how are these forms stored? This is the question to which section 5 will provide a preliminary answer with respect to some variants. For various reasons the answer can be only preliminary. One of these is that not all variants have been investigated and it may very well be that extending the domain of investigation will have effects upon the results achieved so far. In what follows we will pursue the question of what a preposition is, attempting first to find an answer by consulting previous approaches.

---

3 Both may in fact be the case. Although in planning an utterance its meaning is relevant first, during the process of production the choice of one syntactic element may determine what has to come next syntactically in order to produce a well-formed sentence. Thus, whether syntactic or semantic properties are accessed first may depend on how early in an utterance a unit is produced.

3. What is a preposition?

During the development of linguistics, prepositions have been classified in different ways, even in more recent approaches. Within the framework of Traditional Grammar, Structuralism, Case Grammar or the X-bar-Theory the answers to the question "What is a preposition?" are not only different but even contradictory in some sense. However, a close look at each of the approaches leads to the conclusion that none of the answers holds for the set of prepositions as a whole, but rather for a selected subset only. Interestingly enough, these subsets are complementary to a certain extent. Thus the divergent judgements about prepositions may be taken as a starting point for the identification of variants of prepositional forms.

3.1. The following quotation providing a definition of prepositions is representative of the view taken within Traditional Grammar:

> A preposition is a word that indicates a relation between the noun or pronoun it governs and another word, which may be a verb, an adjective, or another noun or pronoun. (Curme 1935:87)

It will be seen that compared to other views this one is the most comprehensive one. It emphasizes the unity of function as a critical property, i.e. the function of expressing a relation. Restrictions are imposed only on the governed category, which is required to be an NP. Thus, the same forms which display different properties of government, for example *before* in (18b) and (18c), are not categorized as prepositions, but as adverbs or conjunctions, respectively:

(18) a. I was here before John.
b. I was here before.
c. I was here before John arrived.

On the other hand, this definition includes all those forms that are in accordance with the given characterization. Thus, not only items of the basic inventory are considered prepositions but also secondary, derived forms, for example denominal derivations such as *across* or *aboard*, deadjectival ones such as *round* or *along*, deverbal ones like *except(ing)* or *during*, compounds like *upon*, *throughout* or *notwithstanding* and phrasal prepositions like *by means of*, *for the sake of*, or *because of* (cf. e.g. Sweet 1891:134f). As a consequence, the following statement is adequate within this framework:

> Prepositions have played a conspicuous role in the development of our language. Their numbers are ever increasing. (Curme 1935:91)

It should be kept in mind that it is the criterion of function together with the constraint concerning the governed category which determines what is and what is not an element of the category preposition in this framework. Another property pointed out is the inability to inflect, a property which prepositions share with adverbs, conjunctions and interjections. For this reason all of these are subsumed under the heading "particle" by Jespersen 1924 and Poutsma 1926, for example.

3.2. A view in many ways opposed to the one held by traditional grammarians is proposed within the framework of Structuralism. Basically three properties are identified as typical of prepositions: First they are function or structure words, second, they have little lexical meaning and third, they are limited in number and hardly change through time. It is claimed that prepositions form a closed set (cf. e.g. Harris 1951:252ff; Fries 1952:87ff; Gleason 1955,[2]1961:156ff).

In Rauh 1990 it is demonstrated that assigning these properties to prepositions as a whole is inadequate. Thus, the claim that prepositions are function or structure words is meant to express that they function as a structural signal at the beginning of a prepositional phrase indicating the construction type they introduce (cf. Quirk 1962,[2]1968:79). The data show, however, that prepositions serve this function only in some of their uses, i.e. as markers of prepositional objects (19) as well as in non-spatial or non-temporal contexts, where PPs are used as disjuncts (20), conjuncts (21) or adjuncts (22):

(19) a. They would insist [$_{PP}$ on a king].
b. *They would insist [$_{PP}$ right on a king].

(20) a. [$_{PP}$ On second thoughts], he was successful.
b. *[$_{PP}$ Right on second thoughts], he was successful.

(21) a. [$_{PP}$ On the other hand], he was successful.
b. *[$_{PP}$ Right on the other hand], he was successful.

(22) a. It found ready application [$_{PP}$ on a much larger scale].
b. *It found ready application [$_{PP}$ right on a much larger scale].

The claim does not hold for spatial or temporal prepositions, which may be specified by a preceding element such as *right* which in this case introduces the prepositional phrase:

(23) a. The house was [$_{PP}$ on a hill].
b. The house was [$_{PP}$ right on a hill].

(24) a. The party was [$_{PP}$ on 1 June].
b. The party was [$_{PP}$ right on 1 June].

(25) a. He arrived [$_{PP}$ on time].
b. He arrived [$_{PP}$ right on time].

(26) a. They rested [$_{PP}$ on a peak].
b. They rested [$_{PP}$ right on a peak].

(27) a. We are like a man [$_{PP}$ on a bicycle].
b. We are like a man [$_{PP}$ right on a bicycle].

In these cases it is not the preposition that structurally marks the construction type and it is therefore not a function or structure word in the sense indicated.

The second supposed property, little lexical meaning, again does not hold for spatial and temporal prepositions. This is evident if one preposition is substituted for another, which inevitably causes a severe change in meaning:

(28) The book is	on	the desk.
	under	
	inside	
	near	

(29) He came	on	1 June.
	before	
	after	

However, the property seems adequate, at least to a certain degree, with respect to prepositions which mark prepositional objects (30) or are used metaphorically, as in (31):

(30) a. Bill is dependent on his friends.
b. They reached an agreement on Berlin.
c. I decided on a frontal attack.

(31) a. They flew on one engine.
b. She hit him on purpose.
c. Older children scored higher on the average.

The same holds for prepositional forms in the context of phrasal verbs:

(32) a. He put on his socks.
b. The party was going on for hours.

In examples like these it is not immediately evident what the preposition contributes to the meaning of the whole construction, nor also, why *on* is used rather than another preposition.

The third property, too, i.e. that prepositions constitute a limited and diachronically hardly changed set, may be identified only in part. Again this characterization is adequate for those prepositions that mark prepositional objects or are otherwise used metaphorically, as well as for prepositional forms in the context of phrasal verbs. These are the prepositions considered primary within the framework of Traditional Grammar. Secondary, complex or derived prepositions, e.g. *near*, *round*, *above*, *because of*, *on account of* do not occur in these contexts. Thus it may be concluded that the characterization of prepositions provided by structuralists captures only a subset of the set identified by traditional grammarians and, furthermore, it is restricted to some of their uses: Primary prepositions marking prepositional objects or used otherwise metaphorically and used as part of phrasal verbs. According to the properties postulated, other elements are not part of the set of prepositions.

3.3. A new aspect of prepositions is focussed on in the framework of Case Grammar as presented by Fillmore 1968, 1969. According to his view prepositions are expressions of underlying V-NP-relations which may alternate with case affixes or postpositions. These underlying "case relations" are determined by (case) frame features of verbs. In the unmarked case a given preposition expresses a given relation and is introduced via a mapping function, such as *by* to express the Agent, *with* the Instrument or *to* the Dative, etc. Temporal and spatial prepositions are introduced lexically. Otherwise they are treated in the same way. (cf. Fillmore 1968:32) According to this view, which has been taken up and further developed by Dirven 1982 and Radden 1982, it is the main function of prepositions to express case relations which are specified by the case frame of a verb.

This characterization is problematic where a preposition obviously expresses a different relation than the one predicted by the case frame of the verb.

(33) The village is over the hill.

In (33) the verb *be* assigns the relation LOCATION to its complement whereas *over* indicates the relation PATH. In the framework of Case Grammar this conflict remains unexplained. It is resolved if one assumes with Rauh 1988 that prepositions do not express relations assigned by verbs but rather assign them themselves to their own complements. This property - amongst others - means that prepositions are more autonomous than case affixes. On the other hand Fillmore's comparison of prepositions and case affixes -

> Prepositions in English - or the absence of a preposition before a noun phrase, which may be treated as corresponding to a zero or unmarked case affix - are selected on the basis of several types of structural features, and in ways that are exactly analogous to those which determine particular case forms in a language like Latin. (Fillmore 1968:15) -

seems legitimate for governed prepositions, i.e. for those cases where for example a verb, adjective or noun requires a certain preposition to mark the following object:

(34) He relied on his strength.

(35) He is dependent on his income.

(36) An agreement on the contract was finally reached.

Thus what is indicated here is a distinction between prepositions which share properties of case affixes and those that do not. However, this is not what Fillmore subscribes to. His representations rather suggest that prepositions are always like case affixes. This is confirmed by the following remarks in which he expresses his satisfaction with having developed a means to eliminate the distinction between NPs and PPs:

> Thus we see that the distinction between noun phrase and preposition phrase is no longer necessary. This is all to the good, of course, since *preposition phrase* has always been a terminological nuisance. We would really like all constituents labeled *X-Phrase* to be constituents having X's as their heads. (Fillmore 1969:367)

No restriction is formulated pointing out that only a subset of uses of prepositions or PPs is affected. But it is exactly this that is suggested by the data. Thus the possibility of replacing a spatial PP by *there* or adding the specifier *right* - both operations not yielding grammatical results with respect to NPs - provides evidence for the syntactic difference between NPs and PPs:

(37) a. He stayed on the hill.
b. He stayed there.
c. He stayed right on the hill.

(38) a. He saw the hill.
b. *He saw there.
c. *He saw right the hill.

Investigating the syntactic behaviour of prepositional objects it turns out that it is more like that of NPs than of PPs, as a comparison of (39) with (37) and (38) illustrates:

(39) a. The boy insisted on his share.
b. *The boy insisted there.
c. *The boy insisted right on his share.

Thus Fillmore's representations suggest that prepositions show syntactic variation. For some of the variants his characterizations are adequate, for others they are not.

3.4. While prepositions are considered subordinate elements in Structuralism as well as in Case Grammar, they are classified as a major category on a par with nouns, verbs and adjectives within X-bar-Theory (cf. eg. Jackendoff 1973; 1977; Emonds 1976; van Riemsdijk 1978; Wunderlich 1984; Bierwisch 1988). They are described by the features [-N,-V]. As major categories, they have projection properties, i.e. they are heads of constructions and may in principle take complements of any maximal projection, as is illustrated in the following examples:

(40) a. Bill was here [$_{PP}$ before [$_{NP}$ Mary]].
b. Bill was here [$_{PP}$ before].
c. Bill was here [$_{PP}$ before [$_{CP}$ Mary came]].
d. Bill came [$_{PP}$ from [$_{PP}$ behind the curtain]].

They also may take specifiers, for example, *right*:[4]

(41) Bill was here right before Mary.

Since they share this property with some traditional conjunctions and adverbs it is assumed that these are to be identified as prepositions with sentential complements or intransitive prepositions respectively (see e.g. Emonds 1976:174). The feature [-N] indicates that prepositions, like verbs, are case assigners. Like verbs, they have a theta grid. As two-place relations they are associated with an internal and an external argument[5] and assign a theta role to each.

Checking these properties with respect to various occurrences of prepositions, it turns out that, again, they hold only for a subset. Thus, PPs which may involve a specifier and complements other than NPs are possible in adjunctposition but not as prepositional objects. However, even in adjunct position there seem to be restrictions on metaphorical uses:

(42) a. *She was brought before court right on a charge of child neglect.
b. *They flew right on one engine.

But:

(43) a. They provide an aerial service right on a commercial basis.
b. The debate was right on a high level.

---

4 This assumption is not generally accepted, however. See, e.g. Fukui & Speas 1986 or Bierwisch 1988 for deviating views.

5 It should be pointed out that "argument" here refers to semantic units and thus differs from the terminology used by Chomsky, for example. Syntactic arguments represent explicit semantic arguments, whereas semantic arguments may also be implicit, i.e. without syntactic representation.

In the context of phrasal verbs the prepositional form exhibits projection properties in post-NP-position, in pre-NP-position it does not:

(44) a. He looked the word right up (in the lexicon).
b. *He looked right up (in the lexicon) the word.

In adjunct position it is possible to identify the internal as well as the external argument via syntactic representation:

(45) a. He wanted the book on the table.
b. He read the book on the sofa.

In the interpretation taken here, the internal argument in each case is represented by the NP-complement of P. The external argument is represented by the left sister of PP, N' in (45a) and V' in (45b). In the case of prepositional objects, however, it is not clear whether there is an external argument at all. Thus it is evident that within X-bar-Theory, too, the statements concerning prepositions refer to a subset of their uses only. This subset, however, differs from those of the other approaches. It is just about complementary to the one relevant in the framework of Structuralism.

3.5. To summarize, the question of what is a preposition will receive different answers depending on the approach taken. What is important is that characterizations like "prepositions are function or structure words", "prepositions are like case affixes" or "prepositions are major categories" do not refer to the complete set but only to subsets. The connexion between these is established by the phonlogical identity of the forms in question. Thus it has become evident that sameness of phonological properties need not imply sameness of syntactic properties. The following section will confirm these results on systematic grounds.

4. Syntactic variants of prepositional forms

The discussion in section 3 suggests that syntactic variants of prepositional forms have to be distinguished. In what follows it will be demonstrated that this, in fact, is the case.

4.1. As a first syntactic variant, prepositional forms as elements of a major lexical category will be identified. Contrary to what Aronoff 1978 or Steinitz 1984 assume in rejecting Jackendoff's 1973; 1977 classification, and contrary to what Emonds 1985 claims in correcting his own assumptions of 1976, the data suggest that some uses of prepositions identify them as lexical heads. If, for example, spatial prepositions as parts of PPs are used adverbially, i.e. as complements of verbs of motion or state or as adjuncts, then they exhibit all those properties which can also be identified with respect to nouns, adjectives or verbs;

syntactic properties
- strict subcategorization
- selection of specifiers
- case properties

semantic properties
- argument structure and theta properties
- inherent semantic features
- selectional properties

As with verbs, variation with respect to strict subcategorization does not necessarily hold for every single preposition but for the class as a whole. Thus *from* takes an NP- or PP-complement:

(46) a. He came from the station.
b. He came from behind the curtain.

Up allows either an NP-complement or it is intransitive:

(47) a. He went up the hill.
b. He went up.

On, on the other hand, takes only an NP-complement if it is spatial:

(48) a. He stayed on the hill.
b. *He stayed on.

In this context sentential complements, which may occur with temporal prepositions, as e.g. Emonds 1976:173 observed,

(49) John arrived before the last speech ended.

(50) I haven't seen him since the party began.

are not found.

Spatial prepositions that mark PPs which are adverbial complements or in adjunct position allow specifiers which specify the relation expressed by the preposition:

(51) a. He went right up the hill.
b. He stayed right on the hill.

(52) a. He lives far beyond the hill.
b. The lamp is hanging 50 inches above the table.

In these positions spatial prepositions also assign case to their complements, namely objective case (cf. Chomsky 1981:172) or accusative (van Riemsdijk & Williams 1986:229), as is illustrated by the pronouns:

(53) a. He went to John.
b. He went to him.

(54) a. She sat behind Mary.
b. She sat behind her.

In these positions prepositions also have an internal and an external argument. They express a relation between these:

(55) a. Bill cooked a meal on the boat.
b. Mary showed John the house on the beach.

In (55a) the category V' *cook a meal* represents syntactically the external argument of *on* and the NP *the boat* the internal one. In (55b) it is the NPs *the house* and *the beach* respectively. This means that in the sense of Higginbotham 1985 and Williams 1987a,b the external theta role of *on* is identified with the event role E of *cook* in (55a) and with the referential role R of *house* in (55b) respectively, whereas the internal role theta marks the complement in both cases. The preposition *on* - like all non-directional spatial prepositions - assigns the THEME role to its external argument and LOCATION to its internal one. Prepositions like *from*, *along* and *to*, however, assign THEME to their external and SOURCE, PATH, and GOAL to their internal arguments.

The inherent semantic properties of prepositions characterize the manner of the relation expressed. *On*, for example, expresses CONTACT (x,y), *in* INCLUDE (x,y). In addition, *on* expresses SUPPORT (x,y), which is complemented by or alternates with the selectional feature EXTENDED (y).

Spatial prepositions investigated in this section are inherently marked by the feature SPATIAL(P). This explains why the PPs in question allow substitution by the proform *there*, which itself is marked the same way:

(56) a. She sat on the chair.
b. She sat there.

(57) a. He bought a house in London.
b. He bought a house there.

Thus the data provide evidence for the fact that spatial prepositions of PPs in adjunct position or as complements of verbs of motion or state exhibit properties of major lexical categories. This observation is well matched by the fact that it is exactly in these positions that derived and/or complex prepositions may occur:

(58) a. Bill lives on the hill.
near
on top of
behind
around
next to
b. He came to the ship.
aboard
in front of

Investigating the behaviour of temporal prepositions as constituents of PPs in the same positions yields similar results. They exhibit strict subcategorization properties (59) as well as case properties (60). Selecting a specifier is possible (61):

(59) a. Bill was here before.
before John.
before John arrived.
b. Bill came here *after.
after John.
after John arrived.

(60) Bill was here before me.

(61) He was here right before Mary.

Like spatial prepositions, they have an argument structure and assign theta roles. Thus, *since*, *during* and *until*, for example, assign to their internal arguments SOURCE, PATH and GOAL and THEME to their external ones. Their selectional properties require arguments which represent events or temporal objects.

The potential proform *then* indicates that an inherent feature, in this case TEMPORAL(P), has to be assumed.

Investigating the syntactic behaviour of spatial prepositions used temporally in the same positions as above reveals certain differences. Thus, for example, TEMPORAL(on) takes a gerundial complement, which SPATIAL(on) does not accept:

(62) On hearing the scream I rushed out.

TEMPORAL(on) shares this property with other exclusively temporal prepositions:

(63) After hearing the scream I rushed out.

Obviously, a correlation exists between strict subcategorization and selectional properties, which for temporal prepositions - including spatial prepositions used temporally - require as complement an argument which represents an event or a temporal unit.

The possibility of selecting a specifier for spatial prepositions is restricted in their temporal use. Thus TEMPORAL(on) allows the specifier *right* only in a few contexts:

(64) a. He arrived right on time.
b. *His birthday is right on 1 June.
c. *Right on his last voyage he visited Rome.

This seems to indicate that the inherent features of temporally used spatial prepositions are rearranged in this context. Thus, *right* corresponds to the feature CONTACT (x,y), which is in focus in (64a). With respect to longer units of time, however, the feature EXTENDED (y) is located higher in the hierarchy of relevance. In spatial uses of *on* these features are at least on the same level.

The properties of spatial as well as temporal prepositions in the syntactic domains investigated suggest that they are elements of a major lexical category. It should be noted that spatial and temporal prepositions exhibit different properties even if the same phonological form is concerned, for example, *on*. This must affect their lexical representations.

4.2. In this section prepositional forms which are governed by other categories, by verbs, nouns or adjectives, for example, will be investigated:

(65) a. Bill insisted on his rights.
b. Mary entered on a liaison with Fred.

(66) a. Their view on the matter was supported.
b. His book on Shakespeare is famous.

(67) a. He was busy on his job.
b. They are dependent on their income.

It is striking that not all the forms which may occur in adjunct position may be used in this context. The set is restricted to elements of the basic inventory, that is the primary, originally spatial prepositions like *at*, *on*, *in*, *for*, *from* etc. These are complemented by a few derived forms, originally spatial also, for example, *about* or *against*. In this context the forms, though originally spatial, are not used spatially.

As opposed to the prepositional forms investigated in 4.1, those examined here do not exhibit the property of strict subcategorization. They are always followed by an NP. They also do not allow a specifier:

(68) *Mary entered right on a liaison with Fred.

(69) *Their view right on the matter was supported.

(70) *He was busy right on his job.

In addition, it is not possible to replace the sequence P + NP by a proform representing a PP:

(71) *Mary entered there/then.

(72) *Their view there/then.

(73) *He was busy there/then.

Coordination with other PPs is not possible either:

(74) *Mary entered on a liaison with Fred and into a contract with a publisher.

These observations suggest that the prepositional forms in these positions are not elements of the major lexical category preposition. They are not heads of PPs and consequently prepositional objects do not form PPs, contrary to what is assumed by Chomsky 1965 and following him Akmajian, Steele and Wasow 1977 or Bresnan 1982, for example. The occurrence of prepositional forms in these contexts rather presents the result of what Lehmann 1985; 1986/7 describes as a process of grammaticalization. Elements of the lexical category preposition enter another grammatical paradigm, in this case that of case forms. Thus, these examples of prepositional forms are indeed - as is claimed in Case Grammar - alternative expressions to case affixes. It does not follow, however, that therefore they are affixes. In contrast to affixes, and like prepositions, however, they themselves assign case: The following NP is case marked. In addition, their position is not the one assumed by affixes. It does not follow either that they simply replace case forms. For their meaning is richer and more specific. This is evident if in addition to a case marked complement of a verb a P-marked complement is possible:

(75) a. The new professor read linguistics.
b. The new professor read on linguistics.

Whereas the NP *linguistics* in (75a) expresses that the whole domain of linguistics is concerned, that is, that the professor was responsible for the subject linguistics, the prepositional form *on* in (75b) selects an area out of a larger domain, meaning in this case, for example, that the new professor presented a lecture on a linguistic topic although his own subject was psychology. The situation is similar in the following examples:

(76) a. I know the problem.
b. I know about the problem.

Whereas in (76a) *the problem* again indicates that the whole problem is concerned, the preposition *about* in (76b) causes the selection of a domain which includes the circumstances of the problem, which itself is now less in focus.

Even though the prepositions in these contexts do not express spatial relations the conceptualizations they induce follow the spatial pattern. Thus prepositions in these positions exhibit the same semantic properties as do their lexical equivalents. The following examples illustrate that the semantic, selective function of lexical prepositions is the same as that in (75) and (76):

(77) a. Bill knocked the table.
b. Bill knocked on the table.

(78) a. They loaded the truck with hay.
b. They loaded hay onto the truck.

Whereas in the (a)-examples *the table* and *the truck* refer to the whole object, in the (b)-examples, due to the prepositions *on* and *onto*, a certain area of the object is selected.

The fact that the semantic properties of prepositional forms as parts of prepositional objects can be compared with those of lexical prepositions indicates that the former are not changed in this respect. Like lexical prepositions they have an argument structure and assign theta roles to their arguments. They also have inherent and selectional properties. Thus, for example, *about* in (79a) and *to* in (79b) differ in that the former assigns the role LOCATION to its complement, the latter GOAL:

(79) a. We talked about John.
b. We talked to John.

Accordingly, *about John* refers to the domain of a message whereas *to John* expresses its goal.

(80a) and (80b), on the other hand, differ in that *in* contains INCLUDE (x,y) as part of its meaning and *on* SUPPORT (x,y):

(80) a. Bill lives in danger.
b. Bill lives on potatoes.

In both cases, the external argument x is syntactically represented by the verb, i.e. the external roles of prepositions are identified with the role of the event argument e of V. The internal argument y is represented by the NP following P in both cases.

It may be concluded that prepositional forms marking prepositional objects to a large extent share semantic properties with their lexical equivalents. However, though originally spatial prepositions, they do not contain the feature SPATIAL(P). In addition, the shared features seem to be restricted to what Herskovits 1986:48ff calls the "ideal meaning".

With respect to syntactic properties, prepositional forms marking prepositional objects and their lexical equivalents differ considerably. Though the former assign case, they do not have projection properties, i.e. they are not the heads of constructions. Amongst other things, this is evident from the fact that selection restrictions of the verbs in this context apply to the N in the construction, which therefore must be considered its head:

(81) a. Bill talked to John.
*the station.
b. Bill appeals to Mary.
*the house.

This is different with respect to lexical *to*:

(82) Bill went to John.
the station.

Additional evidence for the fact that in prepositional object constructions the noun rather than the preposition is the head is provided by the fact that the latter is lexically governed by other categories in the same way as in other languages case affixes are governed, for example the genitive by German *harren* or *eingedenk*.

Further support for the claim that in these constructions the preposition is merely 'attached' to the NP may be derived from the fact that wh-movement into the specifier position of C applies to P and NP together, preserving both categories, i.e. no PP-wh-form is possible:

(83) a. On whom did he rely?
b. *Where did he rely?

The possibility of passivization also supports the claim that N rather than P is the head of the construction:

(84) a. John appealed to Mary.
b. Mary was appealed to.

Leaving behind the prepositional form in passives - a variant also possible in wh-questions -

(85) Who did he rely on?

is accounted for in generative grammar by the process of reanalysis (cf. esp. Hornstein & Weinberg 1981). It illustrates the peculiar double-faced character of prepositional forms pointed out by language historians. Thus, Delbrück 1893:654ff, Brugman 1911:758ff, Behagel 1924:33ff and Wackernagel 1924:153ff claim that prepositions - originally spatial adverbs - have migrated towards NPs on the one hand in order to specify case meanings and towards Vs on the other, where - as so-called pre-verbs - they specify the semantics of verbs. Whereas with prepositional forms in the context of prepositional objects the case specifying function is dominant, it is their specifying of the semantics of verbs which is dominant in the variants to be investigated in the next section. Thus, Selkirk 1982:28 seems right in assuming that reanalysis is possible in English because both constructions exist anyway. This is confirmed by the fact that German does not allow reanalysis,

(86) a. An wen hast du geschrieben?
b. *Wen hast du geschrieben an ?

since German also does not allow the construction discussed in the next section. We will see later that reanalysis is not the only way to capture the facts in English.

4.3. The prepositional form to be investigated in this section occurs in the context of phrasal verbs, as in the following examples:

(87) a. He brought in his suitcase.
b. He brought his suitcase in.

(88) a. He put on his socks.
b. He put his socks on.

(89) a. He switched on the light.
b. He switched the light on.

The prepositional forms which may occur here comprise the set of those that typically mark prepositional objects as well as forms considered adverbial particles in Traditional Grammar, such as *up*, *down*, *across*, *off* etc. What is interesting about these prepositional forms is the fact that they may be located either before or after the NP in the complement domain of the verb. Transformational Grammar has attempted to derive divergent surface structures such as the (a)- and (b)-examples in (87) to (89) from the same underlying structure. Thus, Chomsky 1957:75f suggests inserting phrasal verbs as complex verbs composed of the sequence V_1 + Prt and deriving the post-NP-position of the prepositional form transformationally. Thus the pre-NP-position is base generated. In contrast, Emonds 1972; 1985:252ff suggests considering the post-NP-position as base generated, classifying the prepositional form as an intransitve preposition. Accordingly, the pre-NP-position is derived by movement. A problem both suggestions face is the fact that the prepositional forms in both positions should exhibit the same properties since lexical insertion takes place before movement. However, this is not the case. As Radford 1988:100 points out, the variants differ with respect to projection properties. Whereas the prepositional form in post-NP-position may be accompanied by a specifier as well as a complement, it may not in pre-NP-position:

(90) a. He brought his suitcase right in the house.
b. *He brought right in the house his suitcase.

(91) a. He put his socks right on his feet.
b. *He put right on his feet his socks.

On the other hand, with respect to semantic properties no difference is to be observed. In examples like (87) to (89) in both cases argument structures may be identified, in each case an external and an internal implicit argument. Due to the projection properties of the prepositional form in post-NP-position, the latter may be expressed explicitly in this position, as is illustrated by (90a) and (91a). The external argument in each case bears the theta role THEME, the internal one LOCATION. The inherent properties are the same in each position and correspond to those constituting the ideal meaning of the lexical preposition: INCLUDE (x,y) for *in* and CONTACT (x,y) for *on*. Selectional properties like EXTENDED (y) may be postulated for *on* in (88). They are, however, questionable with respect to (89).

However, with respect to semantic properties of prepositional forms in the context of phrasal verbs, different observations may be made. Whereas in examples like (87) to (89) the meaning of the lexical preposition is preserved in general, in other contexts the forms may assume a meaning of their own or enter the verb meaning in order to constitute an idiomatic expression. In (92) *up* assumes a meaning of its own, different from that of the lexical preposition:

(92) a. He painted up the wall.
b. He cut up the bread.
c. He ate up the banana.

As a spatial preposition, for example, in (93),

(93) a. He went up the hill.
b. They bought a house up the hill.
c. The boys stayed up the hill.

up denotes a vertical, upward and thus directed spatial relation. It exhibits an argument structure, requiring an internal and an external argument. The external argument, syntactically represented by V, bears the THEME role, the internal one, represented by NP, the role PATH. In (92), on the other hand, *up* expresses a direction focussing on the final point. An argument structure of its own seems not to be present, as the following comparison suggests:

(94) a. He brought in the suitcase.
b. The suitcase is in.

But:

(95) a. He cut up the bread.
b. *The bread is up.
c. The bread is cut up.

Whereas (94b), as an implication of (94a), illustrates that *the suitcase* is the external argument of *in*, (95b) - which is not an implication of (95a) - suggests that *the bread* is not an argument of *up*. Since (95c), however, is related to (95a) in the same way as (94b) to (94a), it follows that *up* in (95a) merely modifies the verb meaning.

In examples like (96)

(96) He looked up the word.

no separate meaning can be identified for the prepositional form. The construction V + P is idiomatic.

In spite of their semantic changes in examples like (92) and (96), these prepositional forms may nevertheless occur in post-NP-position and then exhibit projection properties,

(97) a. He cut the bread right up.
b. He looked the word right up in the lexicon.

which are absent in pre-NP-position:

(98) a. *He cut right up the bread.
b. *He looked right up in the lexicon the word.

It follows, that their syntactic properties correspond to those of lexical prepositions although they differ with respect to semantic properties.

Thus, the two possible positions for prepositional forms in the context of phrasal verbs present - independent of their meaning - two different syntactic variants. Whereas the form in post-NP-position behaves like a lexical preposition, the one in pre-NP-position does not. The latter, which is intimately related to the verb, may be described in two ways. First, it may be considered an affix (cf. e.g. Leisi 1974:107;145) and the result a derivative. Second, the V + P combination may be considered a compound. The advantage of the second alternative over the first is that there are other constructions in English which are marked in a similar way. Thus, it is unusual for an inflectional affix to occur as an affix rather than a suffix:

(99) He [$_V$ looked up] the word.

This phenomenon, however, may be found in connexion with other compounds, too, as Selkirk 1982:52 points out:

(100) programs coordinator
human services catalogue
arms race

However, in these constructions the head is always to the right and not to the left as in the examples of phrasal verbs.

It is interesting to observe that these unusual constructions [$_V$VP] have their counterparts in German, as is pointed out by Kunsmann 1973. Thus, separable prefixes - those prepositions which are called "pre-verbs" by language historians - behave just as irregularly in that they turn a prefix into an infix:

(101) a. Er ist ihr nachgelaufen.
b. Er lief ihr nach.

The different position with respect to the verb here is explained on typological grounds. For German as an SOV-language the pre-verbal position of a modifying element is to be expected as is the post-verbal one for English as an SVO-language.

To summarize: Prepositional forms in the context of phrasal verbs represent, depending on their position, two different variants. The first is a constituent of a compound with reduced syntactic and semantic properties. The second is like the lexical category preposition, again with possibly reduced semantic properties.

4.4. A large number of prepositional forms are used in the context of phrases which are either syntactically unalterable or may be altered only under restricted conditions. The following phrases constitute sequences of the prepositional form *on* followed by an NP whose head is a deadjectival noun. The expressions thus formed have a pejorative association:

(102) on the quiet
on the sly
on the cheap

In fixed phrases like these it is impossible to change either the P-constituent or the NP-constituent:

(103) *in the quiet
*by the quiet

(104) *on the stealthy quiet
*on the quiet of the night
*on the silence

For our present discussion it is relevant to determine which syntactic properties the prepositional form in these constructions exhibits. The constructions may be used as adjuncts, but not as complements:

(105) a. He did it on the quiet.
b. A drink on the quiet may be dangerous.

(106) a. *He relied on the quiet.
b. *He depended on the quiet.

The examples under (106) are not acceptable with the same interpretation of *on the quiet*.

A specifier may not be used in these constructions:

(107) *He did it right on the quiet.

Nothing but an NP may occur as a complement:

(108) He did it on the quiet.
*that he was quiet.
*being quiet.
*in the quiet.

Thus, strict subcategorization cannot be identified. Since no specifier is possible either, it may be concluded that the prepositional form in these contexts does not exhibit the projection properties of the lexical category preposition. This is confirmed by the following test, which illustrates that *on* is not the head of the construction:

(109) *Where did he do it?

Compare (109) with (110):

(110) a. He stayed on the boat.
b. Where did he stay?

However, *on* in this context does not behave like the prepositional form similar to case affixes either:

(111) *On what did he do it?

Compare (111) with (112):

(112) a. He relied on his strength.
b. On what did he rely?

The ungrammaticality of (111), which excludes the NP and thus N as the head of the construction, illustrates that this construction is higly marked. Neither of its constituents represents the head. The possibility of forming a question using the question word *how*, on the other hand, indicates shared properties of the construction as a whole with elements belonging to other categories:

(113) How did he do it?

As is illustrated by (114) and (115), these are adverbs or adjectives:

(114) a. He did it nicely.
b. How did he do it?

(115) a. He was nice.
b. How was he?

The co-ordination test in (116)

(116) a. He did it on the quiet and quickly.
b. *He did it on the quiet and in the house.
c. *He did it on the quiet and nice.

suggests that *on the quiet* and an adverb, in this case *quickly*, represent the same construction type. This is confirmed by examples like those under (117), which both allow the specifier *so*:

(117) a. Why did you do it so on the quiet?
b. Why did you do it so badly?

Before drawing conclusions from these observations, further examples will be investigated.

Another type of fixed phrases is presented in (118):

(118) on sale
on show
on trial
on exhibition

Again these constructions are syntactically unalterable and even morphologically and semantically marked. In each case the noun is deverbal and denotes an institutionalized action. The constructions may be used as adjuncts or predicates, but not as complements. The possibility of their use as predicates distinguishes them from those looked at before. Syntactic tests analogous to those presented with respect to the *on-the-quiet*-pattern yield the following results:

(119) a. The books are on sale.
b. *The books are right on sale.
c. *Where are the books?
d. *On what are the books?
e. *How are the books.

(120) a. *The books are on sale and cheaply.
b. The books are on sale and in the window/inside.
c. The books are on sale and cheap.

(121) a. *The books are so on sale.
b. The books are so cheap.

The co-ordination test under (120c) suggests that *on sale* represents an adjective. However, co-ordination with other PPs is also possible, as is illustrated by (120b). But, as (119c) indicates, it is not possible to form a question with a PP-wh-question word. The ungrammaticality of (119e) and

(121a), on the other hand, need not be taken as evidence against adjectival properties since both structures may also yield ungrammatical results with respect to adjectives proper. Thus, the specifier *so* occurs only with gradable adjectives:

(122) She is so nice.
tired.
*pregnant.
*married.

And the question word *how* may also not be used with every adjective, as is illustrated by the examples under (123):

(123) a. How is she?
b. Nice.
Tired.
*Tall.
*Pregnant.
*Married.
*Respected.
Interesting.

It is unclear what the constraints are in this case. What may be derived, therefore, is that *on sale* in part behaves like an adjective and in part like a PP.

A characteristic of another type of fixed phrase is the fact that it can be used only in a position and function called "disjunct" by Greenbaum 1969:

(124) on balance
on second thoughts
on the whole
on the other hand

These phrases, too, are syntactically unalterable. They are, however, morphologically and semantically not as fixed. Syntactic tests to determine the status of the prepositional form as well as of the construction as a whole yield the following results:

(125) a. On balance, the weather was good.
b. *Right on balance, the weather was good.
c. *Where was the weather good?

d. *On what was the weather good?
e. *How was the weather good?

(126) a. On balance and frankly, the weather was good.
b. *On balance and in Italy, the weather was good.
c. *On balance and frank, the weather was good.

(127) a. *So on balance, the weather was good.
b. *So frankly, the weather was good.
c. *So personally, the weather was good.

The tests confirm that *on balance* behaves like an adverb, e.g. *frankly* which, according to Greenbaum 1969, belongs to the class of disjuncts.

Thus it turns out that the fixed phrases of the sequence P + NP, of which three examples have been investigated here, syntactically either behave like adverbs and/or adjectives and only to some degree - as is the case with *on sale* - like PPs additionally. The adverbs concerned do not belong to those that enter the category P as intransitive prepositions under the X-bar-Theory but rather to a set that represents positional variants of adjectives. Together with these adjectives they are therefore subsumed under a single hypercategory by Radford 1988:241ff. Only in predicate position, however, do these phrases behave like adjectives. Within an NP they normally take the postnominal position typical of PPs. The typical position for adjectives in these constructions in English is prenominal. It may be observed, however, that some prepositional, fixed phrases may, in fact, take this position:

(128) a. He is an out of work teacher.
b. He is good at after dinner speeches.
c. He watched an on-line operation.

Thus, obviously, these phrases represent mixed forms exhibiting adjectival or adverbial properties on the one hand and properties of PPs on the other.

A look at contemporary English vocabulary illustrates that these findings are not surprising at all. There are quite a few forms which originated as PPs but are now either adjectives or adverbs or both, as, for example, the following:

(129) a. A: awake, aghast, alive, alert, akin
b. Adv: again, apart, aloud, aboard, ashore, apace
c. A, Adv: alike, ajar, aloof, alone, amiss

This suggests that the phrases investigated are in transitional state between PP and adjective and/or adverb, exhibiting properties of the one as well as of the other category.[6] During the process of change the prepositional head obviously loses its autonomy without the noun becoming the head of the construction. The participant constituents merge to form a new syntactic unit.[7]

So far only the syntactic properties of fixed phrases and the constituent prepositional forms have been investigated. Attention will now be directed briefly at their semantic properties.

In the examples presented the prepositional form involved is always *on*. *On* is of spatial origin but in no case does it denote a spatial relation, as is illustrated by the examples repeated in the following:

(130) He had a drink on the quiet.

(131) The book is on sale.

(132) On balance, the weather is good.

Thus, in no case is the feature SPATIAL(on) present. The prepositional form establishes a relation between an event or an object, syntactically represented by V' or N' in (130) - the sentence is ambiguous - V' in (131) and something abstract, syntactically represented by NP in each case. Thus an argument structure can be identified. The arguments bear thematic roles, the NPs a role determining the domain of reference and thus the role LOCATION; the external argument bears the role THEME. Although inherent and selectional features of prepositions in these phrases are bleached - the impossibility of inserting other prepositions has caused the specific meaning of the given preposition to become a synthetic part of the meaning of the whole - they can nevertheless be identified. Identification may be achieved via a conceptualization test. By inserting other prepositions than the one required, though the result is ungrammatical, it can be tested what the conceptualization would be like in these cases, illustrating the difference between the de-

---

6 See Foskett (this volume) for a similar conclusion concerning *together*.

7 Independent evidence in support of these assumptions is provided by Napoli 1989:45, who points out that prepositional fixed phrases are subject to AP-movement. She provides the following examples:

Happy though he is, he isn't really.
Into art
*In bed

viant and the regular expressions. The test is thus a semantic well-formedness test.

In the example under (133) *on* is replaced by *above*, in those under (134) by *under*, in (135) by *in* and (136) by *at*:

(133) a. *He had a drink above the quiet.
b. *The book is above sale.
c. *Above balance, the weather is good.

(134) a. *He had a drink under the quiet.
b. *The book is under sale.
c. *Under balance, the weather is good.

(135) a. *He had a drink in the quiet.
b. *The book is in sale.
c. *In balance, the weather is good.

(136) a. *He had a drink at the quiet.
b. *The book in at sale.
c. *At balance, the weather is good.

The replacing prepositions have been selected because each of them compared to *on* differs in meaning with respect to exactly one distinctive feature. Thus *above* is marked by the feature NO CONTACT (x,y) as opposed to *on* CONTACT (x,y), *under* by VERTICAL, NEGATIVE (x,y) as opposed to on VERTICAL, POSITIVE (x,y), *in* by INCLUDE (x,y) as opposed to EXTENDED (y) and *at* by NOT EXTENDED (y). Comparing the respective conceptualizations - a detailed description of which would lead too far, the reader should therefore test his/her own intuitions - with those induced by *on* in these contexts illustrates that *on* in these cases maintains the same inherent and selectional semantic features it exhibits as a lexical preposition. However, in these contexts it does not express a spatial but rather a modal relation. It should be emphasized again that identification of these features requires a specific conscious activity. The fixed connexion between the constituents of these phrases, which allows neither replacement of the preposition nor of the NP, normally results in assigning a meaning to the phrase as a whole. In general, these phrases are metaphorical, the metaphor being determined by the preposition, the focus of the metaphor.

Thus, in principle the same properties are to be identified which generally hold for metaphors.[8]

What needs to be kept in mind is that the prepositional fixed phrases investigated here as a whole are highly marked syntactically, morphologically as well as semantically, which is less true of the prepositional forms themselves. We will see in the next section how these facts may be captured in the lexicon.

5. Suggestions for the lexical representation of selected prepositional forms

5.1. The results of the analysis of the data in the previous section may be summarized as follows. Prepositional forms, mostly *on*, have been investigated in different uses with respect to syntactic and central semantic properties. The investigations included prepositional forms as constituents of complements of verbs of motion and state as well as adjuncts - in this case restricted to spatial and temporal uses - as markers of prepositional objects, parts of phrasal verbs and fixed phrases. Assuming that elements of major lexical categories exhibit projection properties, the results suggest a division of prepositional forms into those that represent the major lexical category preposition and those that do not. The first set includes prepositional forms which as heads of PPs may be used to form complements of verbs of motion and state or adjuncts. It turned out that spatial and temporal uses of the same phonological form in these contexts differ with respect to properties of strict subcategorization. Prepositional forms which are part of phrasal verbs in post-NP-position have to be included in this first set. Used in pre-NP-position, however, i.e. adjacent to the verb, they do not exhibit projection properties and may thus not be considered elements of the autonomous lexical category preposition. In this position they are constituents of a complex verb. Prepositional forms which mark prepositional objects also lack projec-

---

8 A promising description may be developed on the basis of the "Interaction theory" presented by Richards 1936 or Black 1962; 1979. According to their view, metaphors are the result of combining in general two elements creating the meaning of the metaphor by an interaction of selected features of either constituent. Thus, it is a critical characteristic of metaphors involving prepositions that only selected features may differ with different nouns.

tion properties and therefore may not be considered elements of a major category. It was shown that in these contexts N is the head of the sequence P + NP. The prepositional form as a governed element has the same function as a case affix but without being one. Finally, prepositional forms which are part of fixed phrases also do not exhibit projection properties and consequently do not represent the major category preposition.

As opposed to projection properties, case properties are present in all the uses of the prepositional forms under investigation. However, in some cases case properties are inferred rather than observed, assuming the validity of the case filter. For, if it is accepted that each lexical NP requires case, then every prepositional form followed by an NP must be able to assign case. But there is no empirical evidence for this property because in English case is visible only with respect to pronouns. In some of the contexts investigated, pronouns are not allowed, as is demonstrated by the following examples:

(137) a. These books are on sale.
b. *How long are they on it?

(138) a. He had a drink on the quiet.
b. *Does he often have drinks on it?

(139) a. He looked up the word.
b. *He looked up it.

But:

(140) a. He sat on the chair.
b. He sat on it.

(141) a. He relied on his brother.
b. He relied on him.

(142) a. He is dependent on his brother.
b. He is dependent on him.

The assumption that in English only pronouns and no other lexical NP receive case and are subject to the case filter would explain the ungrammaticality of (137b) through (139b). It would also explain why phrasal verbs with an NP complement represented by a pronoun allow only post-NP-position for the prepositional form:

(143) a. *He looked up it.
b. He looked it up.

But:

(144) a. He looked up the word.
b. He looked the word up.

The explanation would be that the prepositional form involved has neither projection nor case properties. Therefore, pronouns which need case must occur adjacent to the case assigning verb, whereas other lexical NPs need not.

Assuming that in English only pronouns are subject to the case filter would have far reaching consequences and will not be further pursued. The data show, however, that it is not completely implausible.

Semantic properties of prepositional forms have been investigated only to the extent that they are related to argument structure and theta grids as well as inherent and selectional features belonging to the "ideal meaning". In addition, domain specific properties, for example, "temporal" and "spatial", have been considered. It turned out that argument structure and theta grids may be identified not only when prepositional forms represent the major lexical category preposition but also in those cases where they are governed and thus similar to case affixes, in fixed phrases and as parts of phrasal verbs. In the latter case, however, this holds only if the prepositional form together with the verb does not result in an idiomatic meaning. Inherent and selectional features, too, have been identified not only for elements of the major lexical category preposition but also for the other syntactic variants. It was pointed out, however, that in fixed connexions with other constituents - manifested by the impossibility of replacing the given prepositional form by others - the features are bleached, although recoverable. This holds for governed prepositions as well as for prepositional forms in fixed phrases. Sometimes a change in meaning can be observed, as with respect to phrasal verbs of the type *eat up* or *point up*, sometimes the preposition together with the verb gives an idiomatic meaning.

Domain specific meaning, i.e. "spatial" and "temporal", was identified only with respect to the major lexical category preposition. It would be hasty, however, to conclude that only these two are relevant since non-spatial and non-temporal prepositions in the domain of adjuncts have not been investigated. As far as domain specific features were included in the investigation it turned out that they are involved as inherent as well as selectional features, i.e. temporal *on* requires temporal arguments and spatial *on* requires spatial ones.

5.2. How then, are prepositional forms which are syntactically and/or samantically heterogeneous to be represented in a lexicon designed as a model of the mental lexicon? In contrast to the ideal situation described in section 2, where one phonological representation is mapped onto exactly one syntactic and one semantic representation, in this case one phonological representation is faced with more than one syntactic and (possibly) semantic representation. Does this mean that prepositional forms are represented in more than one lexical entry, that each one forms a lexical unit of its own and has to be learned separately? In what follows a solution will be suggested which, in fact, supports the claim that prepositional forms are introduced in various lexical entries. Since these are designed to be connected in a network fashion it is claimed furthermore, that variants of prepositional forms are not learned like new words but either by changing single properties or by embedding them in new contexts. The suggestions refer mostly to the form *on*.

5.2.1. First, a lexical entry has to be provided which represents the spatial major lexical category preposition. The lexical entry contains the phonological matrix, the syntactic and the semantic representation in roughly the following way:

(145) PHON:	/on/	
SYN:	[-N, -V]	implies e.g. projection properties and case assignment
	[__ NP]	strict subcategorization
SEM:	*on* (x,y)	argument structure and theta grid
	THEME (x)	
	LOCATION (y)	
	SPATIAL(on)	domain specific feature
	CONTACT (x,y)	inherent and selectional features, ideal meaning
	SUPPORT (y,x)	
	EXTENDED (y)	

Based on the results of section 4.1, this lexical entry is designed to assign projection properties to lexical prepositions via the feature combination [-N,

-V], as well as strict subcategorization properties [__NP]. It is very likely that strictly subcategorizing NP represents the unmarked case and need not be mentioned explicitly. Of the semantic properties argument structure and theta grid are presented, the domain specific feature SPATIAL as well as inherent and selectional features of the ideal meaning.

This entry represents the main entry for *on*. This is justified on historical as well as synchronic grounds - the latter related to aspects of linguistic competence. Thus if a native speaker is asked to describe the preposition *on* he/she will first provide examples which illustrate accessing this lexical unit. It remains an open question in what way the set of semantic properties in (145) has to be supplemented. It is not the aim of this paper to offer an answer to this question.[9]

The temporal variant of the lexical preposition *on* differs from the spatial one with respect to semantic as well as syntactic properties. Accessing this variant is achieved via the same phonological representation which has the function of a connective node. From here different paths may lead to syntactic and semantic representation. Compared to the spatial variant, the temporal one contains the feature TEMPORAL instead of SPATIAL. In the unmarked case further changes follow automatically. These affect selectional properties as well as strict subcategorization: Temporal prepositions take temporal arguments and allow CP-complements in addition to NP-complements. In the case of *on* certain restrictions are imposed on the internal structure of CP: It must be infinite, the subject must be PRO and the verb is specified by *ing*. Since the strict subcategorization is marked this way, it has to be represented in the lexicon. This implies that it cannot be derived from general principles and must be learned. Another change affects the inherent semantic feature SUPPORT (x,y), which for principled cognitive reasons is irrelevant in the context of TEMPORAL(on). Therefore it need not be expressed in the lexicon. The remaining features are not subject to change. Thus, in the lexicon only the feature TEMPORAL(on) and in addition the change concerning strict subcategorization need be represented:

(146) TEMPORAL(on)
[__ NP]; [__ $[_{CP}$ ... $[_{IP}$ $[_{NP}$ $[_{VP}$ ing V']]]]]

As a result, temporal *on* does not receive a full lexical entry of its own. The features are connected with the lexical entry for spatial *on*. A single

9 Suggestions concerning the lexical representation of semantic properties of prepositions are presented, for example, by Wege (this volume).

phonological matrix is thus mapped onto two syntactic and two semantic representations, each pair being connected via identical features. With respect to language production it follows, for example, that if accessing starts with the semantic representation a decision concernig the syntactic representation is made simultaneously and vice versa. The path then leads to the phonological form /on/. With respect to language perception it follows accordingly that the path leads from /on/ either to the syntactic or the semantic representation. No matter which one is accessed first, the other one is triggered automatically.

5.2.2. Next we will have a look at prepositional forms that mark prepositional objects. It was demonstrated in section 4.2 that these are lexically governed forms which cannot be replaced by others arbitrarily. It was shown that these forms do not exhibit the projection properties of lexical categories and that semantically also, i.e. on the basis of selectional properties of the governor, they cannot be considered the head of the sequence P + NP. It was concluded that therefore they have to be viewed as semantic specifying elements which have entered the case paradigm without themselves being case affixes. They have to be distinguished from the latter with respect to position and case assigning properties. They share with them the property of being governed, although in English case affixes are governed structurally and prepositional forms lexically. Being dependent on their governor requires of governed prepositions that they are introduced in the lexicon in the lexical entry of the governor. They are represented as conditions on the context of the respective governor, which may be a verb, an adjective, a noun or even a preposition:

(147) a. *depend* [__ $[_P$ on] NP]
b. *angry* [__ $[_P$ about] NP]
c. *refusal* [__ $[_P$ of] NP]
d. *out* [__ $[_P$ of] NP]

It is suggested here that governed prepositions are introduced by representing their category label P as well as the phonological matrix, /on/ for example, in the context of the strict subcategorization of the governor at the linear position they assume in d-structure, i.e. after the V and before the NP. According to this view, the prepositional form in the lexicon neither forms a constituent with the V nor with the NP. In the lexicon its position is only linearly and not hierarchically determined. When lexical insertion applies and lexical information interacts with other parts of the grammar, as e.g. with the principles of X-bar-syntax, syntactically marked sequences like these must be analyzed. There are two possibilities. According to the first, the prepositional form is attached to its governor via Chomsky adjunction, according to the second to the following NP. This results in alternative structures for the VP in sentences like (148), as presented under (149a) and (149b):

(148) Bill depends on approval.

(149) a.

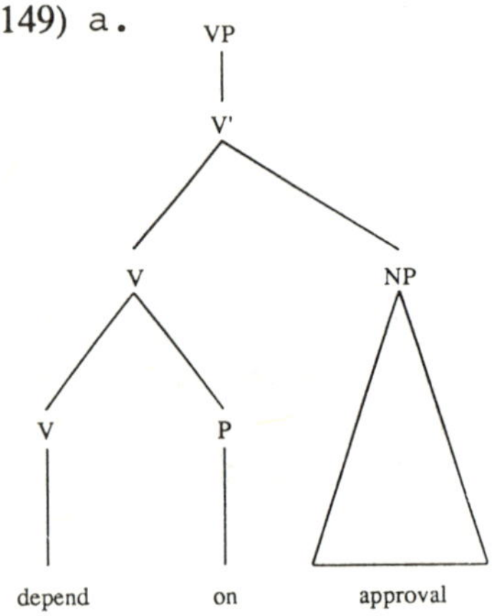

b.

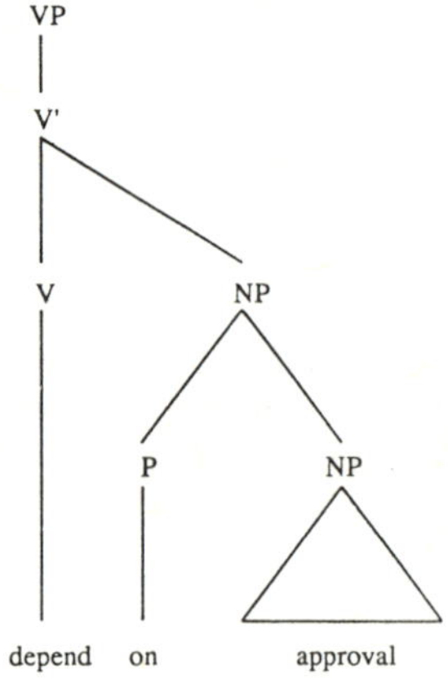

Given this analysis, the wh-movement in (150a) may be derived from (149a) and that in (150b) from (149b):

(150) a. What does he depend on?
b. On what does he depend?

(149a) also presents the underlying structure for passives:

(151) a. The committee agreed on the solution.
b. The solution was agreed on by the committee.

Assuming that governed prepositions are not yet determined structurally in the lexicon has several advantages over the analysis suggested in general, which represents them as constituents of a PP together with the following NP (cf. e.g. Chomsky 1965:96f; 1981:292ff; Hornstein & Weinberg 1981): It avoids some of the problems, solves others and explains relations which are otherwise left unexplained.

For one thing, reanalysis can be dispensed with. It was introduced to reanalyze [$_{V'}$ V PP] as [$_{V'}$ [$_V$ V P] NP] in order to describe passives like (151b). As opposed to the *analysis* suggested here, *reanalysis* changes structures and thus clearly violates the projection principle. Thus the syntax is burdened in an unnecessary way. The lexicon certainly is a better place for marked information. On the other hand, analyzing a sequence not yet analyzed in the lexicon is compatible with the projection principle. What is needed is a slight modification to the effect that lexical information is "non-distinct" through all levels of representation rather than "identical".

Another problem is solved by the analysis suggested here which determines P - in contrast to the view taken generally - as not being a constituent of a PP. As has been demonstrated in section 4.2 - and as has been pointed out in the literature (cf. e.g. Fillmore 1969:367; Czepluch 1981:221ff) - in these constructions N rather than P is the head of the strictly subcategorized constituent. This is predicted by both structures, (149a) and (149b). The analysis assumed generally, on the other hand, inadequately claimes that P is the head of the construction.

In addition, it has been pointed out that in these constructions the prepositional forms are comparable with, though not identical to case affixes. Both forms are governed and syntactically both serve the same function. This insight is captured by structure (149b). The prepositional form together with an NP constitutes an NP, just like case affixes do. Thus the syntactic similarity of case affixes and governed prepositions is described. The differences are related to their respective positions as well as to other syntactic, semantic and phonological properties. These are taken into consideration in the following way.

Information about the position as well as about phonological properties is provided by the lexical entry of the governor. The phonological form, /on/ for example, which occurs in the strict subcategorization frame of the governor, allows access to the information provided by the lexical entry for the lexical category *on*. In this way the governed prepositional form is connected with the lexical category. The category label, in addition to the phonological representation, signifies that this access is legitimate. The lexical entry for *on* then provides the information that the phonological form is linked to certain syntactic properties, for example projection properties and case properties. Since, with respect to governed prepositions, the preceding as well as the following categorial context is lexically fixed, there is no way to realize projection properties. The analysis only allows P. P'and PP are excluded. This explains why in this position and function no specifier and nothing but an NP complement may occur. In fact, the NP following P is not even its complement, as is illustrated by (149b). Unlike projection properties, case properties may be realized. Accordingly, prepositions assign case to the following NP, obeying the requirements of adjacency and government. This may be considered a version of exceptional case marking since the NP is not the complement of P. Thus, another difference between governed prepositions and case affixes is described: Governed prepositions assign case themselves.

The phonological form of governed prepositions also allows access to the semantic properties of their lexical counterparts. This explains why governed prepositions have an argument structure, theta properties and inherent as well as selectional semantic properties. The fact that the latter are reduced compared to those of lexical prepositions is due to the fact that governed prepositions are parts of metaphors. Their being bleached, on the other hand, is a consequence of the fact that governed prepositions often cannot be replaced, so that the meaning the preposition contributes is not evident and tends to become an integral part of the meaning of the whole construction. Wherever alternation is possible, however, the meaning contributed by the preposition is evident, as is illustrated by the following examples:

(152)	a. to talk	to	s.o.
		about	
	b. to linger	on	s.th.
		over	
	c. to think	about	s.th.
		of	
	d. to wait	for	s.o.
		on	

Thus the semantic difference between governed prepositions and case affixes is also explained. The syntactic and semantic differences between the two, which are explained by the connexion of governed and lexical prepositions, provide arguments against a possible alternative to the suggested lexical representation of governed prepositions. Thus it might be argued that governed prepositions have entered the case paradigm and therefore have to be represented together with case affixes but independent of lexical prepositions. However, this would neither explain the difference between case affixes and governed preposition nor, in fact, their similarities. On the other hand, it would inevitably lead to redundancies with respect to lexical prepositions. In what follows it will be demonstrated how the similarities between case affixes and governed prepositions can be explained more adequately, taking into account diachronic aspects.

The similarity of governed prepositions and case affixes suggests an analysis with far-reaching consequences which are, however, as far as can be seen, all desirable. If governed prepositions, loosely speaking, assume semantic differentiating case functions, then it seems natural to consider them inherent case markers, i.e. lexically determined case realizations. As a consequence, a verb governing a preposition in this case does not assign structural, but rather inherent, lexical case realized by the preposition. Looking at the structures (149a) and (149b), here repeated as (153a) and (153b), let us consider the consequences of this suggestion:

(153)

a. b.

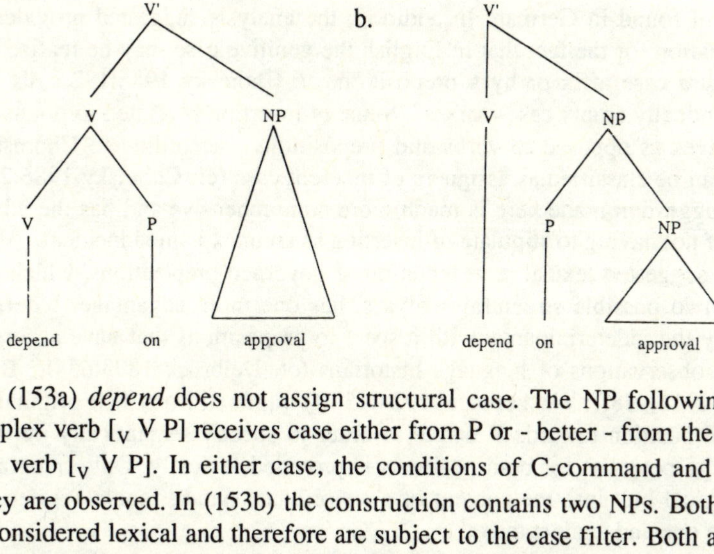

In (153a) *depend* does not assign structural case. The NP following the complex verb [$_V$ V P] receives case either from P or - better - from the complex verb [$_V$ V P]. In either case, the conditions of C-command and adjacency are observed. In (153b) the construction contains two NPs. Both may be considered lexical and therefore are subject to the case filter. Both are, in fact, case marked and the structure is well-formed. The dominating NP is inherently case marked by *on* via *depend*, the dominated one structurally by *on*. It turns out that structure (153b) would be problematic if the governed preposition was not considered an inherent case marker. In this case both NPs would be structurally case marked - the dominating one by V and the dominated one by P - without it being clear what the consequences are for the realization of case. From this point of view assuming that governed prepositions are inherent case markers is not only plausible but necessary.

The suggested analysis has farther reaching consequences, however. Thus, if governed prepositions are inherent case markers there can be no reason why this property should be restricted to selected contexts. (147) provides examples of the well-known fact that in English not only verbs and prepositions govern prepositions, but adjectives and nouns as well. According to the analysis suggested, it follows that all major lexical categories are able to assign inherent case. Thus, the claim that in English only [-N] categories are case assigners can be restricted to structural case. This consequence is all to the good since it solves the problem of having to explain why in modern English, as opposed to Old English and German, adjectives and nouns have lost their ability to assign case without any alternative to replace this ability. There is an alternative, inherent case, realized by governed prepositions. As lexical case this is comparable to lexical case affixes present in Old English and still found in German. In addition, the analysis suggested provides an explanation for the fact that in English the genitive case may be realized either by a case affix or by a preposition, *of*. Chomsky 1986:192 calls *of* a "semantically empty case-marker". Since *of*-insertion is related to nouns and adjectives as opposed to verbs and prepositions - according to Chomsky - they can be classified as assigners of inherent case (cf. Chomsky 1986:202). The suggestion made here is much more comprehensive and has the advantage of not having to stipulate *of*-insertion as an unexplained incident.

The suggested lexical representation of governed prepositions, which provides two possible structural analyses, has one more advantage. It reflects exactly the indeterminancy with respect to prepositions that have according to the observations of language historians (cf. Delbrück 1893:654ff; Brugmann 1911:758ff; Wackernagel 1924:153ff) migrated from their original adverbial position towards V or NP in order to specify semantically the V or NP. The potential for both positions is provided lexically. Only integrating the lexical unit into the context of a subordinate phrase requires a decision for the one and against the other.

5.2.3. In 4.3 it was observed that prepositional forms as parts of phrasal verbs may occur in two different positions - pre-NP or post-NP - exhibiting different projection properties. These differences prohibit considering one of the positions as base generated, the other one as derived. That is, it is not adequate to provide only one lexical representation. It was further shown that there is evidence for analyzing the prepositional form in pre-NP-position as a constituent of the preceding verb, whereas for the form in post-NP-position syntactic properties of lexical prepositions were identified. It follows that prepositional forms as parts of phrasal verbs have to be represented in the lexicon in two different ways, as in (154), for example:

(154) *switch on* [__ NP] : *switch* [__ NP [$_{PP}$ [$_{P}$ on]]]
[$_{V}$ V P]

That is, they are introduced together with the verb under the heading of the verb, providing an alternative between the prepositional form as a constituent of V and as a PP complement, respectively. The entry for *switch on* provides the morphological structure of the complex verb, which describes it as a compound, composed of V and P.

The twofold lexical representation of the syntactic properties of prepositional forms as parts of phrasal verbs indicates that these are marked properties. That this is adequate is supported by the observation that not all phrasal verbs allow both prepositional positions. Some allow only the post-NP-position. Thus, the syntax of these prepositional forms, including their idiosyncratic variation, signals instability, which illustrates with respect to the synchronic state of English diachronic processes, which were also observed with respect to governed prepositions. The pre-NP-position is a result of the migration process already mentioned, which in the case of phrasal verbs ends closer to the verb. If it ends closer to the noun the result is a governed preposition. Since with respect to the latter case one of the two variants has been identified which is structurally identical to one variant of phrasal verbs, this indicates that there is a smooth transition between phrasal verbs and verbs with governed prepositions. That is, it is not always clear whether the landing site of the preposition is closer to the verb or the noun. Prepositional forms of phrasal verbs are connected with the lexical preposition via their identical phonological representation in the same way as governed prepositions. Thus accessing their syntactic as well as semantic properties is possible.

With respect to semantic properties of prepositional forms as parts of phrasal verbs it was noted in 4.3 that at least three different possibilities have to be distinguished. The first one is represented by *switch on.* As part of a metaphor the prepositional form selects some semantic features of the main entry, in this case the argument structure, the theta grid as well as the features CONTACT (x,y) and EXTENDED (y). According to the second possibility, the sequence V + P is idiomatized. Thus accessing semantic properties of the lexical category is blocked. The idiomatic interpretation has to be marked lexically, indicating that it holds for both syntactic variants. For even though the prepositional form exhibits syntactic properties of the lexical preposition in post-NP-position, accessing semantic features is blocked in this case. An example of this variant is provided by *look up*.

The analysis of the third semantic variant of phrasal verbs has farther reaching consequences. It was observed that some prepositional forms have a uniform meaning which, however, differs from that of the lexical preposition. An example is provided by *up* in constructions like *sell up*, *eat up* or *cut up*. In each case the prepositional form contains a perfective element not present in the meaning of the lexical preposition *up*. Thus the meaning of *up* in these contexts cannot be derived via the entry of the lexical category. Since *up* with this deviating meaning and use is not unique - whether it is fully productive or not, however, requires further investigation - it must be assumed that a new lexical unit has developed. In pre-NP-position this unit behaves like a suffix. Therefore it is suggested that it is a suffix deriving perfective verbs from non-perfective ones. However, this derivational suffix differs from others in that it is not the head of the construction and in that it may follow an inflectional subject, which is unusual and thus marked in English. Including *up* as a derivational suffix with an entry of its own in the lexicon, these properties have to be listed. It is very likely that all deprepositional derivational affixes behave in the same way and that these properties should be derived from a general feature characterizing this affix class. A final solution must be postponed. For the time being, the following representation is suggested:

(155) a. *eat up* [-N, +V], [__ NP]
$[_V$ V Af]
b. *up* PHON: /ʌp/
SYN: [+Af]
$[_V$ V $([_{Af}$ Flex]) __]
SEM: PERFECTIVE (x)

The category feature [+Af] is meant to indicate that the affix is not the head of the construction like, for example, *-ness*, which as the nominal head of deadjectival nouns, such as *sadness*, would be described as [+N, -V, +Af]. The strict subcategorization
$[_V$ V$([_{Af}$ Flex]_] signals that *up* as a constituent of a verb follows the verbal head and an inflectional suffix, if present. Optimizing of this representation is probably necessary. Semantic features other than PERFECTIVE have been neglected here. The represententation under (155)

illustrates that in producing and perceiving phrasal verbs in those cases where the prepositional form as a suffix occurs in pre-NP-position the lexical entry of the suffix is accessed via the lexical entry of the verb. This is possible because the lexical entry of the verb contains the phonological matrix as well as the category fature [+Af]. Via this information the syntactic and semantic properties can be accessed. Thus, the prepositional form represented under (155) shares only the phonological form with the lexical preposition. From a synchronic perspective their relation is one of homonymy.

Representing the prepositional forms of the same phrasal verbs in post-NP-position is more complicated. From a semantic point of view the form is a suffix, from a syntactic point of view it is a preposition. Thus, there seems to be no other solution than to represent this highly marked form in two ways, indicating the relation between class membership on the one hand and syntactic or semantic properties on the other. Thus something like (155a') should be added to (155a):

(155) a'. *eat up* [-N, +V], [__ NP] : *eat* [-N, +V], [__ NP, up]/
[$_V$ V Af] *up*: SYN: [-N, -V]
SEM: [+Af]

Via the phonological matrix and the category features it is then possible to access semantic and syntactic properties from different sources.

5.2.4. In section 4.4 it was observed that fixed phrases containing prepositional forms are often marked syntactically as well as semantically and morphologically. The sequence P + NP turned out to be an exocentric construction which as a whole has mainly adjunctival or adverbial properties and only a few PP properties. The phrases are unalterable. Substitution or modification yield ungrammatical results. The constructions are frozen. Thus, apparently these are examples illustrating the process of recategorization through time. The examples investigated can be graded, exhibiting some properties of PPs but mainly those of adjectives and adverbs. Thus, no PP-properties were observed for *on balance* whereas *on sale* is not only used in the typical post-NP PP-position but also co-ordinates with PPs, which is impossible for examples like *on the quiet*. How these phrases as a whole will finally have to be described categorially is not pursued here. It is obvious, however, that the categories involved, adjective and adverb, are just as heterogeneous as the category preposition investigated here. It is also obvious that the diachronic process of recategorization with respect to elements of a syntactic category creates a situation in which applying prototype theory as a method of description seems promising. Thus it appears that there are prototypical elements of a category located at its center which differ considerably from prototypical elements of another category. At the periphery, however, the boundaries are fluid. Prepositional forms illustrate that the boundaries may be fluid with respect to several other categories, adjectives and adverbs on the one hand, case affixes or derivational affixes on the other.[10]

The syntactic and in part semantic and morphological inflexibility of fixed phrases and thus their strong markedness require that during the process of language acquisition they must be learned as a whole. They cannot be generated by general rules. It follows that in the mental lexicon they are stored as complex units. A lexicon designed as a model of a mental lexicon accordingly contains lexical entries for each of these phrases.[11] These entries include the following information, which analyzes the phrases syntactically:

(156) a. *on the quiet*
$[_{Adj/Adv}\ P\ [_{NP}\ D\ [_{N}\ Adj]]]$
b. *on sale*
$[_{Adj/Adv}\ P\ [_{NP}\ [_{N}\ V]]]$
c. *on balance*
$[_{Adv}\ P\ [_{NP}\ N]]$

Analyzing *on* as P connects this representation with the entry for the lexical preposition. Thus accessing the syntactic as well as semantic properties represented in this entry is possible. As in the case of governed prepositions, here, too, projection properties cannot be realized because the context of the prepositional form is fixed. Case properties, on the other hand, can be realized and result in case marking of the following NP, observing the case filter. The possibility of accessing the semantic features of the lexical category explains the fact that even in these contexts semantic features of the prepositional forms can be identified, as is illustrated in section 4.4.

---

10 An investigation of the phenomenon of recategorization related to deverbal prepositions is presented by König & Kortmann (this volume).

11 Coulmas 1985 also points out that the lexicon must contain a rather large number of fixed phrases. This may also be derived from Di Sciullo & Williams 1978.

6. Results

It was the intention of this paper to contribute to answering the question how prepositional forms are represented in a lexicon designed as a model of the mental lexicon, given the fact that a single phonological form is related to more than one syntactic and/or semantic representation. For this purpose, the role of the lexicon and the kind of information it should contain was discussed first (section 2). Since the apparent heterogeneity of prepositional forms requires a fresh look at what a preposition is, section 3 was devoted to the study of previous approaches. It turned out that different classifications of prepositions are presented, which was explained by the fact that different subsets are investigated in each case. This was taken to support the hypothesis that, in fact, prepositional variants have to be identified and that the question raised here is not an irrelevant one. In section 4 syntactic and - in part - semantic properties of selected prepositional variants were investigated. These included spatial and temporal uses of prepositional forms as constituents of PPs in adjunct position or as complements of verbs of motion or state, governed prepositions, prepositional forms as parts of phrasal verbs and fixed phrases. Other variants such as non-temporal and non-spatial prepositional forms in adjunct position were not investigated. Section 5 presented an attempt to develop lexical entries for prepositional variants to adequately reflect the descriptive results.

The results are satisfactory to the extent that they explain why acquiring variants of prepositional forms during the process of language acquisition presents no serious problems. Even if they occur in different lexical entries, the forms are interconnected and therefore need not be learned like new words. The descriptive results suggest that there is a main entry, the spatial variant, which as the head of a PP may occur in adjunct position as well as as the complement of verbs of motion or state. This variant exhibits all the properties of a lexical major category. Closely related is the temporal variant which, too, exhibits all the properties of a lexical major category. It is connected with the spatial variant by a lexical rule which replaces some semantic as well as syntactic properties, maintaining the phonological form. It was shown that governed prepositions are introduced in the lexical entry of their governor and that in this context their phonological form as well as the category features are presented. These establish a connexion with the main entry of the preposition which renders possible accessing the syntactic and semantic properties presented there. Because of the fixed syntactic context of governed prepositions, the projection properties of the lexical preposition - as opposed to case properties - cannot be activated. From the set of semantic properties argument structure and theta grid as well as selected inherent and selectional features are accessed. The selection is determined by the metaphor of which the non-spatial prepositional form used in this context forms a constituent part.

Prepositional forms as parts of phrasal verbs also appear under an alien entry, that of the verb. Phrasal verbs which allow for the prepositional form a pre-NP-position as well as a post-NP-position provide both these positions lexically. In pre-NP-position the prepositional form and the verb constitute a complex verb. In post-NP-position the prepositional form is the head of a PP. In both cases again the form is connected with the entry of the lexical preposition via its phonological matrix and category features. With respect to the pre-NP-position activating projection properties is not possible because of the fixed categorial context. Case assignment is possible, though it is probably the complex verb that assigns case in this context. In post-NP-position, however, projection properties as well as case assignment can be activated. Semantic properties are accessed in both positions in the same way. It was pointed out, however, that with respect to the meaning of the prepositional forms which are part of phrasal verbs three possibilities may be distinguished. The first one was mentioned above. In the second, the combination V + P expresses an idiomatic meaning independent of the syntactic structure. Thus accessing the semantic representation of the lexical preposition is blocked. The idiomatic meaning is itself represented in the lexical entry of the phrasal verb. In the third possibility the prepositional form has assumed a meaning of its own. Since productivity is to be observed at least in part, it was suggested that a new lexical unit with properties of a derivational suffix has developed which requires a lexical entry of its own. The prepositional forms of the affected phrasal verbs are connected with this entry rather than with that of the lexical preposition.

With respect to fixed phrases it was noted that because of their strong markedness they have to be represented as a whole in the lexicon, their syntactic analysis being part of the entry. The prepositional forms in this context are represented by their phonological matrix as well as their category features. These establish a connexion with the lexical preposition and accessing the syntactic and semantic properties represented there is possible. As in the case of governed prepositions, projection properties cannot be activated because of the fixed context, whereas case assignment is possible. Accessing semantic properties is also possible and is performed in the same way as with respect to governed prepositions.

The final conclusion for the lexical representation of prepositional forms is therefore that there are two autonomous entries, the main entry of the lexical preposition on the one hand and the entry for the derivational suffix on the other. A temporal variant is directly connected with the spatial one. The other forms investigated here are prepositional variants, "allo-prepositions", so to speak. Their deviance with respect to the main entry can be explained by their contexts. This explains why these variants need not be learned independently. It became evident, however, that instead the contexts in which these variants occur must themselves be learned as a whole. This result is not surprising. Thus it was shown that governed prepositions represent inherent, lexical case realizations which are therefore phonologically, semantically and syntactically marked. Prepositional forms as parts of phrasal verbs were shown to represent transition phenomena of the process of recategorization, and thus also marked properties. The same holds for fixed phrases.

Some results may be noted which were not the declared aim of the investigation. Thus it has become evident that natural language is always subject to change, to recategorization, creating marked structures which cannot be explained by the general principles of grammar, which must be learned and therefore are represented in the lexicon as complex units. It should be noted that these are not primarily idiomatic phrases, whose representation in the lexicon is beyond doubt, since the interpretation of their meanings clearly does not follow the principle of composition. With respect to the constructions investigated here it is first of all the syntax that is marked. That a natural language makes use of a large number of phrases marked in this way has recently been emphasized by representatives of Construction Grammar (cf. e.g. Fillmore, Kay & O'Connor 1988) and as early as 1976, L. Wong Fillmore called attention to the observation that a large amount of language acquisition does not follow generative principles but is rather to a high degree a learning of fixed phrases. Thus, these lines also provide independent evidence for such observations and postulates without claiming, though, that these phenomena contradict the theory of language developed by the Chomskyan school.

References

Akmajian, A., S. Steele and T. Wasow 1979. The Category AUX in Universal Grammar. *Linguistic Inquiry* 10:1-64.

Aronoff, M. 1978. Lexical Representation. In *Papers from the Parasession on the Lexicon.* Chicago Linguistic Society. 12-25.

Behagel, O. 1924. *Deutsche Syntax*. Bd. 2. Heidelberg: Carl Winter's Universitätsbuchhandlung.

Bierwisch, M. 1988. On the Grammar of Local Prepositions. In Bierwisch, M., W. Motsch and I. Zimmermann (eds.). *Syntax, Semantik und Lexikon*. Berlin: Akademie-Verlag. 1-65.

Black, M. 1962. *Models and Metaphors*. Ithaca and London: Cornell University Press.

Black, M. 1979. More about Metaphor. In Ortony, A. (ed.). *Metaphor and Thought*. Cambridge: Cambridge University Press. 19-43.

Bresnan, J. 1978. A Realistic Transformational Grammar. In Halle, M., J. Bresnan and G. A. Miller (eds.). *Linguistic Theory and Psychological Reality*. Cambridge, Mass.: MIT Press. 1-59.

Brugmann, K. 1911. *Vergleichende Laut-, Stammbildungs- und Flexionslehre nebst Lehre vom Gebrauch der Wortformen der indogermanischen Sprachen*. Bd. 2.2. von K. Brugmann und B. Delbrück. *Grundriß der vergleichenden Grammatik der indogermanischen Sprachen*. Straßburg: Karl J. Trübner.

Chomsky, N. 1957. *Syntactic Structures*. The Hague: Mouton.

Chomsky, N. 1965. *Aspects of the Theory of Syntax*. Cambridge, Mass.: MIT Press.

Chomsky, N. 1981. *Lectures on Government and Binding*. Dordrecht: Foris Publications.

Chomsky, N. 1986. *Knowledge of Language: Its Nature, Origin, and Use*. New York: Praeger.

Coulmas, F. 1985. Lexikalisierung von Syntagmen. In Schwarze, C. and D. Wunderlich (eds.). *Handbuch der Lexikologie*. Königstein/Ts.: Athenäum Verlag. 250-268.

Curme, G. O. 1935. *A Grammar of the English Language. Vol. 2: Parts of Speech and Accidence*. Boston etc.: D. C. Heath & Comp.

Czepluch, H. 1981. *Syntaktische Funktionen im Englischen. Elemente einer 'funktionalen autonomen Syntax'*. Tübingen: Gunter Narr Verlag.

Delbrück, B. 1893. *Vergleichende Syntax der indogermanischen Sprachen*. Bd. 3.1. von K. Brugmann und B. Delbrück. *Grundriß der vergleichenden Grammatik der indogermanischen Sprachen*. Straßburg: Karl J. Trübner.

Di Sciullo, A.-M. and E. Williams 1987. *On the Definition of Word*. Cambridge, Mass.: MIT Press.

Dirven, R. 1982. Spatial Relations in English. In Radden, G. and R. Dirven (eds.). 103-132.

Emonds, J. E. 1972. Evidence that Indirect Object Movement Is a Structure-preserving Rule. *Foundations of Language* 8:546-561.

Emonds, J. E. 1976. *A Transformational Approach to English Syntax: Root, Structure-Preserving and Local Transformations*. New York: Academic Press.

Emonds, J. E. 1985. *A Unified Theory of Syntactic Categories*. Dordrecht: Foris Publications.

Fillmore, C. J. 1968. The Case for Case. In Bach, E. and R. T. Harms (eds.). *Universals in Linguistic Theory*. London: Holt, Rinehart & Winston. 1-88.

Fillmore, C. J. 1969. Towards a Modern Theory of Case. In Reibel, D. A. and S. A. Schane (eds.). *Modern Studies in English*. London: Prentice Hall Inc. 361-375.

Fillmore, C. J., P. Kay and M. C. O'Connor 1988. *Regularity and Idiomaticity in Grammatical Constructions: the Case of Let Alone*. Report Nr. 51, Cognitive Science Program, Institute of Cognitive Studies, University of California at Berkeley.

Foskett, C. this volume. *Together* - a Preposition?

Fries, C. C. 1952. *The Structure of English*. New York: Harcourt, Brace & Comp.

Fukui, N. and M. Speas 1986. Specifiers and Projection. *MIT Working Papers in Linguistics* 8. 128-172.

Gleason, H. A. 1955, ^{2}1961. *Introduction to Descriptive Linguistics*. New York etc.: Holt, Rinehart and Winston, Inc.

Greenbaum, S. 1969. *Studies in English Adverbial Usage*. London: Longman.

Harris, Z. S. 1951. *Structural Linguistics*. Chicago: The University of Chicago Press.

Hawkins, B. W. 1984. The Semantics of English Spatial Prepositions. Diss. University of California, San Diego, Cal.

Herskovits, A. 1986. *Language and Spatial Cognition: An Interdisciplinary Study of the Prepositions in English*. London and Cambridge: Cambridge University Press.

Herweg, M. 1988. Zur Semantik einiger lokaler Präpositionen des Deutschen. Überlegungen zur Theorie der lexikalischen Semantik am Beispiel von *in*, *an*, *bei* und *auf*. LILOG-Report 21. Stuttgart, IBM.

Higginbotham, J. 1985. On Semantics. *Linguistic Inquiry* 16:547-593.

Hornstein, N. and A. Weinberg 1981. Case Theory and Preposition Stranding. *Linguistic Inquiry* 12:55-91.

Hottenroth, P.-M. this volume. Präpositionen und Objektkonzepte. Ein kognitiv orientiertes, zweistufiges Modell für die Semantik lokaler Präpositionen.

Jackendoff, R. S. 1973. The Base Rules for Prepositional Phrases. In Anderson, S. R. and P. Kiparsky (eds.). *A Festschrift for Morris Halle*. New York: Holt, Rinehart & Winston. 345-366.

Jackendoff, R. S. 1977. *X' Syntax. A Study of Phrase Structure*. Cambridge, Mass.: London: MIT Press.

Jespersen, O. 1924. *The Philosophy of Grammar*. London: George Allan and Unwin Ltd.

König, E. and B. Kortmann. this volume. On the Reanalysis of Verbs as Prepositions.
Kunsmann, P. 1973. *Verbale Gefüge. Transformationsgrammatische Untersuchungen im Deutschen und Englischen*. München: Hueber.

Lehmann, C. 1985. Grammaticalization: Synchronic Variation and Diachronic Change. *Lingua e Stile* 20:303-318.
Lehmann, C. 1986/7. Grammaticalization and Linguistic Typology. *General Linguistics* 26/27:3-22.
Leisi, E. 1974. *Das heutige Englisch*. Heidelberg: Carl Winter Universitätsverlag.

Napoli, D. J. 1989. *Predication Theory. A Case Study for Indexing Theory*. London: Cambridge University Press.

Poutsma, H. 1926. *A Grammar of Late Modern English*. Part II: The Parts of Speech, Section II: The Verb and the Particles. Groningen: P. Noordhoff.

Quirk, R. 1962, ^{2}1968. *The Use of English*. London: Longman Group Ltd.

Radden, G. 1982. Die übertragenen Bedeutungen der englischen Raumpräpositionen. In Radden, G. and R. Dirven (eds.). 133-179.
Radden, G. 1985. Spatial Metaphors Underlying Prepositions of Causality. In Paprotté, W. and R. Dirven (eds.). *The Ubiquity of Metaphor. Metaphor in Language and Thought*. Amsterdam: John Benjamins Publ. Comp. 177-207.
Radden, G. and R. Dirven (eds.). 1982. *Kasusgrammatik und Fremdsprachendidaktik* (anglistik & englischunterricht 14). Trier: Wiss. Vlg. Trier GmbH.
Radford, A. 1988. *Transformational Grammar. A First Course*. Cambridge: Cambridge University Press.
Rauh, G. 1988. *Tiefenkasus, thematische Relationen und Thetarollen. Die Entwicklung einer Theorie von semantischen Relationen*. Tübingen: Gunter Narr Verlag.
Rauh, G. 1990. Präpositionen: Eine geschlossene Klasse? Wuppertaler Arbeiten zur Sprachwissenschaft 7, Mai 1990.
Richards, I. A. 1936, ^{2}1971. *The Philosophy of Rhetoric*. London: Oxford University Press.
Riemsdijk, H. C. van 1978. *A Case Study in Syntactic Markedness: The Binding Nature of Prepositional Phrases*. Lisse: The Peter De Ridder Press.
Riemsdijk, H. C. van and E. Williams. 1986. *Introduction to the Theory of Grammar*. Cambridge, Mass.; London: MIT Press.

Selkirk, E. O. 1982. *The Syntax of Words*. Cambridge, Mass.: MIT Press.
Steinitz, R. 1984. Lexikalisches Wissen und die Struktur von Lexikon-Einträgen. *Linguistische Studien, Reihe A*. Arbeitsberichte 116. Untersuchungen zur deutschen Grammatik III. 1-88.
Sweet, H. 1891. *A New English Grammar. Logical and Historical*, Part I. Oxford: At the Clarendon Press.

Vandeloise, B. 1986. *L'Espace en Français. Sémantique des Prépositions Spatiales*. Paris: Editions du Seuil.

Wackernagel, J. 1924. *Vorlesungen über Syntax*. Bd. 2. Basel: In Kommissionsverlag von Emil Birkhäuser & Cie.

Wege, B. this volume. On the Lexical Meaning of Prepositions. A Study of *above*, *below* and *over*.

Williams, E. 1987a. Implicit Arguments, the Binding Theory, and Control. *Natural Language and Linguistic Theory* 5:151-180.

Williams, E. 1987b. NP Trace in Theta Theory. *Linguistics and Philosophy* 10:433-447.

Wong Fillmore, L. 1976. The Second Time around. Diss. Stanford.

Wunderlich, D. 1982. Sprache und Raum. *Studium Linguistik* 12:1-19, 37-59.

Wunderlich, D. 1984. Zur Syntax der Präpositionalphrasen im Deutschen. *Zeitschrift für Sprachwissenschaft* 3:65-99.

The lexical meaning of the French preposition *contre*[1]

Marie-Theres Schepping
(Konstanz)

0. Introduction

Most of the studies on the meaning of prepositions which have recently appeared, e.g. Herskovits 1982, Vandeloise 1986, and Hottenroth 1986, deal with local prepositions.

Analyses of lexical items within a semantic field generally focus exclusively on readings specific to the field. Such studies, therefore tend to show an almost restrictive view of the range of possible readings of a lexical item.

One of the authors who have studied the polysemeous structure of prepositions is Brugman. On the basis of a prototype approach, in her article "The Theory of *over* " 1983 she tried to analyze the different readings of the preposition as derived from its local meaning.

What I want to elaborate in this article is the lexical meaning of the French preposition *contre*.

Although occurrences of *contre* as a prefix, as e.g. in *contredire*, *contre-poison* are excluded, I expect the prefix to share essential meaning properties with the preposition.

What are the reasons for choosing *contre* as the subject of this study?

1. As far as I know, *contre*, as well as its counterparts in Italian *contro*, in English *against*, and *gegen* in German have not yet been studied in detail. I therefore hope to contribute to filling a descriptive gap.
2. In general *contre* is regarded as a local preposition. The question is, whether this is true.
3. The number of readings the preposition allows for is relatively restricted.

The theoretical framework chosen for the analysis of *contre* has been outlined by Schwarze (1989). His approach to lexical meaning is a procedural

1 I am obliged to my colleagues Heike Speitz and Bruce Mayo for carefully reading and correcting my English.

one. He assumes the lexical meaning of a word to consist of an initial meaning ("*Startbedeutung*") and "manipulation rules" ("*Umdeutungsregeln*").

The initial meaning is the reading other possible meanings are most easily derived from. Schwarze argues that the initial meaning will often coincide with the prototypical meaning.

The manipulation rules creating derived meanings are supposed to operate on the initial meaning. They can only apply if certain conditions with regard to syntactic context-structure and semantic restrictions on arguments are met.

Following Schwarze I take the lexical meaning of a word to be interpreted in terms of conceptual schemata. The interpretation of a lexical meaning of a word depends on the context in which it is used.

A conceptual schema or frame representing concepts of objects, events, states etc. in a structured way is built up of attributes and their values ("slots" and "fillers"). The former are constants, the latter variables which can be instantiated in the course of an interpretation process.

According to the basic assumptions of this framework, the aim of this article will be to

a) establish the initial meaning of *contre*

b) formulate the manipulation rules and specify their conditions of application

c) provide conceptual schemata in order to interpret the different uses of the preposition.

In order to achieve this aim I will first of all give a descriptive analysis of the use of *contre*. It will be based on information found in linguistic literature as well as on psychological approaches concerning the concept of force developed by Talmy (1985) and Johnson (1987).

1. The uses of *contre*

In order to elucidate the lexical meaning of *contre* I will start with the information provided by dictionaries, grammars and comments found in linguistic literature.

1.1. Information on *contre* in literature

The dictionary of P. Robert 1975 tries to capture the meaning of *contre* by referring to the notions of proximity or contact and opposition. The dictionary entry reveals at first glance that, while the semantic information is rather pure, many verbs are listed which allow for a complement with *contre*. This is also the case in the *Trésor de la langue française* 1978. The meaning of the preposition is subdivided into three components: 1. local meaning ("sens local"), 2. expression of opposition ("exprime l'opposition"), and 3. indication of exchange, namely a relation between two entities ("marque l'échange, le rapport de deux grandeurs").

This is about all one can find in French dictionaries. Let us have a look at Italian *contro*, English *against*, and German *gegen* in order to complete this information.

The French and the Italian prepositions seem to allow for quite the same range of usages. The semantic distinctions found in the standard Italian dictionary, Zingarelli 1986, in comparison with the French dictionaries, are not only elaborated more precisely; they are also presented in a different order. At the beginning we find: denotes opposition, contrast, hostility ("indica opposizione, contrasto, ostilità"), with examples like:

> la nostra squadra giocherà domani contro la vostra, odio contro cq.;

the second entry says: denotes movement or action directed at someone or something, ("indica movimento o azione diretti verso o adosso a qc. o q.c."), with the example:

> la maccina è andata a schiantarsi contro il muro;

in the third entry we find: "di fronte, davanti (indica un determinato stato o posizione)" with the example:

> stava appoggiato contro la porta.

With reference to *contro*, Hottenroth (1983:120f) points out:

> "*Contro* ist mit der Vorstellung von einer Bewegung auf eine entgegenlaufende Bewegung - oder einen Widerstand zu - verbunden. Es steht daher den direktionalen Präpositionen nahe und ist oft mit entsprechenden Verben kombiniert. Zur Angabe der Befindlichkeit kann es Kontakt oder unmittelbare Nähe bezeichnen."

(With *contro* we associate the idea of movement towards a counter-movement or towards resistance. Therefore the preposition is closely related to directional ones and is often combined with corresponding verbs. With respect to location it can denote contact or immediate proximity.)

The latter observation can be seen in the following example:

> "Il bastone era poggiato contro il muro. "
> (The stick was leaning against the wall.)

Another possibility, Hottenroth points out, is the use of *contro* in contexts where it expresses a relation with a background, e.g. in:

> "Il profilo si disegnò netto contro lo sfondo della parete."
> (The outline stood out clearly against the background of the wall.)

With reference to Engl. *against* Hawkins (1985) postulates surface contact between two objects and, as he calls it, a "dynamic relation of counterforce". Unfortunately further explanations of this concept are missing.

The German *gegen* is not restricted to the domains of usage listed for *contre*, *contro*, against. In addition, *gegen* can be used temporally (Schröder 1986:115-119), as in

> Fritz kommt gegen vier Uhr.
> (Fritz is coming shortly before four o'clock.)

and with comparative meaning as in

> Gegen einen PC ist eine Reiseschreibmaschine ein kleines Gerät.
> (In comparison with a PC a portable typewriter is a small piece of equipment.)

In this paper I cannot study in detail the differences between the lexemes *contre*, *contro*, *against*, *gegen*. The few observations mentioned above are to be taken as a suggestion for further contrastive analysis.

As we have seen, for our purpose the amount of information available in the literature is rather poor.

The next step will be to propose a classification for possible usages of the preposition *contre*.

1.2. Classification of *contre* by usage

We have already seen that verbs play an important, and even crucial role in determining the readings of the preposition.

Consequently, a basis for classification can only consist of general semantic properties of the verbs occurring in combination with *contre*.

1.2.1. States of contact

The preposition *contre* occurring with the copula *être* can refer to a state of contact between two objects. This reading is restricted to expressions where the object specified in subject-position and the object denoted in the prepositional phrase belong to the same object-class. Sentence (1) gives an example:

(1) Sa maison est contre la mienne.
(His house stands right next to/wall to wall with mine.)

The relation between objects of the same kind and *contre*, established by the copula, is a reversible one.
If sentence (1) is true, then (1') is also true:

(1') Ma maison est contre la sienne.

These two sentences only differ in perspective, depending on the choice of the subject. In sentence (1) *sa maison* is the located object, *la mienne* is the localizing one. The reverse holds for sentence (1').
This reversibility reflects our knowledge about physical objects and their forces. A contact between two objects can only be maintained if the physical forces directed against each other are of comparable strength.
A stable contact between objects which do not belong to the same category has to be specified with reference to the position of the object denoted in the subject-phrase, e.g. in:

(2) L'échelle est appuyée contre le mur.
(The ladder is leaning against the wall.)

(2') ?? L'échelle est contre le mur.

can only be interpreted as elliptical.

1.2.2. States of visual contrast

There are marginal usages where *contre* occurs with reflexive verb forms to denote a state, as in:

(3) La tour se dresse contre un ciel bleu.
(The tower rises against a blue sky.)

(4) Son profil se détache clairement contre le fond noir.
(His profile stands out clearly against the black background.)

As non-reflexives, the verbs occuring in these sentences are causatives denoting actions that imply a positional change of the affected object, as in the examples:

Max dresse le drapeau. (Max raises the flag.)

Max détache la photo. (Max detaches the photo.)

Used as reflexives, these verbs require a non-agentive entity in subject-position. The states depicted in (3) and (4) refer to a contrast in size between two objects projected onto one level.

The place occupied by the object in subject-position is contained in the place occupied by the object specified in the prepositional phrase.

In such contexts, the entities involved do not function as physical forces, but as spatial entities contrasted with respect to their size.

The contrasted object is specified in subject-position. The object functioning as the contrasting one is denoted in the prepositional phrase.

1.2.3. Causative motion and events of contact

Another group of verbs cooccurring with *contre* are causative verbs of motion. Examples are:

(5) Max pousse le lit contre le mur.
(Max pushes the bed against the wall.)

(6) Max met l'échelle contre le garage.
(Max puts the ladder against the garage.)

(7) Max se blottit contre la porte.
(Max is crouching against the door.)

(8) Max s'adosse contre l'armoire.
(Max is leaning with his back against the cupboard.)

(9) Max se serre contre sa maman.
(Max snuggles up to his mother.)

The object specified in the prepositional phrases can be characterized - because of the preposition *contre* - as an affected object involved in an event of contact functioning as counter-force.

In the sentences (5) to (7) *contre* can be replaced by a local preposition:

(5a) Max pousse le lit au milieu de la chambre.
(Max pushes the bed to the middle of the room.)

(6a) Max met l' échelle près du garage.
(Max puts the ladder near the garage.)

(7a) Max se blottit dans un coin.
(Max is crouching in a corner.)

The other sentences do not allow for similar substitutions. Apart from the preposition *contre*, *s'adosser* only accepts the preposition *à*, a semantically empty preposition. *Se serrer* does not allow for any other preposition than *contre*.

Let us take a closer look at sentence (5). *Pousser* connected with *contre* is interpreted as an action of motion. Its agent (*Max*) exerts a mechanical force on an object (*le lit*). This object is moved until it gets into contact with the object *le mur* denoted in the prepositional phrase. *Le mur* is a stable, solid object reacting with counter-force only in the case of contact.

Generalizing these observations on uses of *contre* with causative verbs of motion we now can assume:

There is an agent who causes himself or a material object to come into contact with a solid, stable object. It is the physical force of an object in motion which releases the physical force of the stable object.

An agent can make use of such a counter-force in a positive way in order to stabilize the position of an object, to give support or protection.

1.2.3.1. *donner*

There is one marginal use of *contre*, in connection with *donner*, which seems to be very much like the uses studied above.

An example is sentence (10):

(10) Max donne son briquet contre un couteau de poche.
(Max gives his lighter for a pocket-knife.)

Sentence (10) refers to the directed action of giving. The object denoted in the prepositional phrase is the one taking the counter-directed path. It is the received object.

Sentence (10) is interpreted in analogy to (5) -(9), which means that one object functions as directed, the other as counter-directed. This assumption is supported by the fact that a sentence such as e.g.

(11) ?? Max reçoit un couteau de poche contre un briquet.
(Max receives a pocket-knife for a lighter.)

is semantically inadequate.

With *donner* followed by a *contre*-phrase it is not the contact releasing a collision of physical forces that is relevant. What plays the crucial role here is the inherent positive directionality of an act of giving and the reverse directionality of the event of receiving - its counterpart.

1.2.4. Events of Contact

Prepositional phrases headed by *contre* occur not only with causative verbs of motion but also with reflexive verb forms denoting events of contact. In contrast to verbs referring to causative motion, however, there is no agent involved to cause a contact between two material objects.

Still both usages of *contre* - in connection with verbs of causative motion and with reflexive verb forms denoting events of contact - share the following properties:

- The events of contact are the result of a directed motion of an individual.
- The object in motion exerts a physical force.
- The stable, solid object affected by the object in motion reacts as a counter-force.

Examples to illustrate this use of *contre* are:

(12) Les vagues se brisaient contre les rochers.
(The waves were breaking against the rocks.)

(13) L'avion s'est écrasé contre une montagne.
(The plane crashed against a mountain.)

(14) Max s'est heurté contre le poteau.
(Max banged against the post.)

The prepositional phrases in these sentences are not obligatory. Nevertheless, they have to be regarded as phrases governed by the verb.
The preposition cannot be replaced by another one.
In the sentence

Le verre s'est brisé sur le plancher.
(The glass broke on the floor.)

the prepositional phrase with *sur* does not denote the object functioning as a counter-force but as the place where the event has taken place. It is a phrase not governed by the verb. In order to find the object with the counter-force, you have to infer that the floor is e.g. a stone floor.
In sentences (5) to (9), that is in those cases where causative motion is described, the object functioning as counter-force can, as we know from our world-knowledge, be used by the agent for support or protection. In sentences (12) to (14), denoting events of contact, the counter-force is viewed as a resistance or an obstacle to the object in motion.

1.2.5. Non-Causative Counteractions

1.2.5.1. Motions

Examples (5) to (9) have shown us occurrences of *contre* with causative motion verbs describing actions that lead to a contact between one object in motion and another one, stable and solid. As we mentioned above, the contact between the moved object with its force and the stable one causes the latter to function as a counter-force.
Let us now turn our attention to sentences (15) and (16):

(15) Max nage contre le courant.
(Max is swimming against the current.)

(16) Max se raidit contre le vent.
(Max is bracing himself against the wind.)

In these examples the object specified in the prepositional phrase is neither solid nor stable. Instead it is a natural force coupled with directed motion. Due to the preposition *contre*, the actions denoted by the verbs *nager*, *se raidir* are interpreted as directed, namely against the direction of the natural force. In such contexts verbs like *voler*, *courir* are acceptable as well. These verbs denote non-causative motion, motion without agent, but with an individual in the thematic role of a theme. They lexicalize manner of motion but no direction.

Comparing the action expressed in sentences (5) to (9) with those specified in (15) and (16), we observe that the prepositional phrases fulfill reversed functions:

The objects denoted by the prepositional phrases in (5) to (9) function as counter-directed entities.

In (15) and (16) is is an individual's action having this role.

We can now state that *contre* determines either a solid, stable object as counter-force (or contrast) or an action as counter-action.

To the prepositional phrase itself we cannot attribute any function.

Another example will help us to make this point clearer:

(17) Max s'appuie contre l'armoire.

Due to the reflexive verb form, this sentence allows for different readings. In English these can be distinguished verbally as 'lean against s.th.' versus 'brace oneself against s.th.'.

According to the first reading ('lean against'), *s'appuyer* followed by *contre* is interpreted as a causative motion activity leading to a contact between *Max* and *l'armoire*. Within this event of contact, the force *Max* exerts in moving causes the solid, stable object to release its own force, which then functions as a counter-force.

As we know, *l'armoire* can be used by *Max* for support.

In the second reading ('brace oneself against'), *l'armoire* is interpreted as an object in motion. *S'appuyer* followed by *contre* is then meant to denote a non-causative action directed opposite to the motion performed by *l'armoire*. In this reading the action functions as counteraction, thus serving as resistance, e.g. in a situation where the cupboard threatens to fall over.

Appuyer, used as non-reflexive, also allows for a prepositional phrase with *contre*:

Max appuie contre l'armoire.

This sentence clears up the following point:

The interpretation does not depend on whether the object specified in the prepositional phrase is in motion or not, but only on whether the action denoted by the verb is a causative or a non-causative one.

Consequently, the different readings of (17) are not due to the preposition but to the reflexive *s'appuyer*.

Since the syntactic structure offers no device for disambiguation, the adequacy of one of the readings can only be determined pragmatically.

We can now conclude that it is decisive for the interpretation of *contre* to know whether a verb form refers to a causative and/or to a non-causative action. As far as I know, this semantic aspect of verbs has not been studied yet.

A causative action will be characterized by the fact that the verb occurs in its transitive use. This characteristic, however, turns out to be insufficient. Only reflexive forms of verbs that can also be used transitively, such as e.g. *appuyer* in

Max appuie son pied sur la chaise.

seem to be candidates allowing for a causative and a non-causative reading. This assumption is supported by e.g. *se blottir* (cf. sentence (7)), obligatorily reflexive and unambiguously denoting a causative action.

Sentences (15) and (16) can be considered as intermediate cases:

On the one hand, in a situation of contact between two material objects - a state, an event, an event brought about by a causative motion action - *contre* is used to determine the solid, stable object involved in the relation as counter-force or contrast.

On the other hand, as we will see in the following paragraphs, *contre* is used to establish a relation between an abstract entity and an action.

1.2.5.2. Actions

As we have already seen, the object affected by a counteraction can be a material object or a natural force (cf. sentences (15) to (17)). A counteraction may, however, concern persons or abstract entities as well. The action then involves a psychological or social component.

An example illustrating such a use of *contre* is given in sentence (18):

(18) Max a agi contre son habitude.
(Max has acted against his habit.)

Talmy would consider this sentence an example of "intrapsychological force dynamics".

The possessive indicates that the affected entity and the counteraction carried out by *Max* are counterdirected "forces" referring to one single individual. *Habitude* designates one person's typical behavior. The counteraction violates this same behavior.

The following sentences refer to psycho-social counteractions:

(19) Les catholiques luttent contre les protestants.
(The Catholics fight against the Protestants.)

(20) L'équipe de Wuppertal joue contre l'équipe de Düsseldorf.
(The team from Wuppertal plays against the team from Düsseldorf.)

There are two parties involved in the events: One of them functions as an agent acting against someone or something, the other one as an addressee, an affected entity.

Analogously, this also holds for sentence (21):

(21) Max lutte contre l'injustice.
(Max fights against injustice.)

As these examples show very clearly, a counteraction is an action of real resistance. The prepositional phrase denotes the object of attack. Accordingly, the role this object fulfills will be called 'target'.

Here are some more examples denoting a psycho-social counteraction. The target is specified in the prepositional phrase:

(22) Max a plaidé contre l'acquittement de l'accusé.
(Max protested against the acquittal of the accused.)

(23) Max a voté contre Bush comme successeur de Reagan.
(Max voted against Bush as Reagan's successor.)

(24) Max proteste contre l'injustice.
(Max protests against injustice.)

Due to the semantics of certain verbs, counteractions can also serve as precautions.

There are two examples:

(25) Max s'abrite contre la pluie.
(Max protects himself against the rain.)

(26) Max s'est assuré contre l'incendie.
(Max has insured himself against fire.)

1.2.5.3. Emotional processes and states

A phrase governed by *contre* can also function as the target of an emotional counter-process or counter-state:

(27) Max se fâche contre sa fille.
(Max is getting angry with his daughter.)

(28) Max est en colère contre sa fille.
(Max is angry with his daughter.)

An emotional process or state directed against a person is in general not considered as something positive. The sentence

(29) ?? Max est très aimable contre sa fille.
(Max is very kind against his daughter.)

can therefore only be understood as an ironical expression.

Can we deduce from this example that counteractions, processes and states always imply evaluations?

This is not necessarily the case, as the following examples will show:

(30) Max n'a rien contre le directeur.
(Max has nothing against the director.)

(31) Max a des préjugés contre les étudiants de sport.
(Max is prejudiced against sport students.)

(32) Max prend du sirop contre la toux.
(Max takes syrup for his cough.)

Sentence (30) will not be interpreted as depicting a positive attitude towards the director but rather a neutral one.

We can only state a tendency connected with the use of the preposition *contre*: a counter-process or state tends to be evaluated negatively when there is a person in the role of the target involved.

1.3. Summary

Let us summarize our observations concerning the different uses of the preposition *contre*:

1. Connected with causative motion verbs, as well as with the copula *être*, *contre* relates two material objects. The relation *contre* establishes is one

of counter-directed physical forces becoming manifest in the contact of the objects involved. The object denoted in the prepositional phrase is stable and solid; its physical force functions as counter-force. The agent can make use of such an object for support.

2. Combined with verbs used in their reflexive forms - verbs that can be applied causatively as well - *contre* denotes a state of contrast in size between two objects. Their projection on one level allows for the sizes to be measured in comparison. The object designated in the prepositional phrase, including the space occupied by the object specified in subject-position, functions as contrasting object.
3. Cooccurring with reflexive verb forms that denote events implying contact between an object in motion and a stable, solid one, *contre* establishes a relation between one object (the moved one) functioning as force, and the other one having the role of a counter-force. The object specified in the prepositional phrase fulfills the latter role.
4. Used with non-causative motion-verbs, *contre* establishes a relation between two entities exerting counter-directed physical forces. In contrast to 1., the entity denoted in the prepositional phrase functions as a force. It is an entity in motion. The role of the counter-force, however,is filled by an action, an individual in the broader sense.
5. Combined with non-causative verbs of action, as well as with verbs denoting psychological processes or states, the preposition *contre* establishes a relation holding between an entity and a counteraction, a counter-process or a counter-state. The entity specified in the prepositional phrase is a person or an abstract entity functioning as target. This entity is not evaluated positively.

As we have seen, counter-directed physical forces play a crucial role for the uses of *contre*.

The question we are now turning our attention to is whether we can base our semantic analysis of *contre* on a 'force-model': the physical one or a psychological one.

The physical model of actio and reactio turns out to be insufficient for our purpose. According to the principle of equality between actio and reactio (Gerthsen/Kneser 1971), the forces exerted by two objects are of equal strength, and counter-directed to one another.

This principle is only relevant for those cases where *contre* cooccurs with *être* and relates two material objects.

The physical model allows neither for marking one of the forces with reference to the other nor for an imbalance of those forces.

Perhaps we can find more useful suggestions for our purpose if we look at psychological models.

2. The psychological force-models developed by Talmy and Johnson

2.1. Talmy's concept of "force dynamics"

To my knowledge of recent publications, Talmy (1985) is the first author to have pointed out the interaction of physical forces as "one of the preeminent conceptual organizing categories in language" (1985:41).

He develops the concept of "force dynamics" in connection with an analysis of verbs like *keep*, *make, let*, *hinder*, *help* and modal verbs. Within this framework, he also draws attention to the preposition *against*, claiming that the opposition of forces in general could be expressed by the preposition *against.*

According to Talmy (1985:5), the concept of force dynamics is constituted by

1. an Agonist, a focal force-exerting entity
2. an Antagonist, a force opposed to the focal force
3. a force-tendency inherent in the Agonist, that is a tendency towards motion or towards rest
4. a relation of the mutual strength of the forces.

As Talmy emphasizes, there is always a causative component involved in an interaction of forces. We can confirm this assertion, recalling examples where *contre* cooccurred with causative motion verbs. The object denoted in the prepositional phrase, however, does not function as "Agonist", but as counter-force, that is as "Antagonist".

In order to describe the semantics of the preposition *contre*, neither the relation of the strengths nor the force-tendency postulated to be important for the "Agonist" turn out to be relevant.

Talmy shows that the concept of force dynamics plays a decisive role not only in the physical domain of reference but also in its extension to the psychological and social domain, so-called "intra-psychological" and "interpsychological" force dynamics.

One example he gives in order to underline the relevance of this concept in the intra-psychological domain is

"The gang pushed him to do things he didn't want to."
(Talmy(1985:25))

We have already seen examples similar to this except that sentences such as (18) to (26) do not really refer to interactions of forces. A habit, an injustice, a team of players, rain or fire certainly cannot be interpreted as directional entities and thus as forces.

2.2. Johnson's "general gestalt structure for force"

Johnson (1987:44) considers the concept of force a "gestalt structure", a unified whole given in our experience and our understanding. According to Johnson (1987:43f), this "gestalt structure" has the following characteristics:
1. force involves interaction or potential interaction
2. "force has a vector quality, a directionality"
3. there is typically "a single path of motion"
4. "Forces have origins or sources, and because they are directional, agents can direct them to targets."
5. "Forces have degrees of power or intensity"
6. Force always implies "a structure or sequence of causality".

When we studied uses of *contre* in connection with causative verbs, we found corresponding phenomena in more detail.

In addition to the components of force just mentioned, Johnson (1987:45ff) gives a list of seven force structures he considers the most interesting in our experience. Among these we can find:
- The experience of being moved by an external force, such as being pushed against a barrier by a crowd (="compulsion")
- The experience of running into obstacles that block our force, such as running against a wall (="blockage")
- The experience of two equally strong force entities colliding face-to-face, "with the result that neither can go anywhere", such as in a head-on car accident (="counterforce").

In the context of *contre* we have seen functions like support or protection on the one hand, and resistance on the other hand. Both depict important experiences with force which are completely lacking in Johnson's approach.

The "gestalt structures" established by Johnson have a clear disadvantage. They do not differentiate clearly between experiences made by an agent and experiences made by the affected entity. I suppose that such a distinction might also be useful for the description of English modal verbs.

Talmy and Johnson try to describe the semantics of certain selected verbs with respect to the concept of "force dynamics" and the "gestalt structure of force" respectively.

Neither of the authors pays adequate attention to the relating sentence structures. To some extent this link is suggested in Talmy by the fact that "Agonist" and "Antagonist" are to be understood as thematic roles. Talmy, however, does not deal with questions such as what kind of object the "Agonist" and "Antagonist" have to belong to, or in which phrases they are to be specified in surface sentence structures.

Returning to our subject matter, we should ask to what extent psychological approaches to the concept of force can be useful.

As far as I can see they can only be applied to the concept of force involving two force-exerting entities. One of them has to be marked as counter-directed to the other. This confirms our observations stated with regard to sentences (5) to (9), which described causative actions of motion.

Another point relevant for our purpose is the fact that both concepts go beyond the physical concept of force.

The "gestalt structure" labelled "counterforce" in Johnson seems to be motivated physically. He gives no plausible arguments, however, to support a claim that this special concept is connected to our experience or to language: There are certainly very few people who would confirm from personal experience that two forces colliding in a car-accident or in a collision of two footballers - another example given by Johnson - are of equal strength.

Before starting to analyse the lexical meaning of *contre* in the framework chosen to establish the initial meaning and the associated rules, let us briefly consider the semantic structure of *contre* in comparison with local and directional prepositions.

3. The meaning of the preposition *contre* and its interpretations

3.1. The semantic structure of *contre* in comparison with local and directional prepositions

Wunderlich/Herweg (1986) consider the semantic structure of local prepositions to be a relational-functional one. According to this conception the functional component determines an area with respect to an object (the localizing object). A prepositional phrase headed by a local preposition thus refers to a spatial entity, that is an area. The relational component consists of establishing a localization-relation between an object (the localized object) and such an area, the object being localized within that area.

Lang (1988) represents the semantic structure of directional prepositions as a local relation at the end of a path: a relation of inclusion between the space occupied by an object x and the space occupied by an area built up with respect to an object y. In other words: directionality is reconstructed as a relation of localization holding at the end of a path.

As we saw earlier, the function of the preposition *contre* can also be to establish a relation between two objects. It is a directional relation.

As opposed to local prepositions there is neither a function assignable to *contre* of turning an object into an area, nor a function of establishing a local relation. A prepositional phrase introduced by *contre* does not, as has already been pointed out, denote an entity.

Directionality seen as localization at the end of a path has also proved to be inadequate to grasp the meaning of *contre*.

Local prepositions and *contre* commonly cause the objects involved in the relation to be conceptualized in a certain way. It is not the spatial properties of objects that are relevant here, as in the case of local prepositions, but directional properties.

The only property material objects have with respect to directionality is their force.

We know that forces of objects which are counter-directed to one another only become relevant and subjected to experience if the objects interact, that is normally if they are in contact.

The function we can assign to *contre* is to establish a relation of directional opposition between two entities. As we have seen, the preposition can influence the semantics of verbs to the effect that these are to be interpreted directionally. This function can be specified differently according to the verb with which *contre* occurs.

The representation I want to suggest here is to assign one of the thematic roles 'counterforce' or 'target' to the entity denoted in the prepositional phrase.

One argument in the role of a 'counterforce' is assigned to causative verbs, as well as to verbs used in their reflexive form denoting special sorts of events. To the non-causatives - motion, action, emotional process or state - there is assigned one argument in the role of a 'target'.

Prepositions which have a similar function to that elaborated for *contre* are *avec* and *pour*, the latter involving directionality, too. The examples

Max a voté pour Bush.

L'équipe de Wuppertal joue avec l'équipe de Düsseldorf.

illustrate that the preposition pour is used to specify an action - in contrast to *contre* - as a pro-action, while *avec* marks the action as a team-action.

The following sections will deal with the lexical meaning of *contre* and its interpretation.

First of all, I will sketch the conceptual schemata needed for the interpretation of occurrences of the preposition. This step will be followed by determining the initial meaning and the associated manipulation rules. Finally I will give examples for interpretations of *contre*.

3.2. Conceptual schemata

The different interpretations the preposition *contre* allows for are supposed to be representable with reference to different conceptual schemata. The schemata we need are simply postulated. They will only be characterized roughly, without detailed elaborations. Relationships between the schemata will be neglected.

I assume the following schemata:

1. contact
2. visual contrast
3. causative motion
4. transfer
5. motion
6. action
7. emotional process or state.

ad 1

The entities postulated as given are s, x, y. The conceptual schema "contact" will be characterized by the following attribute-value-pairs:
contact: s
involved in s as contacting object: x
class: physical object
involved in s as contacted object: y
class: physical object

ad 2

The entities s, x, y will be given. The schema "visual contrast" will include:
contrast: s
involved in s as contrasted object: x
class: physical object
involved in s as contrasting object: y
class: physical object

ad 3

The given entities will be s, a, x, w, b. The conceptual schema "causative motion" will contain:
causative motion: s
involved in s as agent: a
class: animate
involved in s as "moved object": x
class: physical object
localized object: x
path of x: w
location of x: on w
involved in s as localizing object: b
location of b: at the end of w

ad 4

The given entities will be s, a, b, x. The conceptual schema "transfer" will be characterized by:
transfer: s
involved in s as giver: a
class: animate
involved in s as recipient: b
class: animate
involved in s as gift: x
class: physical object

ad 5

The entities given will be s, x, w. The conceptual schema "motion" will contain:
motion: s
involved in s as "moved object": x
class: animate
localized object: x
path of x: w
location of x: on w

ad 6

The given entities will be s, x. The conceptual schema "action" will be characterized by:
action: s
involved in s as agent: x
class: animate

ad 7

The entities given will be s, x. The conceptual schemata combined here into the schema "emotional process or state" will contain:

emotional process or state: s
involved in s as experiencer: x
class: animate

The subject matter of the next section is the initial meaning with its associated rules, that is, the lexical meaning of *contre*.

3.3. The lexical meaning of *contre*

In order to determine which properties of the preposition can serve best as initial meaning, the question arises whether the initial meaning should be a rather concrete or a more abstract one. Trying to find out properties which would be abstract enough to capture exclusively those properties which are shared by all occurrences of *contre* turns out to be a fruitless business. A property of that sort could only be an unspecified 'reference to directionality', a property not only characteristic of *contre* but also of other prepositions.

Assuming a concrete intitial meaning therefore seems to be an adequate solution.

I suppose that the initial meaning of *contre* is a relation between two physical objects x and y, a relation characterized as follows:

counter-directed to x: y
force: x
counter-force: y

Based on our knowledge in general, we can state that counter-directionality is a function of two physical objects in contact.

The lexical meaning of *contre* is assumed to be made up of the initial meaning and rules associated with it. They are listed below. The conditions allowing for the application of these rules are not repeated here. I will only add short comments that are to be understood as pointers to further information given in 1.2.

rule 1

Cooccurring with reflexive verb forms interpretable with reference to the schema "visual contrast", the initial meaning has to be changed as follows:
- The attribute "counter-directed to x" is replaced by "contrasted to x".
- The attribute "force" is replaced by "contrasted object".

- The attribute "counter-force" is replaced by "contrasting object".

rule 2

Cooccurring with a verb that is interpreted with reference to the "transfer"-schema, the following rule operating on the initial meaning has to be applied:
- The attribute "force" is replaced by "gift".
- The attribute "counter-force" is replaced by "counter-gift".

rule 3

In combination with a verb interpreted with reference to the "motion"-schema, the initial meaning has to be changed as follows:
- The attribute-value-pair "counter-directed to x: y" is reversed into "counter-directed to y: x".
- The attribute"force" is replaced by "counter-action and counter-force".
- The attribute "counterforce" is replaced by "force and target".
- The class x belongs to is that of actions involving physical force.
- The class y belongs to is that of natural forces or physical objects.

rule 4

In the context of verbs that can be interpreted with reference to the conceptual schemata "action" and "emotional process or state" the initial meaning is changed as follows:
- The attribute-value-pair "counter-directed to x: y" is - as in rule 3 - reversed into "counter-directed to y: x".
- The attribute "force" is replaced by "counter-action" or "counter-process/state".
- The attribute "counter-force" is replaced by "target".
- The class x belongs to is that of actions or emotional processes/states.
- The class y belongs to is that of animates or abstract objects not associable with directionality.

Finally, I will try to show what results the application of the initial meaning and the associated rules can have. Some of the examples seen in 1.2 therefore will be interpreted with reference to the schemata postulated.

3.4. Interpretations of *contre*

As I have just pointed out I assume that the interpretation of *contre* depends on the interpretation of the verb in combination with *contre*. I therefore suppose that the conceptual schema adequate for the interpretation of the verb under discussion is already activated. Then the interpretation of *contre* is integrated into it. The integration can only be successful if

1. the variables occurring as values of attributes in the attribute-value-pairs provided by the lexical meaning of *contre* can be identified with variables which are found in the respective conceptual schema;
2. the activated schema allows for adding new attribute-value-pairs.

One of the conditions that has to be fulfilled in order to instantiate a value by a constant is a unification process of variables.

The sentence

(2) L'échelle est appuyée contre le mur.

will be interpreted with reference to the schema "contact" as follows:
contact: *est appuyée*
involved in *est appuyée* as contacting object: *échelle*
involved in *est appuyée* as contacted object: *mur*
counter-directed to *échelle*: *mur*
force: *échelle*
counter-force: *mur*

Here the **initial meaning** of *contre* is supposed to have been integrated into the schema.

The interpretation of sentence (3)

(3) La tour se dresse contre un ciel bleu.

with reference to the schema "visual contrast" can be represented as follows:
contrast: *se dresse*
involved in *se dresse* as contrasted object: *la tour*

involved in *se dresse* as contrasting object: *un ciel bleu*
contrasted to *la tour*: *un ciel bleu*
contrasted object: *la tour*
contrasting object: *un ciel bleu*

Here *contre* was interpreted by applying the **initial meaning** together with rule 1.

The interpretation of sentence (7)

(7) Max se blottit contre la porte.

carried out with reference to the schema "causative motion" will be:
causative motion: *se blottit*
involved in *se blottit* as agent: *Max*
involved in *se blottit* as "moved object": *Max*
localized object: *Max*
path of *Max*: w
location of *Max*: on w
involved in *se blottit* as localizing object: *la porte*
location of *la porte*: at the end of w
counter-directed to Max: *la porte*
force: *Max*
counter-force: *la porte*

Due to the contact presupposed by *contre* in its **initial meaning** the value attributed to the localizing object and to the object functioning as counter-force have to be the same.

With reference to the schema "transfer" sentence (10)

(10) Max donne son briquet contre un couteau de poche.

will be interpretable:
transfer: *donne*
involved in *donne* as giver: *Max*
involved in *donne* as recipient: b
involved in *donne* as gift: *son briquet*
there is a physical object: *un couteau de poche*
counter-directed to *son briquet*: *un couteau de poche*
counter-gift: *un couteau de poche*

The interpretation of *contre* will be due to the application of the **initial meaning** and **rule2**.

The prepositional phrase causes the schema to be modified by addition of one further argument. This allows for the act of giving to take place simultaneously with an act of receiving.

Let us now consider the interpretation of sentence (13)

(13) L'avion s'est écrasé contre une montagne.

supposed to be processed with reference to the "contact"-schema:
contact: *s'est écrasé*
involved in *s'est écrasé* as contacting object: *l'avion*
involved in *s'est écrasé* as contacted object: *une montagne*
counter-directed to *l'avion*: *une montagne*
force: *l'avion*
counter-force: *une montagne*

It is the **initial meaning** of *contre* that is supposed to have been applied here.

The interpretation of the sentence (15)

(15) Max nage contre le courant.

with reference to the "motion"-schema will be represented as follows:
motion: *nage*
involved in *nage* as"moved object": *Max*
localized object: *Max*
path of *Max*: w
location of *Max*: on w
there is a natural force: *le courant*
counter-directed to *le courant*: *nage*
force and target: *le courant*
counter-force and action: *nage*

In order to interpret *contre* in this sentence, the **initial meaning** was manipulated by applying **rule 3**.

The **initial meaning** together with **rule 4** have to be applied in order to interpret *contre* in the following sentence

(19) Les catholiques luttent contre les protestants.

referring to the "action"-schema.
action: *luttent*
involved in *luttent* as agent: *les catholiques*
there are animate beings: *les protestants*
counter-directed to *les protestants*: *luttent*
target: *les protestants*
counter-action: *luttent*

The **initial meaning**, together with **rule 4**, must also be applied for interpretations of sentences containing verbs which have to be interpreted with reference to the schema "emotional process/state".

4. Final remark

The representations of different interpretations not only summarize my observations on the preposition *contre* but point as well to the open questions and difficulties brought about by an attempt to represent sentence interpretations.

Nevertheless I hope to have called attention to the preposition *contre* and to its interpretations as interesting subject matter, whose interpretation and representation deserve further investigation.

References

Brugman, Claudia M. 1983, *Story of over*. Trier: L.A.U.T.

Gerthsen, Ch. and Kneser, H.O. 1971, *Physik*. Berlin, Heidelberg, New York: Springer.

Hawkins, Bruce 1985, *The Semantics of English Spatial Prepositions*. Trier: L.A.U.T.

Herskovits, Anette 1986, *Language and Spatial Cognition*. An interdisciplinary Study of the Prepositions in English. Cambridge: Cambridge University Press.

Herweg, Michael 1989, "Ansätze zu einer semantischen Beschreibung topologischer Präpositionen", in: Habel, Christopher, Herweg, Michael, Rehkämper, Klaus (eds.), *Raumkonzepte in Verstehensprozessen*. Tübingen: Niemeyer. 99-128.

Hottenroth, Priska Monika 1983, "Die Bezeichnung räumlicher Verhältnisse", in Schwarze, Christoph (ed.), *Bausteine für eine italienische Grammatik.* Tübingen: Narr. 11-171.

Hottenroth, Priska Monika 1986, *Die Semantik lokaler Präpositionen. Ein prototypisches Modell für die französische Präposition dans mit einer Analyse der Beziehungen zwischen der Präposition und den Objektbezeichnungen in den Präpositionalsyntagmen.* Univ. Konstanz. Habilitation Thesis.

Johnson, Mark 1987, *The Body in the Mind.* The Bodily Basis of Meaning, Imagination, and Reason. Chicago, London: The University of Chicago Press.

Lang, Ewald 1988, Zur Semantik der Richtungspräpositionen (*vor - hinter, über - unter*). Lecture held at the Colloquium on Prepositions, University of Wuppertal, 25./26. 11.1988.

Schwarze, Christoph 1989, "Polysemie als Prozedur, am Beispiel von frz. *à travers* und *chez* ", in: Habel, Ch./Herweg, M./Rehkämper, K. (eds.), *Raumkonzepte in Verstehensprozessen.* Tübingen: Niemeyer. 310-339.

Talmy, Leonard 1985, "Force Dynamics in Language and Thought", in: *Parasession on Causatives and Agentivity.* Chicago Linguistic Society (21st Regional Meeting). University of Chicago.

Vandeloise, Claude 1986, *L'espace en français. Sémantique des prépositions spatiales.* Paris: Seuil.

Wunderlich, Dieter and Herweg, Michael 1986, "Lokale und Direktionale", to appear in: Stechow, Arnim von and Wunderlich, Dieter (eds.), *Handbuch der Semantik.*

Dictionaries

Imbs, Paul 1978, Trésor de la langue française. Tome sixième. Paris.

Robert, Paul 1973, Dictionnaire alphabétique & analogique de la langue française. Paris.

Schröder, Jochen 1986, Lexikon deutscher Präpositionen. Leipzig.

Zingarelli, Nicola 1986, Il nuovo Zingarelli. Vocabolario della lingua italiana. Bologna.

Getting round to *(a)round*: towards the description and analysis of a "spatial" predicate

Rainer Schulze
(Essen)

0. Introduction

It is a characteristic of human perception and classification that persons, objects and relations of extra-lingual reality can be perspectivized in different ways. Thus, aspects of entities in our (verbalized) experience may be brought into the foreground, others may recede into the background. If linguists accept this assumption as a viable alternative to customary views on the relationship between language and reality, they should also take a closer look at various language structures and question the autonomous status which has been constantly assigned to them by most generativists. If language structures are not to be equated with abstract and autonomous systems, linguists should attempt to discover and investigate the links with extra-linguistic reality which evidently has some bearing on the language user's choice of particular verbal (sub-)structures. Attempts made so far are very promising and have been anchored to a coherent series of statements on the nature of the language/extra-linguistic reality-relationship. Cognitive Grammar (Semantics) is the product of multifarious endeavours to provide us with a more appropriate description of verbal phenomena (Langacker 1987) and is thus opposed to another approach in current lexical semantics in which Bierwisch (1983), Lang (1987) and Bierwisch/Lang (1987) assume the verbal component to be largely independent of any overall conceptual systems, thus claiming a particular representational level of "semantic form" which, as an autonomous component of the module-based language system, governs the semantic composition between the language and the conceptual system.

1. The aim of the paper

Verbal phenomena appear as texts, phrases, constituents, complements or single lexical items. The semantic description of grammatical words, being part of the latter group is, according to Herskovits, "the skeleton in the closet of both artificial intelligence and logical semantics" (1988: 271), thus indicating that these lexical (!) items have been only insufficiently described by various linguistic approaches. Let us pick out one item, i.e. *(a)round*, which may, for example, be used as a preposition and then cannot have as a complement a *that*-clause or a subjective case form of a personal pronoun (Quirk et al. 1985: 658 ff.); moreover, *(a)round* may be used as an adverbial with complements missing, or, to round this short presentation off, as an adverbial particle as part of a phrasal verb. Manser argues that *around* and *round* are synonymous in most of their adverbial and prepositional usages (1988: 19), though claiming a preference for *around* in American English and *round* in British English. His observation leads us to the semantic description and the multitude of various usages of this item. Inspecting a large corpus of *(a)round*-instances, we gain the impression that this item denotes various entities in different event patterns (Lutzeier 1988: 367). The central question, consequently, arises of how it is possible to take account of this observation in a preliminary semantic description of *(a)round.* And, just to complicate matters, more detailed subjects of investigation have to be added to make the basic concern of our paper clear:

a. What do we understand by "variety of *(a)round*-senses"?
b. What are the relationships among various *(a)round*-senses? Are they of a(n) (ir)regular nature?
c. Does *(a)round* display different senses in different (verbal) contexts?
d. Is *(a)round* a polysemous item?
e. Do we have to assign to *(a)round* a basic meaning which unites the potential of different *(a)round*-instances?
f. Is the variety of *(a)round*-senses determined by the "geographical" properties of the entities involved?

The questions raised are going to be partly answered with the help of an admittedly very small sample corpus of *(a)round*-instances, presented to test-subjects with English as their mother tongue.

2. The corpus and the informants

The sample corpus (cf. Appendix 1) is taken from Hill's collection (1968) of 64 *(a)round*-instances, subjectively chosen since one cannot confront informants with more than 20 or 25 instances and then expect their judgements to provide valuable insights into the semantic mechanisms of the item. The test-subjects (45 students from Christ Church College in Canterbury, England) were faced with three experiments, two of which will be described in the following. We take the assumption for granted that the various *(a)round*-senses are, first, derived from basic and spatial senses (Traugott 1978) and, second, reflect the fundamental perceptual patterns the language user applies during everyday (non)verbal interaction in his/her environment (Schulze 1987, 1988, forthcoming).

Experiment 1 takes account of this hypothesis. It is an evaluation task in which the students are presented with 20 sentences which contain *(a)round* in different grammatical functions (cf. Appendix 1). As the instructions show (cf. Appendix 2), the test-subjects are asked to compare the use of *(a)round* in the respective sentences to their own, subjective, and central idea of *(a)round*, and to use the attached seven-point scale in order to mark their choices. The participants are students of foreign languages, and we are aware of the fact that students of mathematics or economics could have offered slightly different judgements. All the data elicited comprise particular items on the mean, variance, and standard deviation for our set of measurements (cf. Appendix 3a, 3b). Additionally, in order to evaluate whether the difference between two mean values is significant, the statistic t is calculated (cf. Appendix 4a, 4b).

Experiment 2 consists of a sorting task, in which the informants are presented with the same set of sentences and in which they are now asked to group the sentences on the basis of the similarity of the different uses of *(a)round* as specified by the sentence context (cf. Appendix 2). The purpose of this task is to obtain an indication of the uses that speakers of British English are able to differentiate on the basis of their lexical knowledge and of the conceptual representations of these as used in their "internal" lexicon (Cuyckens 1988: 319). We make, however, no claim that the test subjects' choices can be interpreted as intuitions about and reflections of the various *(a)round*-senses in their mental lexicon (Aitchison 1987: 190 ff.). Again, the students are given the set of sentences at one time, the order of the sentences being varied from subject to subject by shuffling the slips of paper. The informants are free to form as many groups as they want. The whole session lasts on average thirty minutes. The data set is analyzed with the help of Johnson's (1967) hierarchical clustering schema. If the structure of the data set is rather "stable", the single linkage and the complete linkage methods should be identical or at least similar (Woods/Fletcher/Hughes 1986: 260) (cf. Appendix 5a, 5b).

3. Descriptive tools

The ensuing semantic description and analysis will be based on a descriptive framework which has become known as Cognitive Grammar. Since I assume that the reader is familiar with the basic tenets of this approach, I will avoid any lengthy and verbose presentation of the macrostructure of the grammar. It seems, however, advisable to introduce the most important items of the microstructure.

(A)round in its prepositional or adverbial function constitutes a stative relation; moreover, it profiles a single atemporal relational configuration of an event pattern (Langacker 1987: 220). The predicate in question is a spatial one and can, in its most basic sense, be characterized relative to the domain of physical space, which is a basic one (besides the domains of time, emotion, etc.). If we accept the assumption that the meaning of *(a)round* can be interpreted as interplay between the domain (conceptual context) and the way this is profiled (Dirven 1988: 334), then we should be able to conclude that non-spatial meanings of the predicate have to be attributed to non-spatial, i.e. more abstract domains. It follows that the description and analysis of *(a)round* relative to a number of domains is supplemented by a fair amount of contextual information, which various scholars would exclusively ascribe to the verbal context of the item (e.g. Bennett 1975). Those parts of our predicate's domain which are relevant for its interpretation make up the base of *(a)round.* It is the predicate's necessary context from which a particular profile is selected, the profile thus being a substructure of the base. The descriptive tools to describe atemporal stative relations also comprise the notions of figure and ground (henceforth F and G). Talmý observes that "within a scene, there is ascribed to one element the status of "Figure", with its attentional primacy, and to another element the status of "Ground", with

its function in the background of attention as a reference object for the localizing of the Figure" (1988: 195).

We will now start off by applying Langacker's descriptive tools to *(a)round*, demonstrating incidentally that language in Cognitive Grammar is primarily semantics-oriented, and that the meaning of predicates cannot be derived from a set of necessary and sufficient semantic markers, but rather from a structured whole of word senses, the structure of which provides for and gives account of central and more peripheral senses, but which are still closely connected.

4. The case of *(a)round*

As can be seen from Appendix 3a, sentence (6) shows the smallest mean value, but not the smallest deviation value, which can be assigned to (3). Higher deviation scores can be assigned to (2), (4) and (7). In their judgement of all the remaining sample sentences, the informants have made use of the whole range of the seven-point scale provided. (5) has the highest mean score, and, as all adjacent scores indicate, the test-subjects were almost unanimous in their judgement of this *round*-instance. Nevertheless, we should keep in mind that the elicited scores do not give us a precise idea of whether the informants judged the grammaticality and/or acceptability of the sentences or not. Thus, all the interpretations drawn from the figures merely give us an indication of the tendency of the results and should not therefore be seen as absolute scores. The tendency, however, which becomes obvious when we skim through the numerical data, is the following: a high mean value correlates with the loss of the originally spatial meaning of *(a)round*-relations. Though this conclusion might not be surprising to most of us, the experiments nevertheless reveal that the test subjects are able to discern distinct senses of *(a)round*, that they are able to relate these senses to each other and that they are able to assign different ranks to the item(s) in question. But what is more important is that the assumption that the spatial meanings of prepositions or adverbs are the basic ones, allowing for metaphorical and metonymic extensions into other domains, can be empirically validated (Colombo/Flores d'Arcais 1984), leaving this time aside the historical argumentation which has dominated the debate over central and more peripheral senses so far.

Before leaving the numerical data completely, let us take one final look at the scores resulting from the *t*-test in Appendix 4a and 4b. As can be seen from the rightmost columns in these appendices, the *t*-distribution has been chosen for relatively small sample sizes in order to calculate the statistical significance of the difference between the mean values of two scores: the smaller the value in the right columns, the more reliable is the difference between two mean scores. If the value exceeds the 5 % level (as is the case when comparing (6) to (4)), then the difference is less significant; this value then merely indicates a tendency towards significance. The bearing this score has on our interpretation of the data will be shown in the next section.

What we learn from a close inspection of Appendix 5a and 5b is that the informants' judgements of similarities of meanings result in numerous and distinct clusters. A first cluster, which comprises the paradigm case of the whole sample, includes the sentences (4), (6) and (20). What is common to the samples of this group is that the event patterns denote (in general) a circular movement round a (real or imaginary) centre. F in these constructions is represented by nouns or pronouns which may denote persons or objects, G again for nouns or pronouns which denote all those persons or objects which allow conceptualization as points or axes. Please note that (20), which joins to (4) and (6) in our dendrograms, does not convey the idea of a path which is covered by F; rather, we assume F's current location as an end point of prior movement. The assignment of the roles of F and G seems to follow a particular syntactic pattern, in which F coincides with the subject of the respective sentence and is conceptualized (contrary to our real-world experience) as the agent in the event pattern. G may coincide with the noun of the optional and more complex prepositional noun phrase, but it may also be sub-lexical so that the reference entity (Herskovits 1986: 7) has to be inferred by the language user. This is the case in (4), where *round* gains adverbial status as the result of this "clipping" process. Now, Ewald Lang (personal communication) states that it is at least surprising that the informants group items with different grammatical status together. We have, as must be admitted, no definitive answer to this problem and would like to offer two "explanations":

a. first, we are glad that the test-subjects put "different" items together and thus avoided the impression that their judgements simply mirror grammatical decisions;
b. second, interpreting the students' evaluations as they are, we feel confirmed in our assumption that they have mainly directed their attention to the semantic aspects of the evaluation task.

To sum up: *round* in this cluster constitutes a stative relation. This relation comprises an F-configuration, which can be characterized as indeterminate (thus implying that G is not conceived of as a punctiform entity). This *round* instance requires a primary characterization against the domain of oriented physical space, which is no longer a basic domain of physical space since some orientation is imposed on it. The relational information in the profile of *round* cannot be simply reduced to either separation or coincidence, though the coincidence pattern (i.e. some part of the F-configuration coincides with some part of the G-configuration) seems to prevail. Our interpretation may be diagrammatically specified as in Appendix 6, identified as (4), (6) and (20).

The next cluster comprises (2) and (3). Common to both samples seems to be the concept of near-circular movement, though the idea of movement round a centre seems to be more peripheral here. It is mainly the idea of change in direction which comes to the fore and which has some bearing on the choice of nouns (and objects respectively) in this event pattern. Seen from a grammatical standpoint, again nouns and pronouns are the possible candidates for the F-realization which denote persons and objects in our everyday environment. What is peculiar to these persons and objects, however, is that they have an in-built front and back, i.e. they are intrinsically marked. Thus, persons and ships may turn round and thus face in a different (or most probably: opposite) direction. Taking this for granted, we should be allowed to apply this schema to similarly structured beings and objects such as to most four-legged animals, means of transportation (aircraft, car, train, etc.), objects in everyday use (postcard, envelope, knife, chair, cupboard, wardrobe, book, picture, shirt, etc.) or body-parts such as a hand (it would be an interesting challenge to investigate the relationship between the structure of beings and objects and their respective (verbal) conceptualization in genetically different languages). What has been said so far on the properties of F applies equally well to the properties of G, since F and G are conceptualized in this cluster as congruent entities, i.e. they are perceived as unit-constituting entities. The semantic description of this *round*-instance is reflected in its syntactic counterpart, where those persons and objects which are conceived of as agents in the respective event patterns take the role of the subject in the sentence, whereas all those objects which defy the agent-assignment may take the role of a direct object in such constructions as *She turned the knife round* or *Peter turned the book round* (allowing of course an additional interpretation if Peter turns an open book round so that this verbalized event pattern may require a more deictic explication). To sum up: *round* in this cluster profiles a relation with F in a near-circular movement and F and G as indeterminate entities, or to be more precise, as unit-constituting entities; *round* is again specified relative to the cognitive domain of oriented physical space. Conceptualizing F and G as one and the same unit, we suggest labelling this *round*-instance "reflexive". The diagrammatic specification can again be found in Appendix 6.

The next cluster contains the sample sentences (1), (14), (7), (15) and (16). In presenting these samples in this sequence, we refer to the hierarchical clustering scheme provided by the complete linkage method (Appendix 5b). Here both (1) and (14) and (15) and (16) form "immediate" clusters, the latter moreover bound together with (7). The single linkage method yields a different distribution of *round*-instances: (1) and (14) form the basic cluster and both (15) and (16) add to this one successively; (7) becomes the member of clusters already discussed. These partly contradictory results may be traced back to our choice of the dissimilarity measure, clustering algorithm or cut-off dissimilarity value, thus characterizing the clustering approach simply as an exploratory technique for searching for plausible structures (Woods/Fletcher/Hughes 1986: 260). We think that we are justified in basing our discussion on the complete linkage method, at least for plausible reasons: one of them being that (7) may be attributed to one cluster which is marked by F's near-circular movement (apart from (14) and F being conceptualized as an indeterminate entity) against G as an indeterminate entity. G may sometimes be lexicalized as in (14), (7) and (15), but it may occur in sublexical "position" as in (16) or as a textual antecedent as in (1). Moreover, not only does the distribution of G convey the idea of a heterogeneous sense-group, but also the syntactic pattern(s) which dominate(s) this cluster display(s) some particular properties: we can have F as the subject of the sentence, represented by nouns or pronouns which may stand for persons or objects as shown in (1), (14), (15) and (16), or F may alternatively occur as the direct object of the sentence, represented again by nouns or pronouns exclusively for persons and then followed by a prepositional phrase with G explicitly stated. The palpable diversity in this cluster may be due to the fact that different bases require different interpretations and thus pose the question of whether the cognitive domain of oriented physical space is still the dominant cognitive context for the sense-group at issue. The primary local aspect is obvious in those instances where G stands for nouns which again represent "geographical" specifications such as corners, bays, bridges or bends. These function as obstacles and force F to follow a more circular, less direct, course.

Furthermore, we can assume that F on the way to his/her goal moves away from an imaginary speaker, thus vanishing from his/her sight. Taking the feature "deviation from a direct course" into consideration, we can account for a more metaphorical extension of *round* which is realized in (16): it is the idea of "visit" which comes to the fore and which could be "locally" rephrased as "F moves round an obstacle to get into contact with somebody else". We suggest treating this *round*-instance as an intermediate instance which is localizable between the more basic "spatial" domain and the more abstract one which could be labelled "social encounter". For the interpretations given above, we suggest the diagram in Appendix 6. The sample sentence to which the students assigned the highest mean value is (5), the reason being that most of the students in general doubted the grammaticality of this sentence, at least in British English. As can be determined from the third experiment in our investigation (Appendix 2), most rephrasings by informants included syntagms such as *We planted our garden with thick bushes* (six times), *We planted bushes all around our garden* (three times) and *We planted thick bushes around our garden* (three times). The result of these rephrasings is that we can identify *(thick) bushes* as F and direct object of the sentence and *garden* as G and part of the prepositional phrase, respectively. Moreover, it is not the idea of movement which is conceptualized by the F/G-configuration, but the idea of enclosure. Thus, any multiplicity of persons or objects which may surround something solid is (are) the suitable candidate(s) for F; G may be represented by nouns which denote delimitable areas of land, excluding, in a broad sense, geographical areas which palpably defy any efforts at surrounding. Thus, what is under consideration here is a stative relation with F as a host of indeterminate entities and G as a surface configuration profiled against a base containing the cognitive domain of oriented physical space or enclosure. Taking this interpretation for granted, it is an easy and justified step to accept constructions such as *We can set buildings round the courtyard*, *Several people sat round the table* or *The football field has a fence all around*. The corresponding diagram to this view can again be found in Appendix 6.

All four clusters discussed so far should be interpreted as subschemata or as idealized cognitive models which help the language user "... to organize our knowledge by means of structures" (Lakoff 1987: 68). These in turn are subordinate structures, being dominated by a more abstract schema or superschema which provides for the specification and elaboration of particular F/G-configurations. We suggest identifying the superschema with the prototypical core meaning of *(a)round*. Or in other words: we claim an abstract prototypical core meaning, not dependent on particular F/G-specifications, which contains minimal conditions for the use of *(a)round.* Lakoff introduces the notion of minimal specification interpretation (1987: 420) which allows for the "derivation" of various *(a)round*-instances and confirms at the same time the polysemous character of the item in question. All *(a)round*-instances discussed so far may be conceived of as instantiations (Langacker 1987: 438 f.) or near-instances (Fillmore 1982: 32) of our superschema; in particular, the *(a)round*-instances in (4), (6) and (20) may be identified both as paradigm cases (Fillmore 1982: 32) of the superschema and instantiations or near instances of the whole sample. The various distances between the single subschemata and the superschema, as indicated in Appendix 6, are meant to illustrate the different ranks assigned to the *(a)round*-instances by the informants in our network of related senses.

There is no denying the fact that we have to assume additional superschemata, though not of a prototypical, but of a more abstract nature. These should be seen as derived schemata, i.e. derived from the prototypical one. These abstract projections are again defined without recourse to particular F/G-configurations and act as triggers which set off additional F/G-elaborations.

One of these abstract schemata "generates" a cluster with (9), (19), (17) and (18) as instantiations. Both the single linkage and the complete linkage method reveal that (17) and (18) and (9) and (19), respectively, establish sub-clusters which unite to form an independent cluster in Appendix 5b and which constitute parts of a more complex cluster in Appendix 5a. What is common to all these samples, however, is the idea of proximity which seems to be of a "stationary" nature, i.e. the lack of motion verbs in all four samples suggests the proximity of at least two entities. These are identified as F and G and, to put it in long-known terminology, are both conceptualized as indeterminate configurations profiled against a base which again contains the cognitive domain of oriented physical space. If we examine real-world persons and objects, which may be represented by nouns and pronouns and which may act as F and G in the sentence respectively, we arrive at the conclusion that all those persons and/or objects may be "correlated" that are possibly either within sight of an imaginary speaker (language user) or are part(s) of a search domain and thus can be brought in relation to each other. The dominant syntactic pattern which emerges from this interpretation is one in which F takes the role of the subject and G, if lexicalized, the role of the noun in an optional prepositional phrase as a constituent of a complex structure. If G is sub-lexical, *(a)round* in this cluster acts exclusively as an adverb, not as an adverbial particle. The pictorial representation in Appendix 6 is meant as a plausible representation of the semantic concept discussed and suggests a coincidence relation between F and G in the profile.

Another abstract schema comprises two distinct clusters, one of them being represented by (8), (11) and (10). Both the "nearest-neighbour" and the "furthest-neighbour" approach to our data confirm that (8) and (11) form an immediate cluster before (10) joins. The *(a)round*-instances here evoke the idea of change of place (location), paralleled by the concept of motion in an unspecified direction. F stands for nouns or pronouns which represent persons or two-dimensional areas. Or in other words: G can be described as a surface configuration which includes F as an indeterminate configuration. It is worthwhile noting here that in two opposing prepositional syntagms such as *(dogs run) around the streets* vs. *(dogs run) in the street*, G is conceptualized in two different ways: on the one hand as a surface configuration allowing the possible replacement of *(a)round* by *all over* or *throughout*, on the other hand as a medium configuration (Hawkins 1988: 246 ff.), necessarily dependent on the predicate's choice of the relevant parts of the G-configuration. This example provides conclusive evidence for the assumption that *(a)round* in particular is "meaningful", that it indicates how we structure the everyday world and that it suggests taking account of experiential factors in the adequate description of event patterns. Thus, it is not simply the specification of the noun phrases involved which renders the semantic information of the preposition or adverb; the "verbal" context of *(a)round* only partially reflects the prepositions's or adverb's characteristics. Rather, it is the impact of *(a)round* on the context which should appropriately be accounted for.

After this digression into the basic tenets of Cognitive Grammar as regards the proper treatment of particular lexical items, let us now turn to the last cluster of our investigation. It comprises (12) and (13) and is given identical treatment by both the complete and single linkage method. Again, the idea of F's change of place is dominant, supplemented by the conception of social (sociable) gatherings or interpersonal relationships. This observation is corroborated by the fact that F and G stand for nouns or pronouns which here exclusively represent human beings. Two syntactic patterns seem to emerge: the one presenting F as the subject of the sentence and thus stressing the point that some agentivity on the part of F is implied; the other presenting F as the direct object of the syntagm, leaving F as a primarily non-agentive entity (Talmy 1985: 62 ff.). The last pattern seems to be the most frequent and dominant one in this cluster, being also the pattern for all those extensions in which F does not solely stand for nouns representing human beings, but also for nouns representing inanimate objects, as may be realized in constructions such as *Peter handed glasses round* or *Ruth passed the news round.* Leaving the shape and the structure of F aside, we still have to examine the particulars of G which are dominant in this cluster. Whereas F may be described as an indeterminate configuration in non-circular and non-directional movement, G is conceptualized as a multiplex entity (and is not to be confused with the purely grammatical status of being plural): since we cannot hand glasses round a single person (and thus excluding the interpretation of a marginal event pattern), we have to assume that F is handed over to several bystanders, i.e. successively from one person to another. Thus, G has to be identified as a series of indeterminate entities which, furthermore, occupy a particular territory. This territory is conceptualized as a container for both F and G entities, as can be found in the diagram in Appendix 6. What is different from all the schematic representations given so far is that we have to assume a more elaborate notion of G in this sub-cluster in order to take account of the intricacies of this sample: it is the notion of a secondary ground (Rudzka-Ostyn 1985: 217) which acts as a secondary reference entity and which allows a more precise "location" of F. If we take this interpretation for granted, then we should assume some relational information in the profile of this cluster which indicates that some part of the F-configuration coincides with some part of the G-configuration. The *round*-instances here again require a primary characterization against the domain of oriented physical space.

5. Conclusion

With the help of a fairly small corpus we have attempted to show that particular senses of *(a)round* (in its prepositional and/or adverbial use) cannot be interpreted as idiosyncratic entries in a dictionary. Rather, our preliminary study provides evidence for the fact that the various senses of *(a)round* are interrelated, that these senses form parts of, metaphorically speaking, a network. The senses of this network cannot be appropriately described with semantic features (sufficient and/or necessary) as the main elements of the traditional criterial attribute model in lexical semantics;

instead their "location" in the network is substantially based on particular conceptual (or even perceptual) patterns. It is the Cognitive Grammar approach which rightly takes account of this fact.

Our preliminary study is the forerunner of a more comprehensive one in which *(a)round* is not only going to be described against the cognitive domain of space, but also against more abstract domains in order to achieve a proper treatment of numerous metaphorical extensions of the item. The starting-point is the assumption that metaphorical extensions of *(a)round* should be interpreted as elaborations and derivations from space-oriented schemata (cf. Appendix 6), the derivation being supported by sets of conceptual metaphors or metonymies (Lakoff/Johnson 1980). Future investigations will thus focus on the following: how do we handle verbalized event patterns such as *There is a rumour going round that milk is radioactive* or *I can get round my father to lend us his car* or *This volume has around 450 pages?* Several questions could be raised here:

a. Is it possible to resort to the schemata established in Appendix 6 to describe the *(a)round*-instances?
b. If it is, how can similar meanings be related to each other?
c. How are the particular and "local" F/G-configurations affected by the postulate of semantic neighbourhood?
d. What types of metaphorical extensions do and may occur?
e. What are the effects of the F/G-elaborations on the underlying "local" syntactic patterns?
f. What are the metonymic or metaphoric formulations which account for the extended meanings of *(a)round*?

In answering these questions we might then be able to prove that metaphorical extensions are not a matter of a largely extraordinary and idiosyncratic language, but should rather be regarded as reflections of a well-structured network which governs our thoughts and actions.

References:

Aitchison, Jean. 1987. *Words in the Mind. An Introduction to the Mental Lexicon.* Oxford: Blackwell.

Bahner, Werner et al. (eds.). forthcoming. *Proceedings of the XIVth International Congress of Linguists* (Held in Berlin - GDR, 1987). Berlin (GDR): Akademie.

Bennett, David C. 1975. *Spatial and Temporal Uses of English Prepositions. An Essay in Stratificational Semantics*. London: Longman.
Bierwisch, Manfred. 1983. "Semantische und konzeptuelle Repräsentationen lexikalischer Einheiten". In: Ruzicka, Rudolf and Wolfgang Motsch (eds.). 1983. 61 - 99.
Bierwisch, Manfred and Ewald Lang (eds.). 1987. *Semantische und konzeptuelle Aspekte von Dimensionsadjektiven* (studia grammatica 26/27). Berlin (GDR): Akademie.

Colombo, Lucia and Giovanni B. Flores d'Arcais. 1984. "The Meaning of Dutch Prepositions: A Psycholinguistic Study of Polysemy". *Linguistics* 22. 51 - 98.
Cuyckens, Hubert. 1988. "Spatial Prepositions in Cognitive Semantics". In: Hüllen, Werner and Rainer Schulze (eds.). 1988. 316 - 328.

Dirven, René. 1988. "A Cognitive Approach to Conversion". In: Hüllen, Werner and Rainer Schulze (eds.). 1988. 329 - 343.

Fillmore, Charles J. 1982. "Towards a Descriptive Framework for Spatial Deixis". In: Jarvella, Robert J. and Wolfgang Klein (eds.). 1982. 31 - 59.

Greenberg, Joseph H. (ed.). 1978. *Universals of Human Language*. Vol. 3: *Word Structure*. Stanford, CAL: Stanford University Press.

Hawkins, Bruce W. 1988. "The Natural Category MEDIUM: An Alternative to Selection Restrictions and Similar Constructs". In: Rudzka-Ostyn, Brygida (ed.). 1988. 231 - 270.
Herskovits, Annette. 1986. *Language and Spatial Cognition: An Interdisciplinary Study of the Prepositions in English*. Cambridge: Cambridge University Press.
Herskovits, Annette. 1988. "Spatial Expressions and the Plasticity of Meaning". In: Rudzka-Ostyn, Brygida (ed.). 1988. 271 - 297.
Hill, Leslie Alexander. 1968. *Prepositions and Adverbial Particles. An Interim Classification, Semantic, Structural, and Graded*. London: Oxford University Press.
Hüllen, Werner and Rainer Schulze (eds.). 1988. *Understanding the Lexicon. Meaning, Sense and World Knowledge in Lexical Semantics*. Tübingen: Niemeyer.

Jarvella, Robert J. and Wolfgang Klein (eds.). 1982. *Speech, Place, and Action. Studies in Deixis and Related Topics*. Chicester: John Wiley & Sons.
Johnson, Stephen C. 1967. "Hierarchical Clustering Schemes". *Psychometrika* 32. 241 - 254.

Lakoff, George. 1987. *Women, Fire, and Dangerous Things: What Categories Reveal about the Mind*. Chicago/London: University of Chicago Press.
Lakoff, George and Mark Johnson. 1980. *Metaphors We Live By*. Chicago: University of Chicago Press.
Lang, Ewald. 1987. "Semantik der Dimensionsauszeichnung räumlicher Objekte". In: Bierwisch, Manfred and Ewald Lang (eds.). 1987. 287 - 458.

Langacker, Ronald W. 1987. *Foundations of Cognitive Grammar*. Vol. 1: *Theoretical Prerequisites*. Stanford, CAL: Stanford University Press.

Lörscher, Wolfgang and Rainer Schulze (eds.). 1987. *Perspectives on Language in Performance. Studies in Linguistics, Literary Criticism, and Language Teaching and Learning. To Honour Werner Hüllen on the Occasion of His Sixtieth Birthday*. Tübingen: Narr.

Lutzeier, Peter Rolf. 1988. "A Proposal for Spatial Event Patterns". In: Hüllen, Werner and Rainer Schulze (eds.). 1988. 367 - 379.

Manser, Martin H. (ed.). 1988. *Bloomsbury Good Word Guide*. London: Bloomsbury.

Paprotté, Wolf and René Dirven (eds.). 1985. *The Ubiquity of Metaphor*. Amsterdam: Benjamins.

Quirk, Randolph et al. 1985. *A Comprehensive Grammar of the English Language*. London/New York: Longman.

Rudzka-Ostyn, Brygida. 1985. "Metaphoric Processes in Word Formation. The Case of Prefixed Verbs". In: Paprotté, Wolf and René Dirven (eds.). 1985. 209 - 241.

Rudzka-Ostyn, Brygida (ed.). 1988. *Topics in Cognitive Linguistics*. Amsterdam/Philadelphia: Benjamins.

Ruzicka, Rudolf and Wolfgang Motsch (eds.). 1983. *Untersuchungen zur Semantik* (studia grammatica 22). Berlin (GDR): Akademie.

Schulze, Rainer. 1987. "The Perception of Space and the Function of Topological Prepositions in English: A Contribution to Cognitive Grammar". In: Lörscher, Wolfgang and Rainer Schulze (eds.). 1987. 299 - 322.

Schulze, Rainer. 1988. "A Short Story of *Down*". In: Hüllen, Werner and Rainer Schulze (eds.). 1988. 395 - 414.

Schulze, Rainer. forthcoming. "The Meaning of English *By*: A Cognitive - Semantic Approach". In: Bahner, Werner et al. (eds.). forthcoming.

Shopen, Timothy (ed.). 1985. *Language Typology and Syntactic Description*. Vol III: *Grammatical Categories and the Lexicon*. Cambridge: Cambridge University Press.

Talmy, Leonhard. 1985. "Lexicalization Patterns: Semantic Structure in Lexical Forms". In: Shopen, Timothy (ed.). 1985. 57 - 149.

Talmy, Leonhard. 1988. "The Relation of Grammar to Cognition". In: Rudzka-Ostyn, Brygida (ed.). 1988. 165 - 205.

Traugott, Elizabeth Closs. 1978. "On the Expression of Spatio- Temporal Relations in Language". In: Greenberg, Joseph H. (ed.). 1978. 369 - 400.

Woods, Anthony, Paul Fletcher and Arthur Hughes. 1986. *Statistics in Language Studies*. Cambridge: Cambridge University Press.

Appendix 1: *(a)round*-instances

1. When you get to the corner, go round carefully
2. He turned round and I saw his face for the first time
3. The ship turned right round and began to go back to port
4. The propeller of the aeroplane goes round so fast that you can't see it
5. We planted our garden round with thick bushes
6. The earth goes round the sun once in a year
7. We took our guests round the bay after dinner to see our house from the other side
8. He wandered round until he was quite lost
9. There was a big fire near us last week, and everyone for miles round us saw the smoke from it
10. The students went round France during their holidays
11. In this town, hundreds of dogs run around the streets all the time
12. The servants went round the guests and offered them drinks
13. John took his new wife round the guests, and introduced her to all of them
14. His house is round the next corner
15. The bridge is damaged, so you will have to go round by the lower one
16. After supper, we went round to see our friends the Smiths
17. They were standing around the place talking
18. I want to see Mr. Smith. Is he around
19. His house is somewhere round here
20. The string of my kite is round a branch, and it won't come down

Appendix 2: Instructions

Experiment 1:

On each of the slips in front of you, you will find sentences with items underlined. Please judge which underlined item(s) contained in the sentence(s) fit(s) your idea or image of a *round*-relation better than others. Please use the seven-point scale presented below, where "1" stands for "very similar" (the item(s) fit(s) your idea or image very well) and "7" for "least similar" (the item(s) hardly fit(s) your idea or image at all). Indicate your choice by an X in the respective box.

very similar						least similar
1	2	3	4	5	6	7

Experiment 2:

In your envelope you will find a number of paper-clips and slips of paper. On each of the slips you will find a sentence. This sentence includes an underlined item. Please try to visualize each event or scene as expressed by the sentence(s) on the slips. Group together those slips containing items which you think are similar in meaning. Put a paper-clip on each group to keep the slips together and replace them in the envelope. It is up to you to decide on the groups, how many groups you make and how many slips you put into a group.

Experiment 3:

Language very often enables us to verbalize the very same event or scene in rather different ways, depending, for example, on the language user's perspective or attitude. Thus, we may get "She had a mask on her face" or "She wore a mask" as two largely equivalent sentences, e.g. describing a young girl during a fancy-dress ball. Now, on each of the slips in front of you, you will again find a sentence which includes an underlined item. Please try to visualize the event or scene as expressed by the sentence(s) on the slips. Is/Are there any further or additional possibility/ies which rephrase(s) the event or scene on the slip equally well? If there is/are any, please give it/them at the bottom of the slip. You are of course free to use abbreviations or contracted forms in order to avoid rewriting the whole sentence(s).

Appendix 3a

```
VARIABLE    SATZ1
MEAN          2.689    STD DEV     1.443     VARIANCE   2.083
RANGE         6.000    MINIMUM     1.000     MAXIMUM    7.000
VALID CASES   45       MISSING CASES   0
------------------------------------------------------------
VARIABLE    SATZ2
MEAN          1.911    STD DEV      .973     VARIANCE    .946
RANGE         4.000    MINIMUM     1.000     MAXIMUM    5.000
VALID CASES   45       MISSING CASES   0
------------------------------------------------------------
VARIABLE    SATZ3
MEAN          1.711    STD DEV      .695     VARIANCE    .483
RANGE         3.000    MINIMUM     1.000     MAXIMUM    4.000
VALID CASES   45       MISSING CASES   0
------------------------------------------------------------
VARIABLE    SATZ4
MEAN          1.378    STD DEV      .806     VARIANCE    .649
RANGE         4.000    MINIMUM     1.000     MAXIMUM    5.000
VALID CASES   45       MISSING CASES   0
------------------------------------------------------------
VARIABLE    SATZ5
MEAN          5.111    STD DEV     2.036     VARIANCE   4.146
RANGE         6.000    MINIMUM     1.000     MAXIMUM    7.000
VALID CASES   45       MISSING CASES   0
------------------------------------------------------------
VARIABLE    SATZ6
MEAN          1.289    STD DEV      .869     VARIANCE    .756
RANGE         5.000    MINIMUM     1.000     MAXIMUM    6.000
VALID CASES   45       MISSING CASES   0
------------------------------------------------------------
VARIABLE    SATZ7
MEAN          2.578    STD DEV     1.234     VARIANCE   1.522
RANGE         5.000    MINIMUM     1.000     MAXIMUM    6.000
VALID CASES   45       MISSING CASES   0
------------------------------------------------------------
VARIABLE    SATZ8
MEAN          3.978    STD DEV     2.039     VARIANCE   4.159
RANGE         6.000    MINIMUM     1.000     MAXIMUM    7.000
VALID CASES   45       MISSING CASES   0
------------------------------------------------------------
VARIABLE    SATZ9
MEAN          3.622    STD DEV     2.070     VARIANCE   4.286
RANGE         6.000    MINIMUM     1.000     MAXIMUM    7.000
VALID CASES   45       MISSING CASES   0
------------------------------------------------------------
VARIABLE    SATZ10
MEAN          3.400    STD DEV     1.935     VARIANCE   3.745
RANGE         6.000    MINIMUM     1.000     MAXIMUM    7.000
VALID CASES   45       MISSING CASES   0
------------------------------------------------------------
```

Appendix 3b

```
VARIABLE    SATZ11
MEAN          4.111    STD DEV     2.218     VARIANCE   4.919
RANGE         6.000    MINIMUM     1.000     MAXIMUM    7.000
VALID CASES   45       MISSING CASES   0
------------------------------------------------------------
VARIABLE    SATZ12
MEAN          3.556    STD DEV     1.589     VARIANCE   2.525
RANGE         6.000    MINIMUM     1.000     MAXIMUM    7.000
VALID CASES   45       MISSING CASES   0
------------------------------------------------------------
VARIABLE    SATZ13
MEAN          4.044    STD DEV     1.745     VARIANCE   3.043
RANGE         6.000    MINIMUM     1.000     MAXIMUM    7.000
VALID CASES   45       MISSING CASES   0
------------------------------------------------------------
VARIABLE    SATZ14
MEAN          2.867    STD DEV     1.561     VARIANCE   2.436
RANGE         6.000    MINIMUM     1.000     MAXIMUM    7.000
VALID CASES   45       MISSING CASES   0
------------------------------------------------------------
VARIABLE    SATZ15
MEAN          3.778    STD DEV     1.770     VARIANCE   3.131
RANGE         6.000    MINIMUM     1.000     MAXIMUM    7.000
VALID CASES   45       MISSING CASES   0
------------------------------------------------------------
VARIABLE    SATZ16
MEAN          4.022    STD DEV     2.061     VARIANCE   4.249
RANGE         6.000    MINIMUM     1.000     MAXIMUM    7.000
VALID CASES   45       MISSING CASES   0
------------------------------------------------------------
VARIABLE    SATZ17
MEAN          4.600    STD DEV     2.027     VARIANCE   4.109
RANGE         6.000    MINIMUM     1.000     MAXIMUM    7.000
VALID CASES   45       MISSING CASES   0
------------------------------------------------------------
VARIABLE    SATZ18
MEAN          4.644    STD DEV     2.366     VARIANCE   5.598
RANGE         6.000    MINIMUM     1.000     MAXIMUM    7.000
VALID CASES   45       MISSING CASES   0
------------------------------------------------------------
VARIABLE    SATZ19
MEAN          4.467    STD DEV     2.312     VARIANCE   5.345
RANGE         6.000    MINIMUM     1.000     MAXIMUM    7.000
VALID CASES   45       MISSING CASES   0
------------------------------------------------------------
VARIABLE    SATZ20
MEAN          1.667    STD DEV     1.087     VARIANCE   1.182
RANGE         4.000    MINIMUM     1.000     MAXIMUM    5.000
VALID CASES   45       MISSING CASES   0
------------------------------------------------------------
```

Appendix 4a

VARIABLE	NUMBER OF CASES	MEAN	STAND. DEVIAT.	STAND. ERROR	(DIFF.) MEAN	STAND. DEVIAT.	STAND. ERROR	CORR.	2-TAIL PROB.	T VALUE	DEGR. OF FREEDOM	2-TAIL PROB.
SATZ6	45	1.2889	.869	.130	-1.4000	1.388	.207	.363	.014	-6.76	44	.000
SATZ1		2.6889	1.443	.215								
SATZ6	45	1.2889	.869	.130	- .6222	1.284	.191	.031	.840	-3.25	44	.002
SATZ2		1.9111	.973	.145								
SATZ6	45	1.2889	.869	.130	- .4222	1.033	.154	.141	.354	-2.74	44	.009
SATZ3		1.7111	.695	.104								
SATZ6	45	1.2889	.869	.130	- .0889	1.083	.162	.165	.278	- .55	44	.585
SATZ4		1.3778	.806	.120								
SATZ6	45	1.2889	.869	.130	-3.8222	2.092	.312	.148	.331	-12.26	44	.000
SATZ5		5.1111	2.036	.304								
SATZ6	45	1.2889	.869	.130	-1.2889	1.141	.170	.455	.002	-7.58	44	.000
SATZ7		2.5778	1.234	.184								
SATZ6	45	1.2889	.869	.130	-2.6889	2.353	.352	- .189	.215	-7.63	44	.000
SATZ8		3.9778	2.039	.304								
SATZ6	45	1.2889	.869	.130	-2.3333	2.403	.358	- .203	.181	-6.51	44	.000
SATZ9		3.6222	2.070	.309								
SATZ6	45	1.2889	.869	.130	-2.1111	2.069	.309	.065	.672	-6.84	44	.000
SATZ10		3.4000	1.935	.289								

Appendix 4b

VARIABLE	NUMBER OF CASES	MEAN	STAND. DEVIAT.	STAND. ERROR	(DIFF.) MEAN	STAND. DEVIAT.	STAND. ERROR	CORR.	2-TAIL PROB.	T VALUE	DEGR. OF FREEDOM	2-TAIL PROB.
SATZ6	45	1.2889	.869	.130	-2.8222	2.516	.375	-.170	.263	-7.52	44	.000
SATZ11		4.1111	2.218	.331								
SATZ6	45	1.2889	.869	.130	-2.2667	1.698	.253	.144	.344	-8.96	44	.000
SATZ12		3.5556	1.589	.237								
SATZ6	45	1.2889	.869	.130	-2.7556	1.909	.285	.051	.738	-9.68	44	.000
SATZ13		4.0444	1.745	.260								
SATZ6	45	1.2889	.869	.130	-1.5778	1.803	.269	-.021	.890	-5.87	44	.000
SATZ14		2.8667	1.561	.233								
SATZ6	45	1.2889	.869	.130	-2.4889	1.878	.280	.117	.446	-8.89	44	.000
SATZ15		3.7778	1.770	.264								
SATZ6	45	1.2889	.869	.130	-2.7333	2.359	.352	-.156	.307	-7.77	44	.000
SATZ16		4.0222	2.061	.307								
SATZ6	45	1.2889	.869	.130	-3.3111	2.391	.357	-.242	.108	-9.29	44	.000
SATZ17		4.6000	2.027	.302								
SATZ6	45	1.2889	.869	.130	-3.3556	2.673	.398	-.192	.206	-8.42	44	.000
SATZ18		4.6444	2.366	.353								
SATZ6	45	1.2889	.869	.130	-3.1778	2.622	.391	-.193	.204	-8.13	44	.000
SATZ19		4.4667	2.312	.345								
SATZ6	45	1.2889	.869	.130	-.3778	1.386	.207	.008	.958	-1.83	44	.074
SATZ20		1.6667	1.087	.162								

Appendix 5a

Clusteranalyse "round"

Ähnlichkeitsmaß (0 - 45)

Verkettungsregel single linkage
=Minimum Methode

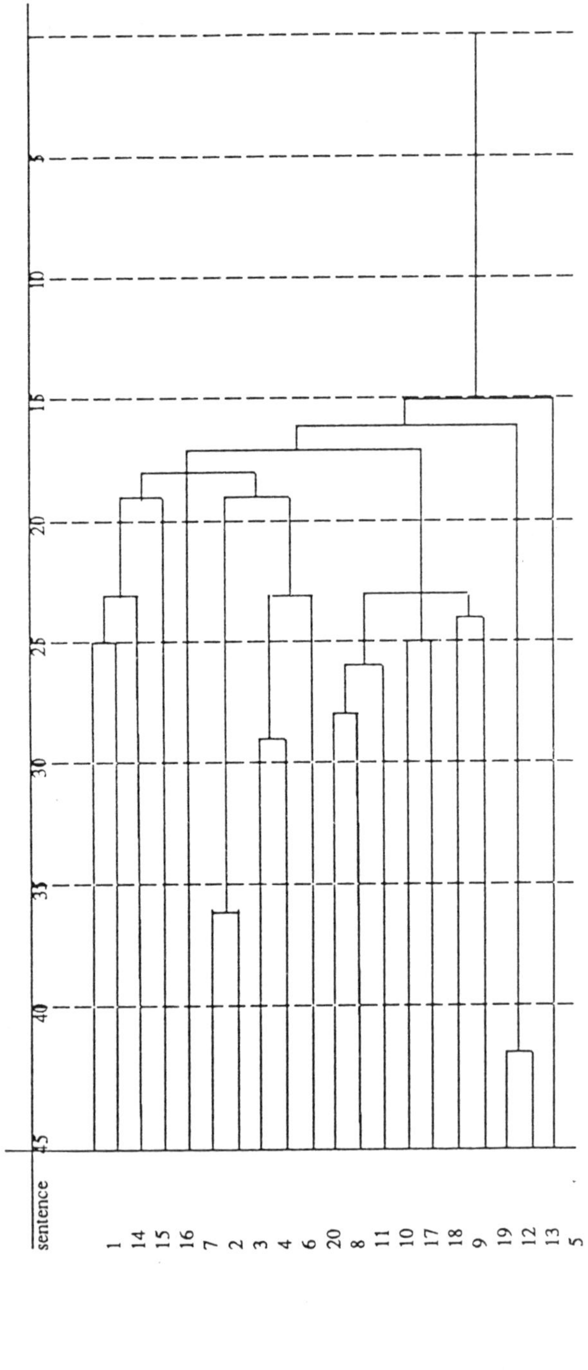

Appendix 5b

Clusteranalyse "round"

Ähnlichkeitsmaß (0 - 45)

Verkettungsregel complete linkage
=Maximum Methode

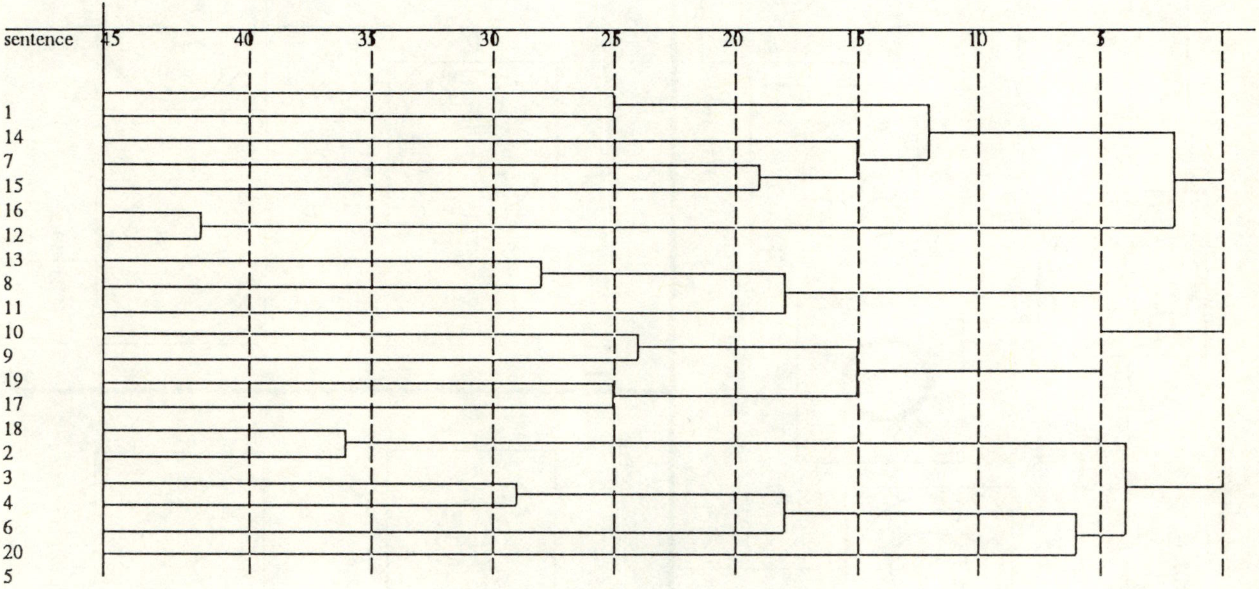

Appendix 6

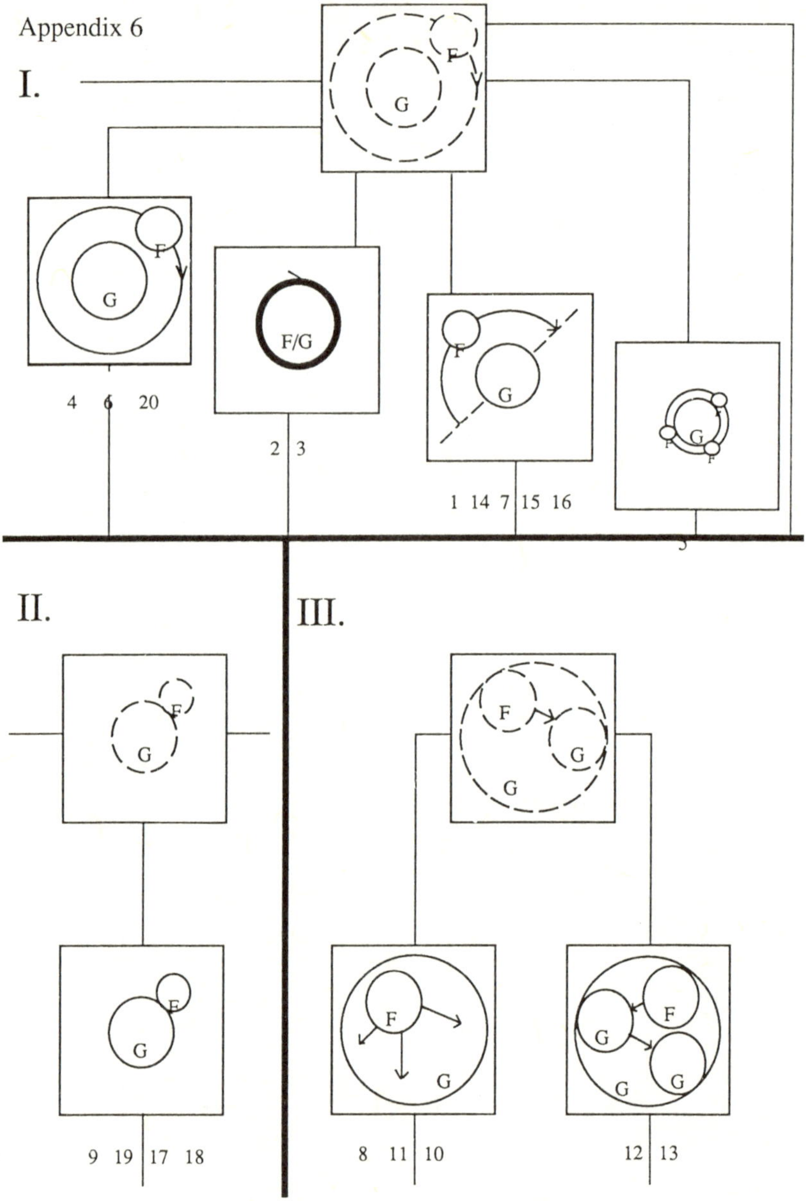
I.
F
G
F
G
4 6 20
F/G
2 3
F
G
1 14 7 15 16
F
G
F
F
5
II.
III.
F
G
F
G
F
G
G
F
G
9 19 17 18
F
G
8 11 10
F
G
G
G
G
12 13

On the lexical meaning of prepositions: a study of *above*, *below* and *over*

Barbara Wege
(Wuppertal)

0. Introduction

It is generally assumed that entries in the mental lexicon contain at least phonological, morphological, syntactic, and semantic information about each lexeme (cf. Schwarze, Ch. & Wunderlich, D. 1985: 13) and this paper is concerned with the semantic part of a lexical entry for prepositions in the mental lexicon. One of the main questions concerning the semantic information in a lexical entry is the role of the context. Should we have contextual information in the lexicon or is it possible to give a context-independent meaning of lexemes, which is then some kind of ideal meaning? Authors such as Brugman 1983, Hawkins 1984, and Herskovits 1982/1986 include contextual information in the lexicon[1], but Bennett 1975 rejects any kind of

---

1 Brugman 1983 and Hawkins 1984 describe prepositional meaning in the framework of Cognitive Grammar and analyse the semantic structure of prepositions in terms of trajector and landmark configurations. By describing properties of the trajector, i.e. the located referent, and the landmark, i.e. the locating referent, they include attributes of the referents, and that means contextual information, in their analyses of prepositional meaning. For example, Hawkins(1984: 201) analyses three predicates, among others, as lexical entries for *over*, which differ in the horizontal and vertical orientation for *hill* in (1), the horizontal orientation for *bridge* in (2) and the vertical orientation for *wall* in (3).

(1) The proud troops marched over the recently taken hill.

(2) The proud troops marched over the recently taken bridge.

(3) The mischievous little boy climbed over the wall.

These attributes of the landmark configuration may be part of the semantic structure of the corresponding NPs, but not of the preposition *over*. This sort of contextual information should not be in a lexical entry for prepositions.
Herskovits(1982, 1986) analyses similar properties of the referents for the semantic structure of prepositions using the concept of *use-types*, which direct the instatiation

contextual information and tries to deduce context-independent meanings of prepositions.[2]

It is assumed here that prepositions have a context-independent meaning represented in the mental lexicon as their *lexical* meaning. *Lexical* meaning refers to the kind of meaning that constitutes the basis for contextual meaning, i.e. it forms the basis for the actual use of a lexeme. The contextual meaning of a word is generated through the combination of different components of the language production process, where linguistic context, world knowledge[3] and situational context play an important role.

For the description of the lexical meaning of prepositions several different aspects have to be considered: inherent and relational characteristics of prepositions as well as the semantic domain. All these aspects have been dealt with already as a consideration of the literature reveals: Hawkins 1984 and Herskovits 1982/1986 have worked on inherent features in the local domain, Bennett 1975, Boers 1987 and Brugman 1983 on inherent features in the local and non-local domain, and they assume that local patterns provide the basis for non-local domains. Bennett 1975, Gruber 1965, Jackendoff 1983 and Rauh 1988 have dealt with relational features of prepositions. Whereas all of these authors handled one or two aspects at a time, this study is concerned with a combining model uniting inherent and relational features and their occurrence in local and non-local domains.

---

of prepositional meaning. The information in the use-types is actually part of a speaker's world knowledge and the appropriate interpretation of a prepositional meaning is the result of a mapping process between semantic structure and world knowledge. Thus, the fact that in (4)

(4) the milk in the bowl

the milk is enclosed by the bowl and in (5)

(5) the crack in the bowl

the crack is part of the material of the bowl so to speak, is a kind of information that a speaker gets when he maps his knowledge about milk, crack and bowl on the meaning of *in* or vice versa.

2 Bennett(1975) posits deep cases and inherent features as components of a lexical entry for prepositions. But he distinguishes between a semantic and a lexemic level and for the lexemic level, which corresponds to some extent to a mental lexicon, he assumes "only such components that are always present in the semantic representation"(1975: 14).

3 The term *world knowledge* refers to non-linguistic knowledge and includes episodic as well as encyclopaedic knowledge as defined by Tulving (1972) and Lüdi (1985).

It will be assumed here that the mental representation of the semantic structure of prepositions is stored in terms of features and not in terms of diagrams as, for example, Brugman and Hawkins assume in the framework of Cognitive Grammar. As a tool in describing *lexical* meaning, the advantages of the feature approach are on the one hand that it is compatible with other types of representations of semantic knowledge like networks and frames (cf. Engelkamp 1985: 294), and on the other hand that it represents all sorts of information in a homogeneous way whereas, for example, in Cognitive Grammar some kinds of information cannot be represented in a diagram and has to be stored in some other way, as Hawkins shows.[4]

The central aim of this paper is the derivation of the lexical meaning of the three English prepositions *above*, *below* and *over*.[5] In the first section a model for the description of lexical meaning will be developed. Some of the components which are considered to constitute lexical meaning are introduced following dataanalysis and native speaker intuitions about the meaning of the prepositions and the situational context in which they are used (section 1.1.). In section 1.2. the connection between context-free meaning and semantic domain will be discussed, and section 1.3. will consider the interdependence of the hypothesis for lexical meaning suggested in section 1.1. and the organisation of the features, their representation and the problem of polysemy.

In section 2 , semantic representations for the prepositions *above*, *below* and *over* will be provided as part of the entry in the mental lexicon for these prepositions. The essential ideas of this paper will be summarized in section 3.

---

4 Hawkins 1984:174 distinguishes *above* from one sense of *over* by using the concept of *search domains*, which are part of the base, while the semantic structure of the prepositional predicates constitutes the profile.

5 In this paper, only lexical prepositions are considered, that is those prepositions that have at least a semantic structure and a theta-grid and that may constitute the head of a syntactic construction (cf. Rauh 1989).

1. Lexical meaning and mental representation

1.1. The lexical meaning of prepositions

Two different kinds of characteristics of prepositions may be derived from data which are assumed to be context-free, i.e. are part of the meaning of prepositions in any contextual use. The derivation of such attributes is exemplified by the preposition *over*.

(1) She laid the blanket over his bed.

(2) the cloth over the table

(3) until my face was over his mouth

(4) He climbed over the wall.

(5) The Smiths live over the hill.

(6) Put the lamp over the counter.

In sentences (1) to (6) the preposition *over* denotes the arrangement of two referents on an imaginary vertical axis where the locating referent is in a *higher* position than the referent to be located. This kind of attribute is called an **inherent** one. If the preposition *over* is replaced by other prepositions like *across*, *on*, *under*, for example, in sentence (1) then the listener/reader conceptualizes the situation in quite a different way due to the inherent feature. Sentences (7a) to (7d) will serve as examples.

(7) a. She laid the blanket {over/across/on/under} his bed.

The second kind of attribute refers to a different conceptual level. Sentences (1) to (3) differ from (4) and (5) in that the PPs in (1) to (3) denote some kind of location, a *place*, whereas the PPs in (4) and (5) refer to a *path* that has to be covered by the object to be located. As Bennett noted, sentence (6) is ambiguous with respect to these two readings for the lamp may be located above the counter or it may be moved to the other side of the counter. Jackendoff 1978, 1983 postulates two hypercategories PLACE and PATH for prepositions to account for these differences and Rauh 1988 assumes two conceptual schemata, the schema of rest (*Ruheschema*) and the schema of motion (*Bewegungsschema*), to which prepositions correspond. Besides **inherent** features prepositions are therefore considered to have a second kind of attribute at a higher level of conceptualization and these are called **relational** features.

As can be seen from sentence (5), relational features for both syntactic categories, preposition and verb, can be assumed, and these may differ from each other in that *live* as a locational verb demands some notion of place, whereas the PP *over the river* may be conceptualized as a path and, therefore, it is the preposition *over* and not the verb *live* that determines the interpretation "path" for this sentence.[6] Such a conflict between the relational attributes of the preposition on the one hand and the verb on the other hand leads to the interpretation of 'orientation'.

From the anaylsis of the sentences (1) to (6) it follows that the preposition *over* has to be classified as ambiguous with respect to its relational attributes because *over* may indicate 'place' as well as 'path'.

The description of inherent and relational characteristics of prepositions as part of their lexical meaning is based on the model of Rauh 1988, which accounts for the data of prepositions in a more appropriate way than the models of Bennett 1975, Gruber 1965 or Jackendoff 1983. Rauh distinguishes three kinds of attributes: inherent, relational and selectional ones. Selectional attributes are useful, for example, in the description of the meaning of *at*, *on*, and *in* because these prepositions highlight particular dimensional aspects of the locating referents, such as *the door* in (8):

(8) John put the key {at/on/in} the door.

In the phrase *at the door*, the dimension of the door is of no interest to the speaker. But *on the door* tells the language user that the key is to be expected on some kind of surface of the door, probably the top edge, which indicates that the door must have a two-dimensional property. In using the phrase *in the door*, the speaker refers to the door as having volume, i.e. as a three-dimensional entity. As (9) indicates, *on* may not be used with NPs that refer to an entity of which no part relevant to the situational context may be conceptualized as two-dimensional:

(9) * He put the glass on the pencil.

On these grounds, the preposition *at* is assumed to have a selectional feature [_ [0dimensional]], *on* requires [_ [1/2dimensional]] and *in* requires [_[3dimensional]].

---

6 Rauh(1988: 379) argues that a verb assigns a theta-role to a PP in this case and that the preposition itself assigns a theta-role to the NP.

For the description of prepositions referring to the vertical axis there is no need to state such selectional features because they do not refer to particular dimensional attributes of the locating referents as (10) shows.

(10) A plane flew {above/over} the
{hill/bridge/wall/sea/town/table/...}.

Rauh 1988 defines relational attributes as corresponding to conceptual schemata which are characterized as grids that organize reality: "Raster, die die außersprachliche Wirklichkeit ordnen." (Rauh 1988: 332) In describing prepositional meaning two of these conceptual grids are assumed to be relevant, the schema of rest (*Ruheschema*), which involves the thematic roles 'affected object' and 'location', and the schema of motion (*Bewegungsschema*), which involves the thematic roles 'affected object', 'source', 'path', and 'goal'. According to these conceptual schemata, prepositions assign the role 'affected object' to their external argument and they assign either the role 'location' or one of the three roles 'source', 'path', or 'goal' to their internal argument.

It follows from the analysis of the examples (1) to (10) above that the lexical meaning of the preposition *over* should be assigned an inherent feature of verticality and two relational features including the thematic roles 'location' and 'path' and, therefore, constituting two different meanings of the preposition. The well-known problem of polysemy and homonymy will not be discussed here, but there are some aspects to be considered from which it may be inferred that *over* should be regarded as showing polysemy rather than homonymy.[7] For this reason, *over* will be treated as polysemous with at least two meanings, dependent on the relational features (In section 2. it will be demonstrated that the semantic structure of *over* demands a more differentiated description).

We must first consider whether the lexical meaning of prepositions has more types of features than those referring to an arrangement of two or more entities and those corresponding to a a conceptual schema.

---

7 Traugott 1986: 540 claims that semantic change may be derived and explained more easily for polysemous items than for homonyms. Thus, she prefers to assume polysemy rather than homonymy in cases of doubt.

1.2. Lexical meaning and the semantic domain

As far as the semantic domains are concerned, the data show that either prepositions may determine the domain of a phrase or that the context may impose a semantic domain on the preposition. In sentences (11a), (11b), and (11c) it is the preposition that determines the semantic domain of the PP.

(11) a. He met him *at* the conference.
b. He met him *during* the conference.
c. He met him *because of* the conference.

The NP *the conference* is interpreted as a place in (11a), as a time-span in (11b), and as a cause or reason in (11c) and these interpretations are determined directly by the preposition. From this it follows that nouns like *conference* occur in different domains, although, in isolation they may be characterized as occuring in one particular domain, in the case of *conference* in the abstract domain.

Turning to non-local prepositions, it might be claimed that temporal prepositions either occur in temporal contexts as in (12a) to (12c).

(12) a. I'll start some time after 3 o'clock.
b. There were two big wars during John's lifetime.
c. Stay here until tomorrow.

or determine a temporal interpretation as in (11b) and (13a) to (13c):

(13) a. He always has the newspaper after me.
b. During sleep, we sometimes dream of ...
c. John was in the Seventh Division until Sicily, but then he was transferred to the Fifty-First.

and that 'abstract' prepositions either occur in abstract contexts or determine an abstract interpretation as in (11c).

Interestingly, local prepositions may **not** determine a local domain for a sentence if they occur in a non-local context.

(14) a. He met him at the corner.
b. He met him at 3 o'clock.

(15) a. The book was on the shelf all day.
b. The book was on my mind all day.

The prepositions *at* and *on*, for example, are considered to be local prepositions, having the feature for the local domain in their entry in the mental lexicon. But in (14b) the domain for the whole sentence is determined by the final NP, *3 o'clock*, which determines the temporal interpretation of the sentence and, thus, the preposition *at* only seems to be temporal. Sentence (15b) is interpreted as abstract due to the NP *my mind*. Here we find the local preposition *on* determined by an abstract context.

On these grounds it may be assumed for all prepositions that the semantic domain in which they occur originally, constitutes one component of their lexical meaning. The fact that local prepositions may occur in temporal and abstract contexts where their semantic domain is determined by other lexical entities, may be seen as the result of a transfer process - a metaphor. Boers 1987, Brugman 1983, Radden 1981/1983 and Rauh 1989, among others, have demonstrated that local prepositions generate metaphors in non-local contexts, which means that their lexical meaning, which conveys the feature of the local domain, forms the semantic basis of their use in non-local contexts.

It follows from these considerations that prepositions may be described by three kinds of features: an inherent one concerning the arrangement between two entities, a relational one corresponding to a conceptual schema, and a third one concerning the original semantic domain.

How can these features of the lexical meaning of a preposition be arranged in the mental lexicon? And how can we describe polysemy and the lexical access of polysemous items? These questions are discussed in the next section.

1.3. Lexical meaning, mental representation and polysemy

In discussing a model for entries in the mental lexicon we have to ask about the mental representation of such a lexicon and its entries. Whereas linguists tend to assume a static list of several attributes such as phonological, morphological, syntactic, semantic and even pragmatic properties (cf. Fillmore 1971) for a lexical entry, psychologists like Leuninger 1986: 237 and Engelkamp 1985: 313 and computer scientists like Habel 1985: 468 as well as linguists like Schwarze 1989: 510 suggest including procedural aspects in the lexicon and assume for lexical entries:

> daß Lexikoneinträge nicht ausschließlich statische Daten sind, die von Sprachverarbeitungsprozessen 'abgerufen' werden, sondern, daß Lexikoneinträge Prozesse aktivieren können bzw. selbst als aktivierbare Prozesse aufgefaßt werden können.(Habel 1985: 468/9)

To give lexical information about a word in terms of a list may thus be considered as stating a theoretical construct in which several items of information about a lexeme are combined which are to be stored in different places in memory and perhaps even in different ways.

Concerning the lexical meaning of prepositions and its mental representation, it is assumed that the semantic structures of different lexemes may share the same semantic elements in a semantic store. This assumption is based on an idea of Flores d'Arcais 1986: 135, who suggests that different word meanings may be connected with the same semantic elements, as can be seen from figure 1.

Fig. 1

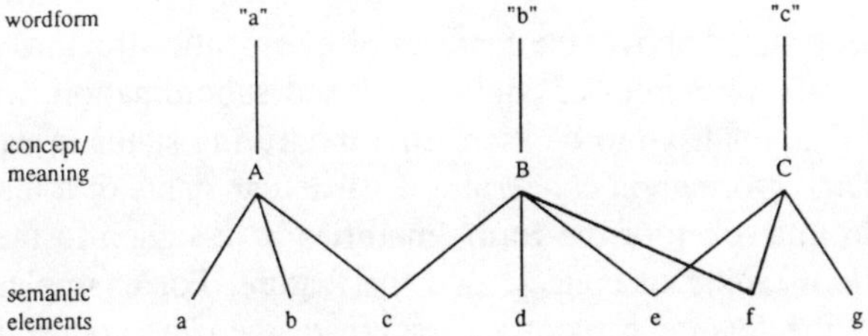

In this way the store capacity might be reduced to give a more economic model although this does not imply that each semantic element is stored only once in the sense of Katz & Fodor 1963. This idea of simple storage and multiple connections is seen as part of the mental representation of true antonyms like *above* and *below* (cf. section 2.1). Flores d'Arcais gives no precise information about the semantic elements and it is assumed that these are features which are arranged according to the principles of equivalence and subordination, where subordinated features have a modifying function (cf. Rauh 1988: 322).

Besides the meanings of different lexemes the different meanings of a polysemous item may also be accounted for by this approach of multiple connections betweeen meaning and semantic elements. A polysemous word may be considered as being connected with a set of semantic elements where each meaning of the word is connected with the corresponding semantic elements, as figure 2 shows.

Fig.2

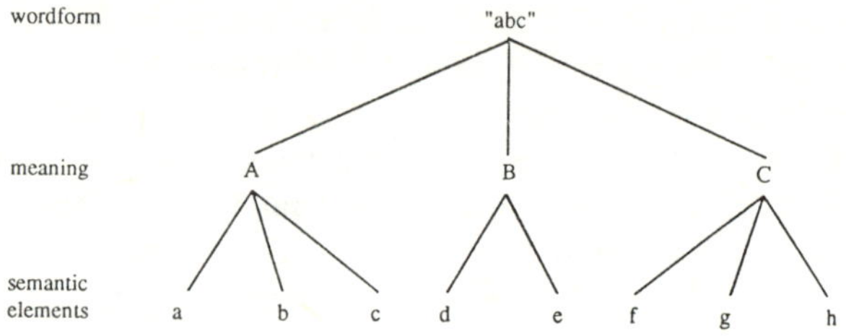

As has been stated above, the features of a semantic structure are arranged according to the principles of equivalence and subordination, which implies that single features have to be ascribed a modifying status in case of subordination. This information concerning a particular status of a feature may be retrieved from a token of the form "modifies x" assigned to the connection between the meaning or concept and the feature. For example, if with the meaning A the feature *b* modifies feature *a*, then the connection between meaning A and feature *b* carries the token "modifies *a*".

Fig.3

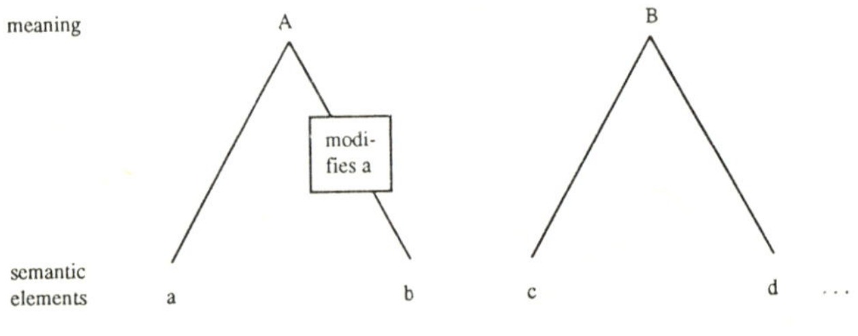

This approach to polysemy differs from that of Caramazza and Grober 1976, who suggest a model with an abstract core meaning and instruction rules that instantiate the core meaning. A core meaning underlying **all** meanings of a polysemous lexeme is far too abstract in character to be stored permanently. Instead, it seems more plausible to assume the reconstruction of an abstract core meaning when required. This claim might explain the difficulty in describing the meaning of a word without using an example. For, as soon as we use an example, we describe the instantiated core meaning and not the core meaning itself.

The considerations above imply the following requirements for the description of the lexical meaning of prepositions:

- the derivation of inherent features for all meanings of a lexeme
- the derivation of relational features for all meanings of a lexeme
- the stipulation of a domain feature
- the assignment of a particular modifying status to a connection between a meaning and a feature if required.

These implications will be applied to the investigation of English prepositions in the next section.

2. The lexical meaning of the prepositions *above*, *below*, and *over*

It is the aim of this section to describe the lexical, that is context free meaning of the three English prepositions *above*, *below* and *over* on the basis of the model developed in section 1. The data are taken from Hill 1968, Heaton 1965 and the LOB-Corpus 1978.

2.1. *Above* and *below*

Above and *below* seem to be prepositions with a simple meaning compared, for example, with *over*. The semantic structures of these two prepositions are assumed to consist of the inherent features [verticality, positive], [no contact], [spatial] and the relational feature [aff_loc] for *above*; and [verticality, negative], [no contact], [spatial] and [aff_loc] for *below*.

The derivation of these features is exemplified by sentences (1) to (6).

(1) The sky above our heads was blue.

(2) moved at the sight of the elderly figures above her

(3) the water was already above our knees and rising

(4) He waited below her window.

(5) there was sea below me

(6) it is just below my knees

Both prepositions, *above* and *below*, refer to an imaginary vertical axis. The point of reference, i.e. the position 'zero' on the imaginary axis, is indicated by the NP in the complement position of the preposition. *Above* and *below* determine the conceptualization of reality in terms of two levels. Dirven 1981 has indicated this interpretation in stating

> The two neutral items *above* and *below* denote neutral altitude (...) and they do not imply that things are in a direct line with one another. In fact, they only denote the notion of a different level than that of the reference point ... (Dirven 1981: 116)

Thus, it is of no relevance whether the two referents are arranged in a direct vertical line or whether they are shifted to either side, such information may be part of the semantic structure of other prepositions like *over*, *under*, or *underneath*, but it is of no importance for *above* and *below*.

The impression of two "levels" with *above* and *below* is caused by the interaction of two components: the vertical axis on the one hand and the separation, i.e. lack of contact between the two referents on the other hand. These components lead to the interpretation of two points on a scale, which are related to one another. In stating this assumption it has to be taken into account that only a particular kind of knowledge is involved, i.e. *lexical* knowledge and not encyclopaedic knowledge. To give an example, the preposition *above* is considered to convey the inherent feature [no contact] in sentences (1) to (3) and even in sentence (7).

(7) The rock was half under the water and half above.

Although, of course, the object to be located, *the rock*, actually constitutes a unit and is in no way divided by the locating object, *the water*, nevertheless, the interpretation of sentence (7) leads to a conceptualization of the rock as separated into two parts, the upper one, as it were, 'hovering' over the surface of the water. It is in examples like these, that language reveals its image building power.

Both prepositions, *above* and *below*, occur originally in the local domain, which is indicated by the inherent feature [spatial]. In their relational feature, both prepositions correspond to the schema of rest and thus assign the relations 'affected object' and 'location' to their arguments.

As indicated, *above* and *below* may occcur in non-local domains, the measure domain and the abstract domain.[8] Sentences (8) to (14) illustrate different subdomains of the measure domain, sentences (15) and (16) present examples for the abstract domain.

(8) the absence of ventilating equipment above floor level

(9) as is situated below high-water mark

(10) pupils above the age of 16

(11) pupils below the age of 16 are not allowed to see this film

(12) can be kept well above freezing point

(13) a lieutenant colonel ranks above a major

(14) the temperature was below freezing point

(15) She thinks herself above criticism.

(16) the observed scores were well below expectation

It is claimed that *above* and *below* convey all those features in the non-local domains that have been found to constitute their lexical meaning in the local domain (cf. sentences (1) to (6)). Concerning the measure domain, it is assumed that the feature [verticality] indicates the scale on which two values are related to one another and the feature [no contact] introduces the level-interpretation. The feature [spatial] indicates for all non-local occurrences of the two prepositions that they are used as metaphors.

In this section, it has been shown that the lexical meaning of *above* and *below* may be described as consisting of the features [verticality, positive], [no contact], [spatial] [aff_loc] and [verticality, negative], [no contact], [spatial], [aff_loc] respectively. This analysis agrees with that of Bennett, who describes *above* as 'locative higher' and *below* as 'locative lower' (Bennett 1975: 84), and with that of Hawkins, who analyses *above* and *below* as expressing a configuration of an indefinite trajector and a landmark that are separated (Hawkins 1984: 367/373). The analysis presented here goes even further in combining the descriptions of Bennett and Hawkins and

8 So far, no coherent theory of domains and their interrelationships has been put forward. The measure domain and the abstract domain are taken as hyperdomains here, where the abstract domain is a sort of collective field to which all items are assigned that are not considered as spatial, temporal or measure expressions. The measure domain can clearly be divided into spatial, temporal or 'abstract' measure because it cross-cuts the other domains.

in adding the transfer component with the feature concerning the semantic domain. As has been proposed in section 1.3., *above* and *below* are considered to have some semantic elements in common as can be seen in figure 4.

Fig.4

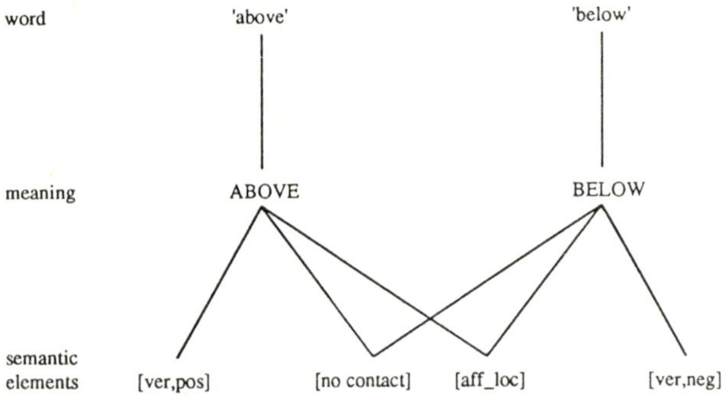

2.2. *Over*

Compared with *above* and *below*, the preposition *over* occurs in a variety of different contexts and seems to have a semantically rich structure.

The prepositions *over* and *above* have one property in common, namely, that they refer to the upper part of a vertical axis where the upper part is defined by a speaker's eye level or a particular reference point (cf. Bühler 1965[2]). But *over* differs from *above* in that it highlights a space along a vertical axis, whereas *above* refers to the whole space above the horizontal axis, or as Brugman puts it:

> *Above* is neutral with respect to the degree of closeness of the trajector and the landmark, that is, the first can be any distance vertical to the second. *Over*, on the other hand, implies a greater physical closeness between trajector and landmark ... (Brugman 1983: 41/2)

Hawkins(1983: 174) tries to capture this phenomenon by assuming different search domains for the two prepositions. Sentences (17a) and (17b) illustrate this difference.

(17) a. There was a shadow *over* her head.

b. There was a shadow *above* her head.

The preposition *over* highlights in sentence (17a) that the shadow is in a direct vertical line above the head, and *above* in (17b) indicates that the shadow is at a level higher than the head. Because *over* refers to the vertical axis in a more direct manner than *above*, we derive [verticality, positive & direct] as one inherent feature for *over*. There seems to be another inherent feature which is distinct from the one stated above. This second feature indicates an embracing relation where the entity to be located embraces the locating entity. Sentences (18) to (20) illustrate the meaning of *over* which is referred to by the inherent feature [embrace].

(18) She laid the blanket over his bed.

(19) He had a coat over his arm.

(20) She hung the rope over the table.

The embracing relation is not specified concerning its location in space. As, however, the *upper* entity embraces the *lower* entity, the feature [embrace] has to be specified by the subordinated feature [verticality, positive & direct]. The verticality feature has to be subordinated in this case because of its modifying function. So, *over* has two meanings, which differ in one inherent feature: one meaning of *over* has the feature [verticality, positive & direct] (cf. (17a)) and the other meaning of *over* has the feature [embrace: verticality, positive & direct]. (Subordination is indicated by a colon).

The preposition is also ambiguous concerning its relational features (as has been shown in section 1.1) because it may correspond either to the schema of rest or to the schema of motion. In sentences (21) and (22) *over* corresponds to the schema of rest and in (23) and (24) to the schema of motion.

(21) a clock hanging over a jeweller's shop

(22) He threw a rug over her.

(23) The storm went over us.

(24) She looked over the fence at us.

As far as the combination of inherent and relational features is concerned, three meaning variants are possible for *over*. The preposition may correspond to the schema of rest and either have the inherent feature [verticality, positive & direct] as in (21) or the inherent feature [embrace: verticality, positive & direct] as in (22). Or, the preposition may correspond to the schema of motion and convey the feature [embrace: verticality, positive &

direct], as in (23) and (24). Thus, *over* is considered to be polysemous with three related meanings.

All three meanings may be transferred to non-local domains. The meaning with the features [verticality, positive & direct] and [aff_loc] occurs in the same non-local domains as *above*, i.e. the measure domain and the abstract domain, as sentences (25) to (28) show.

(25) It is over 700 yards long.

(26) It takes over an hour to get there.

(27) You are seriously over weight.

(28) He gave us preference over the others.

In sentence (25) *over* occurs with a local measure phrase, in (26) with a temporal measure phrase, and in (27) with an abstract measure phrase. The verticality feature gives a kind of scale here, on which the NP in the complement position of *over* identifies a particular value. In that respect the prepositions *above* and *over* are alike in that both express 'more than' in the measure domain. But they differ from each other because *above* has the second feature [no contact], and the verticality feature of *over* is specified by [direct]. This difference in features may account for the difference in the interpretation of sentences (29a) and (29b).

(29) a. It is *over* 700 yards long.
b. It is *above* 700 yards long.

In using *over*, the speaker seems to involve a particular expectation, which is around 700 yards, and the phrase *over 700 yards* highlights the length of 700 yards and more. By using *above* in (29b) the speaker clearly indicates that the length is greater than the 700 yards level. In figure 5 the difference is illustrated.

Fig.5

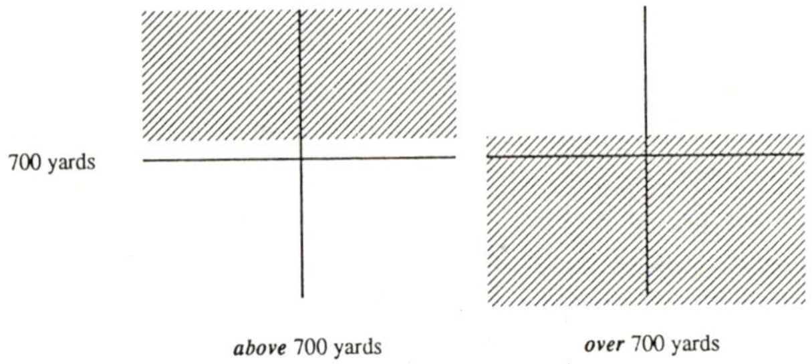

As this example shows, *over* and also *above* keep their lexical meaning in the measure domain. This holds for all inherent and relational features. The feature [spatial] indicates the transfer and the relational feature [aff_loc] indicates that *over* corresponds to the schema of rest in the measure domain too and assigns the relation 'affected object' to *it* in (25) and (26) and to *you* in (27), and the relation 'location' to *700 yards* in (25), to *an hour* in (26) and to *weight* in (27). The same arguments hold for the abstract domain as shown by sentence (28).

The meaning with the features [embrace: verticality, positive & direct] and [aff_loc] may be transferred to the abstract domain only, as (30) and (31) show.

(30) A curious happiness came over him.

(31) her influence over her brother-in-law

In neither sentence can *over* be replaced by *above*.

(32) ? A curious happiness came above him.

(33) ? her influence above her brother-in-law

From this it follows that sentences (30) and (31) contain *over* in its meaning with the feature [embrace]. As with the first meaning, *over* keeps its lexical features when the second meaning is transferred to the non-local domain, in this case the abstract domain only. *A curious happiness* in (29) and *her influence* in (30) are assigned the relation 'affected object', and *him* and *brother-in-law* are assigned the relation 'location'. The feature [spatial] gives the original domain.

The third meaning of *over* with the inherent feature [embrace: verticality, positive & direct] and the relational feature [aff_pa] may be transferred to the temporal and the abstract domain.

(34) We'll stay over Wednesday.

(35) You made me angry but I'm over that now.

In both sentences *over* denotes an embracing relation. In (34) the time-span of the event, *we'll stay*, extends beyond the second temporal unit, *Wednesday*, and thus may be said to embrace it on an abstract level. In (35) the speaker indicates that one event, *you made me angry*, is a kind of obstacle that has been overcome and thus, embraced by the second event (not in a temporal sense, of course). Neither sentence can be used with *above*.

(36) ? We'll stay above Wednesday.

(37) ? You made me angry but I'm above that now.

The modifying feature [verticality, positive & direct] is of no importance in those cases when the meaning of *over* with the features [embrace] and [aff_pa] is transferrred to a non-local domain, because in the temporal and in the abstract domain this meaning of *over* need not be delimited from a concept referring to the negative part of the vertical axis. This is the case with the other two meanings of *over*, as something may be *over* or *under* a particular value in the measure domain and someone or something may have influence *over* someone or something, or someone or something may be *under* the influence of someone or something.

Concerning its relational features *over* assigns the role 'path' to *Wednesday* in (34) and to *that* in (35) just as it assigns the role 'path' to its internal argument in the local domain (cf. sentences (23) and (24)).

This analysis of *over* differs both from Brugman's and Hawkins' analyses on the one hand, and from Bennett's analysis on the other hand. Both Brugman and Hawkins analyse *over* as a polysemous item in contrast to Bennett 1975: 54, who states as the only meaning of *over* "'locative superior'" . But they both assume far more than three meanings for *over*. Furthermore, they suggest an internal structure of the category OVER in terms of prototype theory. Brugman posits as the prototype of the category OVER that meaning of the preposition which includes both the meaning of *above* and that of *across* in equal parts as in (38):

(38) The plane flew over the field.

She describes this meaning of *over* by means of the components [+vertical], [-contact] and [+boundary-traversal] (Brugman 1983: 24). Brugman assumes that several meanings of *over* may be derived by extension from the prototype, i.e. by changing particular components as in (39a) and (39b).

(39) a. Boris walked over the hill.
b. Boris climbed over the wall.

Sentences (39a) and (39b) focus on the *across*-component of *over* in that [-contact] is changed to [+contact], as Brugman 1983: 24 assumes. She indicates that the property 'contact' is part of the meaning of the verb: "*walk* encodes that the trajector [Boris] be in contact with the landmark [the hill]"(Brugman 1983: 22 [B.W.]). Therefore, it seems implausible to analyse

[+contact] as a component of *over*. Furthermore, the relation expressed by *over* remains the same if we change the verb and think of someone moving over the hill, hovering a few inches above the ground.

(40) Superman hovered over the hill.

Firstly, [+/- contact] is of no importance for *over* and, therefore, *over* in (38), (39a) and (39b) and (40) expresses the same relation and has to be analysed with the same meaning, i.e. *one* meaning instead of two senses. Secondly, Brugman's analysis of *over* includes components that are part of other lexical items, for example the verbs, and so she has far more senses for *over* than the analysis given here results in. She even considers the meaning of *over* in non-local domains as related but *different* senses (Brugman 1983: 9/10) although, as could be demonstrated in 1.2, non-local items select the appropriate domain and determine the interpretation of the preposition, which is a context-dependent process. Thus, the senses of *over* in the local and in the non-local domains are not only related but are the *same* in different domains, i.e. in different contexts (this assumption is restricted to the senses of *over* studied in this paper).

For all three meanings of *over* it has been demonstrated that the preposition maintains its lexical meaning when it is transferred from the local domain to non-local domains. Furthermore, it has been demonstrated that all three meanings may be transferred to the abstract domain, while *over* with the features [verticality, positive & direct] and [aff_loc] may also be transferred to the measure domain and *over* with the features [embrace] and [aff_pa] may also be transferred to the temporal domain.

Fig. 6

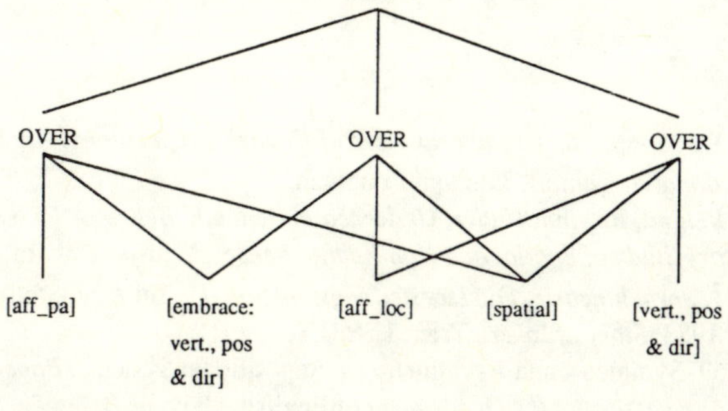

As the analyses show, prepositions do have a context-free meaning, and this lexical meaning may be accounted for by the feature model presented in this paper. The inherent, relational and domain features discussed constitute a part of a lexical entry for a preposition. There may be more features that have to be considered as constituting the mental lexicon, but for the prepositions discussed, inherent, relational, and domain features seem to be the most important ones.

3. Resumé

In the first section a model for the semantic part of an entry (for prepositions) in the mental lexicon is developed. It is demonstrated that prepositions have different types of context-free properties that can be stated in terms of features (1.1.). It is further demonstrated that local prepositions may be transferred from their original domain to non-local domains such as the abstract, temporal, or measure domains, and that this process may only be derived if the original domain is stored together with the lexical meaning of a preposition (1.2.). A model for the representation of the semantic properties of prepositions is introduced and it is claimed that different meanings of a polysemous item may have semantic elements in common (1.3.).

With the help of this model developed in section 1, the lexical meanings of the prepositions *above*, *below*, and *over* are described and the semantic structure of these prepositions is presented as part of the entry in the mental lexicon.

References

Bennett, D.C. 1975. *Spatial and Temporal Uses of English Prepositions: An Essay in Stratificational Semantics*. London: Longman.

Boers, F. 1987. *Behind, Beyond, Under, Underneath, Beneath, Below: A Descriptive and Explanatory Study of Spatial and Non-Spatial Senses*. Wilrijk: Univ of Antwerp.

Bühler, K. 1965^2. *Sprachtheorie: Die Darstellungsfunktion der Sprache*. Stuttgart: Fischer.

Brugman, C.M. 1983. *Story of 'over'*. Trier: L.A.U.T.

Bugarski, R. 1969. Symmetry and Asymmetry in Prepositional Systems. *Papers to Mark the 40th Anniversary of the Department* of English. Univ. of Belgrade. 57-69.

Caramazza, A. and Grober, E. 1976. Polysemy and the Structure of the Lexicon. In Rameh, C. (ed.). *Semantics and Application*. Georgetown: UP. 181-206.

Dirven, R. 1981. Spatial Relations in English. *Anglistik und Englischunterricht* 14: 103-132.

Engelkamp, J. 1985. Die Repräsentation der Wortbedeutung. In Schwarze, Ch. and D. Wunderlich (eds.). *Handbuch der Lexikologie*. Königstein/Ts.: Athenäum. 292-313.

Fillmore, C.J. 1968. The Case for Case. In Bach, E. and R. Harms (eds.). *Universals in Linguistics*. New York: Holt, Rinehart and Winston. 1-91.

-----. 1971. Types of lexical information. In Steinberg, D.D. and L.A. Jakobovits (eds.). *Semantics. An Interdisciplinary Reader in Philosophy, Linguistics and Psychology*. Cambridge: UP. 370-392.

Flores d'Arcais. 1986. Konzeptuelle Strukturen und das mentale Lexikon. In Bosshardt, H.-G. (ed.). *Perspektiven auf Sprache: Interdisziplinäre Beiträge zum Gedenken an Hans Hörmann*. Berlin, New York: Walter de Gruyter. 130-148.

Gruber, J.S. 1976. *Lexical Structures in Syntax and Semantics*. Amsterdam, New York, Oxford: North Holland Publ. Comp.

Habel, Ch. 1985. Das Lexikon in der Forschung der Künstlichen Intelligenz. In Schwarze, Ch. and D. Wunderlich (eds.). *Handbuch der Lexikologie*. Königstein/Ts.: Athenäum. 441-474.

Hawkins, B.W. 1984. *The Semantics of English Spatial Prepositions*. Ph. D. Diss., Univ. of California. San Diego.

Heaton, J.B. 1965. *Prepositions and Adverbial Particles*. London: Longman.

Herskovits, A. 1982. *Space and the Prepositions in English: Regularities and Irregularities in a Complex Domain*. Ph. D. Diss., Stanford Univ.

-----. 1986. *Language and Spatial Cognition: An Interdisciplinary Study of the Prepositions in English*. London, Cambridge: CUP.

Hill, L.A. 1968. *Prepositions and Adverbial Articles: An Interim Classification Semantic, Structural and Graded*. London: Longman.

Jackendoff, R. 1978. Grammar as Evidence for Conceptual Structure. In Halle, M., J. Bresnan and G. Miller (eds.). *Lingustic Theory and Psychological Reality*. Cambridge, Mass.: MIT Press. 201-228.

-----. 1983. *Semantics and Cognition*. Cambridge, Mass.; London, Engl.: MIT Press.

Leuninger, H. 1986. Mentales Lexikon, Basiskonzepte, Wahrnehmungsalternativen: Neuro- und Psycholinguistische Überlegungen. *Linguistische Berichte* 103:224-251.

Lüdi, G. 1985. Zur Zerlegbarkeit von Wortbedeutungen. In Schwarze, Ch. and D. Wunderlich (eds.). *Handbuch der Lexikologie*. Königstein/Ts.: Athenäum. 64-101.

Radden, G. 1981. Die übertragenen Bedeutungen der englischen Raumpräpositionen. *Anglistik und Englischunterricht* 14:133-179.

-----. 1983. *Spatial Metaphors Underlying Prepositions of Causality*. Trier: L.A.U.T.

Rauh, G. 1988. *Tiefenkasus, Thematische Relationen und Thetarollen: Die Entwicklung einer Theorie von Semantischen Relationen*. Tübingen: Narr.

-----. 1989. Präpositionengesteuerte Metaphorik. In Habel, Ch., M. Herweg and K. Rehkämper (eds.). *Raumkonzepte in Verstehensprozessen: Interdisziplinäre Beiträge zu Sprache und Raum*. Tübingen: Niemeyer. 249-282.

Schwarze, Ch. 1989. Polysemie als Prozedur am Beispiel von frz. *á travèrs* und *chéz*. In Habel, Ch., M. Herweg and K. Rehkämper (eds.). *Raumkonzepte in Verstehensprozessen: Interdisziplinäre Beiträge zu Sprache und Raum*. Tübingen: Niemeyer. 310-338.

Traugott, E.C. 1986. From polysemy to internal semantic reconstruction. *Proceedings of the 12th Annual Meeting of the Berkeley Ling. Soc., Feb. 15-17*. Berkeley, Cal. 539-550.

Tulving, E. 1972. Episodic and Semantic Memory. In Tulving, E. and W. Donaldson (eds.). *Organization of Memory*. New York: Academic Press. 382-403.

List of contributors

FOSKETT, Colin

Bergische Universität - Gesamthochschule Wuppertal
Sprach- und Literaturwissenschaften
Anglistik/Amerikanistik
Gaußstr. 20
Postfach 10 01 27
5600 Wuppertal 1

FRIES, Norbert

Seminar für Deutsche Philologie der
Georg-August-Universität Göttingen
Humboldtallee 13
3400 Göttingen

HOTTENROTH, Priska-Monika

Universität Hamburg
Romanisches Seminar
Von-Melle-Park 6, VI
2000 Hamburg 13

HUPPERTZ, Angelika

Bergische Universität - Gesamthochschule Wuppertal
Sprach- und Literaturwissenschaften
Anglistik/Amerikanistik
Gaußstr. 20
Postfach 10 01 27
5600 Wuppertal 1

KÖNIG, Ekkehard
Freie Universität Berlin
Institut für Englische Philologie
Gosslerstr. 2-4
1000 Berlin 33

KORTMANN, Bernd
Freie Universität Berlin
Institut für Englische Philologie
Gosslerstr. 2-4
1000 Berlin 33

LANG, Ewald
Bergische Universität - Gesamthochschule Wuppertal
Sprach- und Literaturwissenschaften
Germanistik
Gaußstr. 20
Postfach 10 01 27
5600 Wuppertal 1

RAUH, Gisa
Bergische Universität - Gesamthochschule Wuppertal
Sprach- und Literaturwissenschaften
Anglistik/Amerikanistik
Gaußstr. 20
Postfach 10 01 27
5600 Wuppertal 1

SCHEPPING, Marie-Theres
Universität Konstanz
Fachgebiet Sprachwissenschaft
Postfach 5560
7750 Konstanz

SCHULZE, Rainer
Universität Essen
Fachbereich 3
Universitätsstr. 12
4300 Essen

WEGE, Barbara
Bergische Universität - Gesamthochschule Wuppertal
Sprach- und Literaturwissenschaften
Anglistik/Amerikanistik
Gaußstr. 20
Postfach 10 01 27
5600 Wuppertal 1